YOUTH
IN THE THIRD MILLENNIUM

CARLOS MIGUEL BUELA

YOUTH
IN THE
THIRD MILLENNIUM

Revised and Updated

IVE Press

New York – 2010

Translated from the original Spanish
"Jóvenes en el tercer milenio"

Imprimatur
✠ **Andrea Maria Erba**
Bishop of Velletri-Segni
January 20, 2006

IVE Press
  113 East 117th Street
  New York, NY 10035

  Ph. (212) 534 5257
  Fax (212) 534 5258

  Email ivepress@ive.org
  http://www.ivepress.com

ISBN 978-1-933871-28-8

Library of Congress Control Number: 2010927063

Printed in the United States of America ∞

TABLE OF CONTENTS

PREFACE

Dear young people, today we stand before a culminating moment in the history of humanity, one of those stages of "fracture" in which it is possible to radically change the orientation of the life of the spirit, the existence of men. We have just crossed the frontier of the third millennium.

You who must fulfill a predominant role in the new rhythm of the march that the world must acquire. You must be the true protagonists of this phase of history.

Our world is not on the right path. One does not have to be subtle to notice it. War, hunger, misery, envy, materialism, seeking after secondary things, immaturity, depression, anguish, the crisis caused by "escapism," insecurities, and relativism of the truth all bear witness to the state of the world.

Our world is not on the right path.

If our world is not on the right path, we cannot take a cowardly position, like *punks* do under the slogan of "The world is rotten...who cares." They hide their heads in the face of danger like an ostrich, facing adverse circumstances. We have no right to sit with our arms crossed when God Himself has died with His arms open in order to infuse us with confidence in victory.

If our world has gone bad, it is because it has not followed the path that it should have followed. So the world must change its course and *we* have to make it change course.

Dear young people, what is the new path the world needs?

The world is a great enigma and Jesus Christ is the only answer and solution.

He is the man who divided history in two; the man who nobody can truly know and not love, the man of the heart pierced for love of men. The God-man.

For this reason, dear young people, I want to accompany you on the first steps of this millennium, this moment of history that is so important. I want to do this calling to mind the Great Pope, John Paul II, who with his life and death marked the course to follow in the third millennium.

In this book, you will not find matters pertaining to science or literature. There are some reflections with very old origins, some lectures that I have given, sermons that I have preached... I simply want to offer you the freshness of the message from Christ to souls like yours, dear young people, who are called to do great things. In vain, then, will you seek quotes or references from different authors, but you will find the values and principles that must take precedence in the life of those who raise the standard of Jesus Christ, Lord of history.

I want to thank Fr. Christian Ferraro, I.V.E., and the group of seminarians at the Institute of the Incarnate Word, who work with youth and young adult ministry, for the help they have given me in the development of this book.

May the Virgin Mary make the pages of this book fruitful in the hearts of youth.

The Author

CHAPTER 1

The Meaning of Life

You Have the Words of Eternal Life"
(Jn 6:68)

"I ask you, youth of Ecuador!
-Do you want to commit yourselves before the Pope to be living members of the Church of Christ?
-Do you wish to commit yourselves to surrender even your life for the good of others, especially the poor?
-Do you want to fight against sin, always carrying the love of Christ in your heart?
-Do you want to employ your youthful vigor in building a new society according to the will of God?
-Do you want to renounce violence, building up fraternity and not hatred?
-Do you want to be permanent powers of justice, truth, love, and peace?
-Do you want to bring Christ to other young people?
-Do you want to be faithful to Christ, even if others are not?
You have answered yes. If you are faithful, I say to you, with the Apostle St. John: 'you have conquered the evil one. [1] *"*

John Paul II,
Address to Youth in Olympic Stadium in Quito, Ecuador,
January 30, 1985.

---

[1] *1 Jn* 2:14.

1.

THE MEANING OF LIFE

"Life is a gift of a certain period of time in which each one of us faces a challenge which life itself brings: the challenge of having a purpose, a destiny, and of striving for it. The opposite is to spend our lives on the surface of things, to 'lose' our lives in futility (...)

Too many young people do not realize that they themselves are the ones who are mainly responsible for giving a worthwhile meaning to their lives. The mystery of human freedom is at the heart of the great adventure of living life well."

John Paul II, Manila, Philippines.
January 14, 1995.[2]

I could not begin these pages without first trying to answer a fundamental question: What is it that distinguishes a human being from the rest of Creation?

In other words: What is Man?

I find this question very important because many times in our daily language, as said by the great author Gilbert Keith Chesterton,[3] it seems that man is no more than a "strange animal." For example, we might say, that Juanita talks like a parrot, that Peter is a beast in the soccer game, that Joseph is as

---

[2] All the epigraphs belong to John Paul II. From now on we will simply give the reference of time, place and/or document. Unless otherwise noted, all quotes from John Paul II and Church documents are taken from the Vatican website: www.vatican.va.

[3] To facilitate reading we will give references only for citations from the Bible and statistics, in other cases we will give them if we consider it opportune.

dumb as an ox, etc. Either these terms are metaphors, or there is no difference between Juanita and the parrot, Peter and the beast, or Joseph and the ox.

Man has similar characteristics to animals in that he has a body with ears, legs, eyes, etc., like other animals. Though we may place man next to animals, we also know that man is superior to them. Man *thinks*, man is *able to sustain love forever*, able to *create works of art*, and able to *become a hero*... This, my young friends, does not occur because he has a body like the animals. Man can do these things because he has a soul, a spiritual and immortal soul that is the image of God.

The reality of the soul is something we count on every day. The soul is always present and, because of that, we sometimes fail to realize it. Every time we see an elderly person with energy and inner youthfulness, we reflect upon ourselves, on the "I," which, like the air, we do not see but is there. Every time we recall our past, which by being *past* no longer exists; every time we consider our future, which by being *future* is not yet in existence; every time we do something like this, we come into contact with the reality of the soul. The soul is spiritual, not bound to the corporal, and does not depend on time and space.

The soul, in Latin *anima*, is what animates the body, gives it life and movement, and what makes it *know* and *love*. Man is capable of knowing and loving because his soul has two capacities (or *faculties*) called *intelligence* and *will*. He knows with the intelligence and loves with the will. With the intelligence he *looks*, he *sees* what he can do, and with the will he *decides*, he *chooses* to do it. This is why man, unlike animals, is *free*. For example, a bird will never plan to make a nest with three floors; or a dog write a book on the one hundred ways of seasoning a bone; or a horse design aerobic exercise classes to stay in shape. Animals will always act in the same way, each one according to the impulse of its instinct, exactly as dictated by nature. Man—who possesses freedom (by having intelligence and will)—can progress or regress by personal decision.

✠   ✠   ✠

This means that man is a being who is capable of setting for himself objectives and goals to reach. Man is a being who is intentional. Man is a being who will be either *good* or *bad* according to the ends he proposes for himself and the means he chooses to reach them. There are different types of ends, some are good and others are bad. If I intend to be a great scientist in order to create a bomb capable of destroying a large part of humanity, I will be proposing a goal that does not dignify me. If I intend to have a lot of money to give myself pleasures without worrying about others, I will be taking the wrong path. However, if I want to form a good family, marked by fecundity, so as to be an example for my future children, I am choosing an objective that will truly fulfill me as a person.

Certainly, all our actions have an end, but the most important end is the one that gives meaning to all of life, *the end of ends,* the *ultimate end.* In other words: happiness.

For this reason it is not enough to know *what* man is. It is also necessary to know what man is *for,* to know the meaning of his journey through this world.

If you were to conduct a survey on the street asking people why they do what they do, you may receive thousands of answers. But behind all of them will be only one desire: TO BE HAPPY.

What is happiness? This is the fundamental question of our existence and the personal answer each person will find with the unfolding of his own life. The answer is difficult but valuable.

Dear young people, throughout these pages we will try to offer a wide view so as to respond with full maturity and freedom. Nothing makes us as free as knowing. May the words of Eva Lavallière, the applauded actress from Paris, never be said by us: "I have gold and silver and all that one can have in this life, and I am the most unfortunate of all women." Nevertheless, she was later able to re-orient her life... In Rosario (a city in Argentina), a wealthy person once told me, "Father, I have everything and I lack everything."

Fundamentally, there are two roads in the existence of man: one that is difficult and one that is easy; one that makes us happy and another that makes us unhappy. In order to reach true happiness it is crucial to choose the appropriate path; e.g., if I walk toward Antarctica, I will not arrive at the moon.

Unfortunately, many people choose the easy road. This road is chosen by those who live this life because the air is free; or govern their lives solely by what the majority says and does without caring whether it is good or bad. They live their lives without discernment or critical thinking, blown by any wind and influenced by any fashion because they don't know why they live, where they come from or where they are going. These are the men of the "masses," who lack high ideals or desires for virtue and, consequently, find only emptiness in their lives.

Those who choose this road end up being resentful and mistreated by society. They are easily disgusted and their days are full of tedium and insipidness. **They get tired of life.** They seem to be poisoned and seek to poison others with their "depressions and pessimisms." Maybe they do not possess the physical beauty they desire or sufficient money. Perhaps they have to study harder than others do or are unable to obtain a girlfriend, a boyfriend, a job, etc. Whatever the case, everyone else is blamed, including their parents, friends, siblings, society, and, most seriously of all, God.

This path has a key characteristic we should always keep in mind: It is a path marked by deceit and lies. This is a path that makes promises, but never keeps them, that presents imaginary and fictitious things as being real. What is actually ordinary is presented as exceptional and serves to distract us from more important things. Examples of this abound in TV soap operas that toy with the sentiments of those who follow them by creating fictional anxieties, happiness, sadness and other emotions that unbalance people's affectivity. In other words, soap operas present imaginary things as real, and ridicule reality or present it as utopian. Some examples of this include the idea that purity is impossible, i.e., virginity before marriage and mutual respect in a courtship are unattainable ideals; that the current state of society precludes the possibility of solutions; that there is no other life after this one, nor is there a final judgment where we will have to account for all our actions to God... In fact, what this "easy" path offers us is a life of total disregard for God, forgetting Him and covering our ears so that we do not even hear His name and His call to us. This is a path that denies God in order to justify the errors and defects no one wants to correct.

St. Paul the Apostle says, *it is full time now for you to wake from sleep.*[4] We should not allow ourselves to be deceived or to allow the lies that circulate in our society to make us feel fed up with life. Life is beautiful and deserves to be lived. What is real is possible. It is possible to live life in its plenitude. For instance, we know that thousands of young people live purity in its fullness as true Christians, and they are not abnormal, or physically or psychologically impaired. These young people are as happy and full of life as it is possible to be. They are willing to deny themselves for the good of others, to live the great ideals and refuse to be carried away by what the majority does. There are more of them than you might think...

The path laid down for us by God is not publicized or advertized in our society and is not very popular at the present time. However, it has something that the other standard paths presented to us do not have. **This path will never deceive us and it will never leave us empty.**

Following Christ is a road that demands sacrifice and renunciation. It demands the soul of a hero and the strength of the youth. It is the path of those who, in the middle of everyday occupations, know how to raise their eyes and see the bigger and nobler things worthy enough that we should give our lives for them. Those who choose this difficult path can say "no" when the majority says "yes." Those who are on the right path do not try to escape reality or deceive themselves, but overcome obstacles like athletes full of energy. They do not cover their eyes

---

[4] *Rom* 13:11.

like ostriches before the first difficulty. They become passionate about and fall in love with great things, and live and die for great things. This path is for those who have "the soul of a prince," those who live with firm principles and carry out the demands of these principles to their ultimate consequences. It is to these youths of noble souls, pure eyes and hearts enamored with goodness and truth, that the beautiful is made visible.

If I told you that obtaining happiness comes by being good professionals, I would be lying to you: there are many famous professionals who are unhappy and miserable.

If I told you that happiness can be obtained by not injuring anyone, I would be incorrect: there are many who do not injure anyone and are still unhappy.

If I told you that you will find happiness in alcohol, drugs, and unbridled living, I would be gravely lying to you.

Youth are made for greater and nobler things. Youth are not made for pleasure, but to fight to obtain arduous and difficult things... for heroism.

2.

THE HEROIC GENERATION

"A gift is, obviously, 'for others': this is the most important dimension of the civilization of love."

Letter to Families Gratissimam Sane.
February 2, 1994.

Not all youth are martyrs, nor are they young priests in the missions, or lay Catholic militants, or seminarians.

I plan to develop this topic in four points:

I

What is meant by calling this generation insipid? We speak of insipid in the sense of tastelessness, dullness, blandness, as if to say, disgust, heaviness, displeasure. The nocturnal youth—at least nocturnal on Saturdays— according to studies of an Argentine sociologist, Mario Margulis, can be classified according to four kinds: those who attend night clubs, rock fans, those who identify themselves with *bailanta,* and the modern ones.

Margulis says that, "Each generation constructs signs of their own identity. The youth communicate among themselves, they form groups, and they display customs different from those of other times. Adults are not *native* to the nocturnal culture; we are separated by the generational gap. In order to speak with the *natives* we must make an effort to recognize their codes as legitimate. In the universal imagination, a person organizes his own party in order to free himself from dominating powers through laughter, through that which is grotesque, through masking... [On the other hand] the commercial party, which is sold to the youth, is organized by others. It is a *simulacrum*,[5] and the liberation is relative: those powers are present, notorious and oppressive."[6]

a- The night club scene: "The night club is a prototype of the simulacrum of a party, an authoritarian place, full of norms and restrictions, with racial criteria. They are places of exclusion where prestige is proportional to their capacity to discriminate."

This prototype has led to testimonies like that of a 22 year-old young man who sometimes goes to Pachá or Caix (two night clubs in Argentina). He does not feel comfortable in that atmosphere. He says: "I go with my girlfriend and in a group; going alone is anguish. The music is loud; communication, nil. It is a display case to look into and to be looked at, a hysterical, narcissistic game, where there is no contact. People attend in non-mixed groups, *each one in their own group*, like autistics. They resemble the mating rituals of animals shown in documentaries. But, in this case, it doesn't go anywhere and it ends up a pathetic spectacle."

b- The modern crowd: They identify themselves with the *new avant-garde bohemia*. It is a Buenos Aires movement that began to acquire its identity beginning with the First Biennial of Youth Art in 1988. It includes young intellectuals and artists, who organize their own network of connections: exhibitions, bars, recitals, private parties (...). "Cultural identity is a necessity for adolescents, and *tribes* are figures proper to the modern city."

c- *Bailanta* (a mix of tropical and typical music from Argentina): "It is mainly for the lower classes. Usually the clubs are located in the vicinities of rail stations. It is a social

---

[5] *Simulacrum*: a mere pretense, sham.

[6] "Notas cotidianas," *La Nación*, 14 July 1995. *La Nación* is a daily Argentine paper. Unless otherwise explicitly stated, all of the following quotes will be taken from this article. (Editorial translation).

phenomenon that embraces other practices from that neighborhood. For them, tropical music is the way to distinguish them from the upper-classes."

d- Rock: "Rock is itinerant, more democratic, popular and less selective than other genres. It is the most politicized, although its potential opponent has become a conditioned product by the media and the *star system*."

A member of a rock band says: "I do not consider myself a rocker; that is a very limited vision of life and there are other things that interest me. *Rock no longer scares anybody*, it stopped being genuine when insult, transgression, rebellion became governed by the system. It is *no longer heroic*, it does not speak about a stance on life." For these reasons he continues: "*there is insipidity among youth;* and today, more than ever, being seventeen years old is not easy." *It is the insipid generation*, disgusted with everything or almost everything.

II

The depressed generation. In New Milford, Connecticut, a situation occurred that was similar to what happened in Villa Gobernador Gálvez, south of Rosario, Argentina. In a lapse of five days, as attested by the authorities, eight girls were taken to the hospital of New Milford due to suicidal attempts.

Some of the girls' testimonies included statements like: "*I was simply fed up with everything, and also with life.*" This girl was only 12 or 13 years old...!

More seriously, according to a local journalist, "several of the girls maintained that they formed part of a suicidal pact."

Many adolescents had the phrases "Life is disgusting" or "Long-live death" written on their arms. The majority of these girls "go to therapy sessions and list off brands of anti-depressants like they can list brands of shampoo. A 14 year-old redhead said she took Zoloft for her depression, Ritalin to pay better attention—that is to say to be a little more attentive—and Trazadone in order to sleep."

23

"Her 15 year-old friend commented that: 'All the girls I know have been to 6 West (the psychiatric ward for adolescents at Danbury Hospital). We don't belong to the generation X, *we are the depressed generation.*"

"About her three friends who tried to commit suicide, Emily mentioned that one had family problems, the other was 'upset that day' and the third 'was just against everything that was happening.'

"A doctor said: "What is happening in New Milford is not a unique case. We have seen it happen in Argentina as well. This culture of desperation can be found anywhere. But, among adolescents the tendency to suicide can become a 'contagious virus.'"

It is not the entire generation; but there are large numbers of youth who are on the brink of, or who have fallen into depression and we know that we cannot sit on our hands, because these things happen and we must, as far as we are able, look for a solution.

III

The so-called *"lost generation."* This is the desperate generation. "Desperate, because they calm their anxiety by violence: 2000 aggressive attacks and killings in 1994 in Los Angeles." That is five violent acts per day. What reasons or events provoked them?

"In the most deprived district in Chicago, thanks to drug-trafficking, a 15 year-old adolescent can have a brand new car of his own. Joseph, a 13 year-old, says: 'Why should I work, when by selling dope in ten seconds I make three times the salary of a doctor?' He says this in a hole of the stairwell of low-income housing, surrounded by needles. The same kid says: 'At 6, we have fun whistling at police cars. At 9, we want to prove to the older ones that we can smoke like them, and can run and catch a handbag in the air—that is to say, mug people. At 12, we want weapons to defend ourselves.'"

This does not only happen with those who are marginalized. Evidently there are cases where this epidemic of irrational violence reaches youth belonging to well-formed families. "Eric Smith, eleven-and-a-half-years-old, lived with his family in a rich neighborhood of New York State. Last summer, for reasons unknown, he strangled his four-and-a-half-year-old neighbor, Derrick. In the televised trial, he clearly stated that he did not regret anything."

In Louisiana's high security prison, Mark, a 16-year-old, declares that he finally understood that what he was doing was wrong. "He explains that he no longer wants to have an 'easy' life. At eleven years of age, a drug dealer gave him his first revolver 'to deliver to clients.' Before being arrested for murder, he admitted he had shot at dozens of people. Now it seems that he converted because he said: 'But now it is over.'

In northern California, where 250,000 adolescents were imprisoned in 1994, a law prohibits teenagers from forming groups with more than two people or wearing a cap backwards because this indicates that they belong to a gang.

"In a culture where weapons symbolize power, psychiatrists agree that 'kids want to resemble the heroes on TV,' whom they see committing an average of 8,000 crimes and 100,000 acts of violence before they reach the age of ten. Every week this culture of violence produces a new martyr, like Twelve-year-old David Kareen, one of the best students in a school in the Bronx. He pursued an engineering career. After leaving school, one of his schoolmates approached him and asked him to hand over his leather jacket. He refused and they argued and quarreled. Kareen received a knife wound and died on the patio of his house. The murderer, a twelve-and-a-half-year-old, later explained that he dreamed of having a jacket like that one.

A manager of a funeral home says: "This week is my third funeral involving youth killed by youth." She appeared to be "resigned to see these coffins with youth inside." Two months later, the day the trial began, the boy who killed David Kareen said: "I really wanted that leather jacket. Life... *what does it matter in today's world?*"[7]

IV

The Heroic Generation. Faced with the *pseudo* morale of the defeated, the mediocre, the losers, and the failures... we, **the heroic generation,** must **oppose** them with strength and courage, following the example of the Blessed Martyrs of Barbastro.[8]

Today, half-hearted efforts are not enough. It is not enough to give aspirins to a patient with cancer that has spread all over his body.

Today, the only thing that can provide a solution to such aberrations is **the young generation of heroism.**

We must raise the noble standard of Christian ideals. The incisive mandate of our Lord must again resonate in the hearts of the youth: *Be perfect, as your heavenly Father is perfect.*[9] If Jesus said it, it is because perfection and sanctity are possible.

We must transmit all the great ideals we have by the grace of God in a convincing manner with strength and courage, (not like false saints, who pretend to be righteous).

We must demonstrate what Paul Claudel said so beautifully: *"Youth has not been made for pleasure, but for heroism."*

We must be convinced that we are *all* called to heroism in the position where God has placed us: whether as priests, religious, wives, husbands, lay consecrated or not consecrated, but always committed to apostolic labors. Heroism is not only lived in the maximum degree, as in the case of the Martyrs of Barbastro; it is

---

[7] "Notas cotidianas," *La Nación,* 13 July, 1995: 9.

[8] Group of seminarians and priests from Barbastro who gave their lives in the Spanish Civil War for fidelity to Jesus Christ.

[9] *Mt* 5:48.

also lived in the everyday heroism of the disposition of the soul to give life and not compromise faith. Our martyrs were killed because they refused to stop wearing the cassock; not just because of the material aspect, but because, in those circumstances, taking off the cassock meant an apostasy of faith.

We must also be prepared to give our lives rather than to renounce or cast doubt on our faith. But to do this we must possess the virtues to a heroic degree. It is not enough to be good more or less (more or less good ends up being bad, and later on, ends up being perverse).

We must live the virtues to a heroic degree. What does "to a heroic degree" mean? Four conditions required to achieve these heroic virtues are:

1. The matter—the object of the virtue—has to be arduous or difficult, beyond the ordinary strength of man;

2. Its actions must be prompt and easily accomplished;

3. It must be accomplished joyfully as a conscious offering of sacrifice to the Lord. Youth must strive to live purity in this civilization. To live purity is mandated by the commandments of the law of God but, in the present age, it is something so arduous and difficult that it entails an offering, a sacrifice to the Lord.

4. It must be accomplished with a certain frequency, whenever the occasion presents itself.

We will be called crazy as Christ was crazy before us!

Some will say that it is too exigent... Christ was asked to come down from the cross but He did not!

They will shout that it is impossible... Christ tells us: "Do not be afraid," with my grace *nothing is impossible!* Let us look to our brothers, the Martyrs of Barbastro!

3.
THE IDEAL

*"Men should understand that with adherence to Christ,
not only have they nothing to lose,
but they have everything to gain,
since with Christ man becomes more man."*

Homily in Rome, March 15, 1981. [10]

One of the characteristics of the present time in which we live is the general loss of ideals. Nowadays, many live a dragging, boring, unfulfilling life, without knowing why their lives have no savor.

What is an ideal? It is something that is *great, superior, worthy and valuable.*

1. An ideal is something ***great*** that is capable of filling a life. It is never a small, selfish, trivial pastime or *hobby*. It is something worthwhile, great in quality (not in quantity). The formation of an authentic Christian family, where the love of Christ reigns, and the spouses are mutually faithful, generous in transmitting life, while educating their children according to the school of Christ, is an ideal because it is great and worthwhile.

In August of 1995, journalist Graciela Römer,[11] asked 1,165 university students between 18 and 25 years of age, about their commitments regarding marriage with the following results:

– 10% plan to live together and then get married;

---

[10] *The Teachings of Pope John Paul II,* computer software, Harmony Media Inc., 1998, Multimedia Viewer, version 2.00, Windows, 3.1x or 95, CD-ROM.

[11] Cf. AGUSTINA LANUSE, *La Nación,* August 1995: 16.

– 17% plan on getting married right away;

– 33% plan to live together and not get married (to cohabitate);

– 40% responded as having no plans yet.

It is frightening to see only 17% want to get married. And the statistic would be graver if they were asked whether they planned on getting married in the Church, as God commands.

The increase of cohabitation and divorce reveals the fear youth have of commitment. Cohabitation has increased because youth see the spread of divorce. In the United States of America, two out of three couples divorce. However, by the evidence gathered, cohabitation does not prevent the rupture of a future marriage.

2. An ideal must be something **superior, excellent, and sublime,** and would include forming an authentic Christian family; being a good man or woman; a worthy professional, a businessman who employs many, or an honest worker. An ideal is evolving towards perfection (it is not an ideal for a man to be lazy or foolish, a thief or a vandal). For this reason, our Lord teaches: **Be perfect just as your heavenly Father is perfect,**[12] which is to say, **be a saint.** As Leon Bloy would say, "there is only one error in life: not to be saints." There is no ideal more excellent than to desire to be a saint, an imitator of Jesus Christ.

3. Striving toward an ideal **dignifies** the human being. It is a **prototype, model or exemplar of perfection** towards which all the strength of our soul must tend, without letting itself be diminished or be frightened by the difficulties that will certainly appear. Truth, goodness and virtue are the hallmarks of an ideal. To be a drug addict, an alcoholic, impure or a terrorist is not an ideal—it is to follow the "ideals" of the devil. The authentic ideals serve others and give joy, happiness, profound convictions, and

---

[12] *Mt* 5:48.

security. They are for the edification of all and are harmful to no one.

4. Ideals are extremely **valuable**. The best definition I know is: "The ideal is that for which we live and that for which we are ready to die if it were necessary." One only lives or is willing to die for something **valuable**.

And, who unites in himself these characteristics of being *great, superior, worthy and valuable?* Who unites them better than Jesus Christ?

Jesus Christ is the summit of the highest and most sublime ideals that have ever been imagined by humanity, even when adding all the healthy ideals of all men from all time. He infinitely exceeds them.

Jesus is the great and insurmountable ideal towards whom we must tend with all our strength if we do not want to waste our time and err in the path of life and eternity. We must work for Christ to reign in our intellect by truth, in our will by goodness, in our sensibility by beauty, and in our nature by grace. He must reign in us individually, and in our families, schools, labor unions, universities and hospitals; across all political, economic and social spectrums, on national and international levels. Ninety percent of youth polled do not participate in politics, and this is not good for a nation. Lack of participation by youth can be explained by the corruption in politicians: 78% of youth reject corruption and 38% are not interested in politics because of rampant corruption in politics. The great endeavor is to form virtuous leaders, lay leaders, good men and women to take responsibility in the public arena. If we fail to do this, we pave the way for ongoing corruption, allowing delinquents to triumph. Youth must become passionate about great things and great causes and free themselves from the juvenile anesthesia provoked by the poor examples of their elders. *"The blood of the youth has become cold."* Unfortunately, this may be true in many cases. Nevertheless, there are youth of clear purpose and ardent hearts who consecrate themselves to Jesus Christ and follow His commandments in virginity and the sacredness of marriage.

With all the strength of my voice and my wish to reach youth worldwide, I invite all youth to realize that there is no greater ideal than Jesus Christ who never fails and does not allow Himself to be outdone in generosity by anyone.

4.
FREE LIKE THE WIND...
SLAVES, NEVER

"Man of our time!
Only the resurrected Christ can totally satiate
your irreplaceable thirst for freedom (...)
Forever!"

Easter Message, April 15, 1991.[13]

Chesterton says that windows are fascinating. He is right in that—windows always have an air of mystery, they send us towards something beyond, something the wall prevents us from seeing.

I like windows very much because I get so much pleasure looking through them and want to enlarge them in order to see more. The joy my windows produce, along with the curiosity they generate, could cause me to desire that my house be all window. To live in a window is like living in something infinite, without limits or borders, without coercion or restriction, without frames or measures.

Without frames? Would it be possible to have windows without frames?

If I wanted my house to be all window, I would find that I would no longer have a house; much less a window.

---

13 Editorial translation.

✠   ✠   ✠

Freedom is like a window. Through it, we can breathe the fresh air of life, and, living in freedom, our life becomes plentiful and reaches unsuspected dimensions.

Frames are essential in order to have windows. They are also essential for freedom.

For this reason, dear friends, love freedom; love the frames.

Sacred Scripture says: *Before a man are life and death...whichever he chooses will be given to him.*[14] When a youth decides to look at the reality of life and then turns his back to God, everything changes. The transparent becomes clouded, the certain becomes confusing, and the day becomes night.

Youth carry within them an enormous potential for energy, which can make them rebellious. This rebelliousness is a very good thing.

"To be at odds with oneself, to feel the necessity to destroy, to build, to fight, is one of our greatest moral and human treasures...resigning oneself to be satisfied with everything as it is, is no more nor less than to be buried alive."[15]

Youth cannot be conformist; they must be rebellious. This rebelliousness is, at heart, the same as that original impulse called freedom, but it must be well-directed. It is necessary to rebel against evil, but not against the good, and a framework is needed. Without a framework, rebelliousness is anarchy and has nothing to do with freedom. Without a framework, rebelliousness is licentiousness.

Licentiousness is a false freedom. True freedom is what compels man to the responsible attainment of good which is based on the truth: in other words, if the goods are not real, the values that regulate freedom are false.

---

14 *Sir* 15:17.
15 JOHN PAUL II, *Cruzando el umbral de la esperanza.* (Editorial translation).

Licentiousness is the slavery that makes man a slave of his passions, submitting his will to what is low, despicable and inferior. It is like a drug for the soul, under the pretext of a "hallucinating" freedom, binding the spirit in darkness and blinding it to the limits or frames that would inform it.

It is very easy to be deceived. In fact, all humans have the tendency to evil, a vicious consequence of original sin. Today, there are many who deceive themselves, just living and letting time pass, without values, and without knowing what to aim for.

It is painful to see that so many, who are ready to attack, and destroy evil and sin, fall under the deception of licentiousness and stumble powerless into the humiliating slavery of a life without depth. There are many who give in to alcohol and drugs that present a way for them to escape their problems and demonstrate their freedom from "frames" without a fight. Youth who are not motivated to heroically fight the battle for purity and do not know how to respect their own bodies, believe that irrational violence is the best way to show strength of will. They spend hours before that electronic babysitter that is television or uselessly risk their lives pretending to reach velocities never before reached in their cars. They are not motivated to defend truth until death and they search for the answers in magic, sects, and sometimes in the demonic; all forms of escape.

On October 1, 1979, John Paul II said to the American youth, faced with the great problems of the present...

"many people will try to escape from their responsibility:
escape in egoism:
escape in selfishness,
escape in sexual pleasure,
escape in drugs,
escape in violence,
escape in indifference,
and cynical attitudes.

"But today, I propose to you the option of love, which is the opposite of escape. If you really accept that love from Christ, it will lead you to God. Whatever you make of your life, let it be something that reflects the love of Christ."[16]

The consequences of a life not lived in freedom are disastrous. We summarize them in just one expression from Pope John Paul II: *the culture of death.* Concrete examples abound: abortion, euthanasia, AIDS, resentment, loneliness, and suicide. This is what we will continue to present in the following chapters.

A great romantic poet said:

"Two roads diverged in a wood, and
I took the one less traveled by,
And that has made all the difference."

Would you be capable of living your life in freedom even if it means you would have to take a risk? Jesus Christ once said that the Spirit is like the wind: you can feel it, but you do not know where it comes from or where it goes.[17] The same can be said of every youth who truly lives in freedom.

The great rebels of their times were the saints. They were rebels against what the world wanted, in order to be faithful to God. Jesus Christ is freedom: *Now the Lord is the Spirit, and where the spirit of the Lord is, there is freedom.*[18]

Either you decide to be a pilgrim of the Absolute, or you become a pilgrim of nothing. It is a matter of motivating oneself to choose the road less traveled.

---

[16] Speech to youth in Madison Square Garden, USA. (Editorial translation).
[17] Cf. *Jn* 3:8.
[18] *2 Cor* 3:17.

CHAPTER 2

Addictions: "The Opposite Meaning of Life"

"His own people did not accept Him" (Jn 1, 11)

"Sometimes it is heard: I have tried everything and nothing fulfills me.

Be alert, that is not true. You have not tried everything. You need to go to the source that can quench your thirst: If anyone thirst, let him come to me and drink, Jesus said. All who have tried know what truth is."

Speech in Lima, Perú, June 5, 1988.[19]

---

[19] Editorial translation.

1.
SLAVES OF ALCOHOL?

"The human being does not have the right to harm himself,
nor must he ever abdicate the human dignity
that has been given him by God."

Speech to the Conference on
Drug Addiction and Alcoholism,
November 23, 1991.[20]

Alcohol is one of the greatest dangers threatening youth and society today. It causes grave evils and misfortunes for the person and his friends and family. Other addictions, such as drugs or irrational violence that may arise with it, increase the risk of alcoholism rather than diminish it. Today, alcoholism goes hand in hand with drugs and violence.

Alcoholism is defined as a chronic sickness or a behavioral disorder, characterized by the repeated ingestion of alcoholic beverages in an amount that exceeds the norm. Alcoholism eventually harms the health of the individual and alters the order of the family and of society.

Alcohol is a toxic substance called "ethyl alcohol" or "ethanol." Paradoxically, ethyl alcohol is a powerful depressant of the central nervous system. The euphoria that it unleashes in acute intoxication is explained by this active mechanism: what it actually does is inhibit the moral restraints of the subject. In high doses, it acts as a narcotic, producing a lack of muscular coordination, delirium and coma.

---

[20] Editorial translation.

There are several stages that lead to alcoholism. The first stage is occasional acute alcoholic intoxication or common "drunkenness." An occasional drinker, every so often and in differing circumstances can become a habitual drinker. The second stage develops when the consumption of alcohol is transformed into a habit. From here one moves, almost inevitably, to the third stage, which is properly called "alcoholism." In this last stage, the subject is incapable of restraining himself once he has started (loss of control). If he stops drinking for a couple of hours, symptoms of withdrawal appear, similar to what happens in drug addiction.

The indiscriminate consumption of alcohol produces very harmful effects ranging from alcoholic psychosis or delirium, serious problems with heart and liver, disruptions to the central and peripheral nervous system, amnesia, loss of concentration, and psychological dependency in which the individual thinks that he cannot be without alcoholic beverages.

The tragedy of alcoholism is not foreign to any cultural class. It encompasses all socio-cultural classes and is present more often among teenagers and adults (20% of the population older than fifteen years old), followed by adolescents, women and children. In Argentina, there are approximately one million alcoholics. Due to the repercussions of alcoholism in families and society, the number of directly or indirectly harmed people increases to approximately four million.

Some of the causes that lead a person to alcoholism conform to diverse inclinations:

– *Personal causes:* Lack of confidence in solving everyday problems, loss of the meaning of life, different failures and weak and submissive personality; some people drink just because others do it.

– *Family:* Serious family conflicts, family separation and dissolution of marriages.

– *Social causes:* Partaking in tasks that require the manipulation of alcoholic beverages, cold or warm places with a lot of alcohol consumption, parties, failures in social or work settings.

More particular causes exist among the youth. Their inclination to drink sometimes stems, with dreadful consequences, from new trends or from the environment in which they find themselves. Recall, for example, the competitions involving tequila consumption held a while ago in some of the night clubs in Buenos Aires, that ended in the deaths of several youth. The need to be considered "cool" or "larger than life" is behind the desire to drink excessively in many cases. Many begin "following the example" of some older "friends" and they end up hooked on it…

Idleness and the failure to know great ideals contribute to dependence on alcohol. Not being employed or studying can lead to drinking. Without a firm "north," or a working compass, the youth is left with what is proposed by those who are incapable of aspiring to great things and expanding the horizons of their hearts.

Slavery, frustration and unhappiness are the consequences of being unable to value what matters. For a young alcoholic, reality without alcohol is insupportable. This is a path to nothing.

The attitudes of contempt and reproach, indifference and isolation are not helpful to alcoholics. They lead the alcoholic to feel misunderstood and humiliated and accentuate his tendency to escapism. It is very important to consider the multiple aspects that directly or indirectly affect the beginning of alcoholism: family, society, work, etc. It has been proven that, with the help of doctors, social workers, priests and rehabilitated alcoholics, 90% of alcoholics recover.

Another effective method is to help them see their condition as a sickness that requires the help of a doctor. When an individual first begins on the path of alcoholism, he hides his disease and conceals his symptoms from the doctor. However, if the problem is averted in its initial stages, it is easier to cure.

If the alcoholic has entered the stage of dependency, social, medical and spiritual assistance, support and understanding of relatives, friends and partners will be crucial. It is necessary to make the person aware of his sickness in order to be able to initiate treatment. If the patient does not voluntarily collaborate and recognize his sickness, recuperation is impossible.

The key point of all treatment is to help the sick person realize that he can face his problems without having recourse to alcohol and that it is one of the worst traveling companions he could have chosen because it does not liberate but enslave. Alcohol is another one of the sad courtiers of death.

Those who suffer from this disease must learn to see how beautiful life is. It deserves to be lived. We were not born to be slaves, but to be lords. We must always remember the words of Mother Teresa of Calcutta, a completely free woman, who consecrated her life to God for the good of others:

What is...?

—the most beautiful day? Today.

—the easiest thing? To make a mistake.

—the biggest obstacle? Fear.

—the biggest error? To abandon oneself.

—the root of all evils? Egoism.

—the most beautiful distraction? Work.

—the worst defeat? Discouragement.

—the best teachers? Children.

—the first necessity? To communicate.

—what makes you most happy? To be useful to others.

—the biggest mystery? Death.

—the worst defect? Irritability.

—the most dangerous person? One who lies.

–the most malicious feeling? Resentment.

–the most beautiful gift? Forgiveness.

–the most essential thing? Home.

–the fastest way? The correct path.

–the most pleasing sensation? Interior peace.

–the most effective defense? The smile.

–the best remedy? Optimism.

–the greatest satisfaction? The fulfilled duty.

–the most powerful force in the world? Faith.

–the most necessary people? Parents.

–the most beautiful thing of all? LOVE!

"That's it: love! In the name of Christ, the Church proposes an alternative answer for drug addicts, victims of alcoholism, families and communities suffering because of the weakness of its members: *the therapy of love*. God is love and whoever lives in love, lives in communion with others and God. *He who does not love remains in death.*[21] Whoever loves savors life and remains in it!"[22]

---

[21] *1Jn* 3:14.

[22] *Speech to the Conference on Drug Addiction and Alcoholism*, 11-23-1991. (Editorial translation).

2.
A "HALLUCINATING TRIP"?

*"To take drugs is always illicit because it is an unjustified
and irrational renunciation
of thinking, willing, and acting as free persons."*

Speech to the Conference on
Drug Addiction and Alcoholism,
November 23, 1991.[23]

Clearly, drug addiction is one of the most serious problems of
the world today. This is not only because of the great extent of
this phenomenon and because it is found, in fact, among the
younger sections of society, but because of what it implies, entails
and proclaims.

The phenomenon of drug addiction demonstrates the misery
of those who do not know where to find the peace they are
seeking and need. Because drugs are incapable of delivering the
much yearned for peace, the result is a truly shattering interior
emptiness that consumes the life of the one who walks that path.
It is a path to nothingness. Consequently, the phenomenon of
widespread drug abuse illustrates that our world is not on the
right path, because the values it proposes and the criteria of
action that it teaches do not provide people with the necessary
answers life presents.

Before considering the causes and consequences of this
terrible slavery, we would like to present, at least briefly and in

---

[23] Editorial translation.

broad strokes, some technical concepts that will guide us in our discussion.

What do we mean by drugs? Strictly speaking, they are defined as any chemical substance that produces harmful or beneficial effects in the organism. However, because of their widespread use, drugs in general have become synonymous with drugs that produce addiction, which we will define next.

What is drug addiction? It is a state of chronic intoxication generated by drugs that produce "withdrawal symptoms" because of physical and psychological dependence that the drug itself causes. The habit, which often in colloquial language is called a "vice," does not imply a physical dependence, but addiction does. This means that what at first might have been a habit or a custom, little by little reaches such a magnitude and intensity that the body itself demands the adequate dosage, which will always be increasing.

There are various types of drugs. Generally, they are classified in three fundamental groups: psycho-stimulants (such as amphetamines or antidepressants), psycho-depressants (such as hypnotics—barbiturates or not—inhalants, tranquilizers), and psycho-dyslexics (hallucinogens, like LSD, "ecstasy," etc.). Out of these drugs, opium, as well as morphine, heroin, marijuana, cocaine, crack, LSD, and inhalants, are all capable of producing addiction.

Drugs produce a psychological dependence first and then a physical one. The one causes the other through an interior coherence, by the logic of the phenomenon of drug addiction. The first stage begins with a feeling of satisfaction or a psychological impulse that becomes more urgent over time, demanding the regular or continuous administration of the drug in order to produce pleasure or to avoid discomfort. In the beginning, the drug user often thinks that he controls the dosage, does it freely and knows exactly where the limit is. In the beginning this is true. However, there comes an imperceptible moment in which he finds that he cannot stop using drugs. This is the moment in which, by wanting to cross all barriers to reach pleasures and hallucinations ever more stimulating or satisfying, the person finds that the drug has destroyed the equilibrium of his nervous system and has created a dependence on it. He needs it to live. This point in time marks the passage to the second stage of dependence mentioned earlier, the physical dependence.

Physical dependence is confirmed by the appearance of intense physical imbalances called "withdrawal syndrome," when the administration of the drug is interrupted. Withdrawal syndrome is generated by the phenomenon of tolerance, a progressive adaptation of the organism to the drug, resulting in the need to constantly increase the dosage in order to continue to experience the strong reactions that were present with the initial dosages. This is precisely why there are many cases of deaths due to overdose.

The fundamental characteristics of the drug addict are: "tolerance" and "withdrawal syndrome," but, there are other characteristics that permit us to delineate, generally, the psychological profile of the drug addict.

Under the appearance of rebellion, strength and freedom, there hides a submissive, weak and enslaved personality. Generally, a young drug addict is a person who does not have the courage to take on adverse situations; i.e., since he cannot change the world, he wants to change his perception of the world by generating "parallel universes" and "alternative worlds."

For this reason, the psychology of the drug addict is intimately united with the phenomenon of evasion and escape from a reality that causes him anguish, by generating an illusion of omnipotence.

The drug addict lives in a DELIRIOUS state, which from the psychiatric point of view, has various characteristics:

* 1. It cannot be reversed by appeals to experience;

* 2. It cannot be reversed by the logic of real thought;

* 3. It lacks consciousness of the sickness;

* 4. Drugs become an ideology of life.

For example, a musician can develop his talent by means of study and practice. However, he believes that if he drugs himself, he will do things better. Immersed in a delirious psychotic state, neither the example of experience, that is to say evidence, nor real logic is of use to him. It is impossible for him to comprehend reality.

Every addict is, as previously stated, a potential suicide due to the enormous capacity for self-destruction he possesses. In addition, the addict is often a potential criminal (the crimes committed by CRACK consumers are characterized by violence). One of the most notable effects of drugs at a social level is the increase in the crime rate. According to police statistics, drug addicts are perpetrators of the most violent assaults and crimes. Among other factors, this can be explained by the price of drugs: in the USA, for example, a heroin addict needs $500 to $1000 to buy drugs; with few exceptions, this money can only be obtained by theft or murder. Sometimes a lower price for drugs in certain places is due to a kind of "promotion"; it is sold for less to initiate and create more addicts.

The consequences of drug addiction are horrifying and play a leading role in what Pope John Paul II called "the culture of death." One who drugs himself does not cultivate life; he cultivates death, not only for himself, but for others. A potential suicidal addict may not only destroy himself, but also the people he loves most. A seminarian once told me that while he was on mission a young man about thirty years old called him. It had been ten years since drugs had begun to consume his life and he asked the seminarian to please help him to get out of that slavery. At one moment, with tears in his eyes, he said: "I am killing my mother; I am killing my two little girls."

If drug addiction has such serious consequences, why has it spread? What are the causes of this plague afflicting our times?

Parts of the answer have been outlined above:

-a weak personality that is easily influenced by others while pretending to be part of a deceitful and false rebellion;

- the search for freedom at the margin of truth and reality;

-the incapacity to solve different problems and the inability to find meaning in life;

-the desire to imitate current models and heroes of our times who have walked and continue to walk the same path (many rock stars!);

-being in environments and company where handling drugs is common;

-using the false excuse: "I'm an adult, I know how to take care of myself, I know very well what I'm doing."

What is not realized is that the majority of those who consume drugs in these environments use the same arguments. Additional causes of drug addiction are: the desire for success, attention, to come out on top, to be considered worldly or experienced and curiosity to experience something different.

The reactions of those who could help the drug addict can, sometimes, make the tendency and impulse to evade treatment stronger. Rejection from loved ones can cause a young person to lock himself up in his own world, created by him and by the drugs he uses. Oftentimes a false understanding (permission to continue on that path) sharpens the crisis. An example of false understanding is Letten train station in Switzerland, where the government financed a refuge for drug addicts where they can go to inject themselves however and whenever they want. The police arrest the distributors only. The place is still in operation. According to European philosophers, this is licit because it deals with "the inalienable right to exercise individual freedom." Our opinion is that of an Argentinean psychiatrist who visited the place: "...the Swiss solution is the greatest example of human imbecility."

The same rejection that sometimes comes from loved ones also comes from society. Marginalization, indifference, and incomprehension are attitudes that are often seen to incite drug addiction.

We have intentionally spoken of the "incitement" of drug addiction. A society whose system of values is dominated by the erotic, and promotes the primacy of technology over ethics and well- being over life, fails to understand man and his meaning in the world. A culture that promotes the value of "feeling good" where standard phrases such as "if he likes it," "if he feels it," "it's his life" are used, incites drug addiction by fostering these anti-values. All subsequent campaigns against drug addiction are band-aids that may alleviate pain, but will never be a real cure.

Treatment to cure a drug addict must be directed toward the family of the drug addict as much as to the drug addict himself and not solely focused on the medical or socio-medical aspects. Effective treatment must encompass all aspects of the drug addict as a person, including root causes at the familial and individual levels. Exploring these underlying issues will help him to confront himself and his problems. In addition to detoxification and reintegration into society and the labor force, his spiritual dimension must be given primary attention because it is a key element in the recovery process. If God does not occupy His proper place in a life, all the other elements will be deranged. It is statistically proven that when people have recourse to human means only (pharmacological treatment, group therapies, etc.), the percentage of recovery is very low, less than 30%, and the percentage of relapse is very high.

John Paul II said:

The behavior (of the drug addicts) is morally unacceptable, but they must be considered **victims and sick people** before being considered criminals. This phenomenon is caused by a climate of human and religious skepticism, hedonism, which in the end leads to frustration, to existential emptiness, to the conviction of the insignificance of life itself, degradation, and violence. Sometimes, the instability of the family is a cause of drug addiction, but not always. Many families who have tried to educate their children in the best way are innocent victims of this painful phenomenon. The State must embody a serious policy that seeks to solve difficulties on personal, familiar and social levels, to implement education on the value of life and health.

We need formation to be able to use freedom positively and to respect persons, allowing for the introduction of the ideals of family, sincere love, brotherly charity and work. Behavior in opposition to the common good, that threatens one's own health, disturbing the mental balance with terrible consequences for self and others, cannot be morally accepted.

I would like to finish this chapter by offering you the testimony of a young drug addict:

"I am sorry, dad, I think this is the last conversation I will have with you.

"I am really sorry.

"You know... it's time for you to know the truth that you never suspected.

"I will be brief and clear:

"DRUGS HAVE KILLED ME, MY DEAR FATHER!

"I met my murderer when I was fifteen years old. It is horrible. Isn't it, dad?

"Do you know how we met?

"Through a very elegantly dressed man, really very refined and well-spoken, that introduced me to my future murderer: «DRUGS».

"I tried over and over to refuse it, but this man won me over by saying that I was not a man.

"There is no need to say anything else, is there...?

"I entered the world of the drug addict. At the beginning was giddiness, then came dizziness and soon after darkness. I did not do anything without drugs being present. Later came the lack of air, fear, hallucinations; then euphoria again.

"You know dad... when I started I found everything ridiculous, just fun and meaningless, I even thought God rather ridiculous. Today, in this hospital I recognize that God is the most important being in the world. I know that without His help I would not be writing what I am writing.

"Dad, you have to believe me, the life of a drug addict is terrible; one feels torn up on the inside. It is horrible and everyone young should know it so they do not fall into it.

"I can't take three steps anymore without getting tired. The doctors say that I am going to be cured, but when they leave the room, they shake their heads.

"Dad... I am only nineteen years old and I know that I do not have any chance to live; it is too late for me. My dear father, I have a last request to ask you: tell all the youth you know about my situation and show them this letter.

"Tell them that behind every school door, in each classroom, in every hallway, any place at all, there is always a well-dressed man, well-spoken, who wants to show them their future murderer, the destroyer of their lives, which will lead them to insanity and death, like it lead me.

"Please, do this, dad, before it is too late for them.

"Forgive me, father...

"I have suffered a lot...

"Forgive me for making you suffer because of my stupidity.

"Goodbye my beloved father!"

After this letter, the youth passed away on May 23, 1995 in Sao Paulo, Brazil.

3.
INVERSION IN DANCE

*"Respect your body (...) It belongs to you because God has
given it to you. It was not given to you as an object that you can use
and abuse. It is part of your person, an expression of yourself, a
language to enter in communication with others in a dialogue of
truth, respect and love. With your bodies you can express the most
secret part of your soul, the most personal meaning of your life:
Your freedom, your vocation.
Glorify God in your body (1Cor 6:20)."*

*Rome, Italy, (O.R.),
June 22, 1984.[24]*

Whether we like it or not, we live in an order immersed in the
supernatural. If it is not the supernatural *of God*, it will be the
supernatural *of the devil*, who always looks to subvert the work of
God: God creates being, the devil wants "the annihilation of
being."[25] The devil wants to invert the transcendentals of being.
For example, rather than radiating the *beauty* of things which are a
reflection of the infinite Beauty, which is God, the devil seeks
things that radiate *ugliness*.

This statement is not a mere intellectual digression, a topic for
books, but a reality that includes the totality of being and doing,
from theology to politics. It is found in all manifestations of
culture and art, including paintings, music, culture, movies, TV,
theater and literature.

---

[24] Editorial translation.
[25] ALBERTO CATURELLI, *La Iglesia y las catacumbas de hoy*, (ed. Al-Almena:
Buenos Aires, 1974), 94.

We will exemplify this inversion with one of the manifestations of man: modern dance taken from a *formal aspect* and not from a moral point of view.

Our grandparents danced the waltz, the minuet, the two-step; and if we compare these forms to classical or folkloric dance to contemporary dances such as heavy metal, or other progressive styles, we see a very significant degradation and an extremely marked inversion. (The same comparison could be made by looking at the folkloric dances in many cultures compared to their modern dances).

Dancing used to be an art that reflected man's nobility. The frenzied, convulsive movements, spasms and contortions now seen on the dance floor show the most coarse uncouthness and vulgar animalism. In some dances where the spirit reigns over the body, the movements are full of grace and charm; in others where it is all about the "movements of the body," savagery, roughness, and agitation take control.

The ability of the dancer used to consist in moving in a rhythmic form; modern forms of dance, on the other hand, often consist in the initial movements of the sexual act (for example, John Travolta), or the dancers are almost immobile, as if they were wearing scuba diving flippers on their feet instead of shoes.

Formerly, the man *invited* the woman to dance, but now they bump and grind in a series of animalistic sexually-driven acts. Dancing used to take a man out of himself to a state of *ecstasy,* transporting the soul towards something superior (for example, Zorba, the Greek). Now it is predominately the sense of touch that acts, extending throughout the body and remaining "especially to be corrupted and infected"[26] in the fierce search of *entasis*, in which the ego is turning back into oneself, lowering the soul and trapping it in the enthusiasm of its own self-worshiping affirmation. The soul is debased. A substantial part of dancing

---

[26] SAINT THOMAS AQUINAS, *Summa Theologica* I-II, 83, 4 (Christian Classics: Allen Texas, 1948).

used to consist in dialogue, but now, talking while dancing is impossible. The noise is too great, the dancers are too far apart (or too close together), and they are focused on themselves. The only contact is on a physical level. For some, dancing was something stylized, but for others, it is animalistic.

In the past, people danced with their hands raised, as if addressing God, their feet barely touching the ground, and their faces reflecting the happiness of the soul. Now, people's hands are not raised to God and their feet, in slow dances, are tied down to the floor as if by a powerful magnet. Instead of looking at each other, they are immersed in themselves. In past times, the whole community participated in the joy of the dancers. In present times, there is only a formless mass of dancers engaged in the most egotistical individualism.

When people used to dress up to go dancing, the atmosphere was chivalrous, but today's dancing venues are populated with people who dress with indecent and vulgar negligence and their souls reflected in their appearance.

In this brief comparison, the deformed nature of dance on the popular and youthful level is made clear. The fingerprints of the devil are seen in these examples because we know that harmony order, beauty and symmetry, reflections of the perfections of God, are anathema to him. The devil's hatred towards God is so great that he even tries to erase that which is in man as *image and likeness* of God.[27]

Modern music which renders cult to what is cacophonous, ugly, unpleasant, and chaotic is another deformity. It is often used as "a tool for social and political change,"[28] and "produces nervous tension, irritability, impotence and aggressiveness."[29] It also causes "intestinal spasms... aggression and neurosis."[30] It

---

[27] Cf. *Gen* 1:26.
[28] T. W. ADORNO. (Editorial translation).
[29] *Medical Tribune*. (Editorial translation).
[30] Medical magazine "*Selecta*." (Editorial translation).

causes progressive deafness due to the high volume at which it is listened to. Modern music also transmits "to those initiated in the vocabulary of hippies, incitements to drug consumption, sexual promiscuity and rebellion."[31] By adding the example of the deformity of modern music, we will have a more adequate notion of the inversion in dance, one aspect of the annihilation of being.

When our youth know how to defend themselves from those who want to commercialize their happiness, better days will come for our Country and the Church.

---

[31] Cf. ALBERTO BOIXADÓS, *Arte and subersión*, (Ed. Areté: Buenos Aires, 1977). (Editorial translation).

4.
SEX WITHOUT RESPONSIBILITY

*"Man's system of values has suffered many changes at losing
its relationship with definitive value, which is God (...)
The longing for happiness thus becomes a longing for pleasures,
ever easier and more fleeting.
At the end of this road, instead of the hoped for fullness,
man finds weariness, interior emptiness and distaste for life."*

Homily in Gurk, Austria,
June 25, 1988.[32]

Man shares many things with animals, including sex.

However, man must not behave like an animal in his sexuality, or in the other things he shares with them.

It is noticeable how human beings try to imitate animals, which is precisely what marks the profound difference that separates man from animals: to wit, animals do not try to imitate man because they cannot.

Man, however, is able to imitate animals and can become even more of an animal than the animal itself. In other words, man can act against his instincts in such a way that his conduct makes him similar to animals. To the degree that he acts in this way, he will be less *human*. Man is a "rational animal" in spite of the choices of many to behave like an "animal."

What does man have in common with animals?

---

[32] Editorial translation.

His body is the obvious similarity. Man also has this in common with rocks, but there is an important difference. We must learn to behave like a real human being and what the consequences will be if our proper essence is not respected.

The ancient Greeks, who were extremely wise, said that man is a "microcosm," a small universe. They based this observation on the fact that all the perfections of things are found summarized in man.

Man shares corporeality with rocks, but his corporeality is not equal to rocks, which do not have their body structured in such a way to permit growth, breath and nourishment. Rocks do not have life.

The principle that gives life to a body is called *soul*, which means "something hidden." In Latin, the soul was properly called *anima*, because it animates the body and gives it life. When we talk about "animated" drawings, we mean drawings that have "life."

Plants have life, thus, they have a soul that is called "vegetative," because its only principle is vegetative vital actions: giving nourishment, growing, reproducing, and breathing. These actions are invariably made in union with the body and when the body is destroyed, so is the soul.

Animals also have life, but it differs from vegetative life. They enjoy a "sensitive" life in that they see, smell, hear, touch, taste, imagine, and feel affection. They have "sensibility."

There are two fields that define the sensibility of animals. One is sensitive knowledge, referring to sight, imagination, listening, etc.; the other is affection, referring to instinct and tendencies. Both aspects work together and involve the body. For example, the animal *sees* the food and *desires* it; when it *hears* its owner's voice, it *rejoices* and goes in search of him. The sensitive soul dies when the body dies.

Man also has life and feels; he has sensibility and so is similar to other living beings, according to their degree of perfection. But man is different from other living beings because he thinks and loves, and therefore, has a soul that is altogether different. He is superior.

The soul of man does not die when the body dies, because it does not depend on matter or time or space like the souls of irrational beings. Man can, for example, consider his past, not only his personal past, but those of others so that man can write history. He can grasp things that cannot be seen or touched, such as love and kindness. He is capable of studying other beings; other beings cannot study man. He can pray and converse with God and he can think and love like God because he has a spiritual and immortal soul, similar to the souls of angels. In Baptism, sanctifying grace is given to that soul, which likens man to God and makes him a son of God.

It seems that man is a stranger on earth. Moreover, if he really lives like a human being, he is a stranger because he is passing through; he is a pilgrim, and an outsider. Earth is not man's destiny, but Heaven.

✠　　✠　　✠

If you have paid attention, dear youth, you will have realized that man really is a "microcosm" who has things in common with rocks, plants, animals, and also with angels and God.

Consequently, man can decide to act according to those things he shares with inferior beings, or to those things he shares with superior beings such as angels and God. He can choose to lean toward zoology, to live as an animal, or toward theology, to live as a child of God. What happens when man only lives according to his "animalism"? As a man, he falls into self-destruction by letting his instincts and passions dominate him. God made man an ordered being; he is a something like the rocks, made to live like the plants, made to feel like the animals; made able to know and love like the angels; made to be a true child of God. He is made to know and love in order to pray. However, there are human beings who let sex guide their thinking and place their thoughts at the disposal of their animalism.

If a person wants to use a handsaw, he has to check if it is good and respect its proper end which is to cut. When the proper end is not taken into account, it will be used incorrectly and produce no results; i.e., one cannot drink soup with a handsaw, or paint a portrait with it.

Similarly, men know that sex is good, that it is created by God and is for man's use. But not everyone respects it, or values its dignity. Its final goal is often distorted and used for personal egoistic objectives.

What does the egotist think? He has an excessive love for self which makes him focus on his own interests and to forget about others. He says: first me, second me and third me. The egotist makes other people into things, objects for his own benefit. The standard principle that regulates the actions of all egotists is: "Does it work for me? I'll take it. Doesn't work for me? I'll leave it." This is man reduced to the genital, man upside down, with his passions on top and his most noble faculties at the bottom. He is an animal, if not in his being, then in his actions.

People today want to separate pleasure from love and separate the surrender of their bodies from the surrender of their souls. They want to make human love an animal love, a commercial commodity, a business. Human love is threatened because it is a source of life but our society follows in the footsteps of the murderer, Cain. Human love is not valued because the culture of death reigns in our society. Evidence:

– Semen Banks;

– In-vitro fertilization;

– Artificial insemination;

– Rentable uteruses, etc.

And so we have two conceptions of sex. The first idea is that man is made for sex; the second is that sex is made for man, with the former considering a human being as an object or a thing and the latter holding that man is a *human being* superior to other beings.

Those who hold to the first conception will not have any problem justifying abortion, prostitution (including child prostitution), masturbation, pre-marital relations, pornography, etc. St. Paul calls these people *enemies of the cross of Christ...their god is the belly.*[33] Sex becomes a god. They become murderers, or at least, defenders of murderers, supporting abortion, etc.

The proposal that sex can be used without responsibility, commitment or love, misuses God's gift and warps its intent. For that reason, belief in this premise will promote ideas that go against life, seeking to block ovulation and implantation with contraceptives because, clearly, cooperating in giving life is not the goal. The side effects that these pills have, are kept hidden including: hyperglycemia and the increase in cholesterol level, thrombosis, hypertension, sexual dysfunction, decrease of pleasure in the sexual act, deformations, anomalies and, often, sterility in women.

In the past, the stated purpose of condoms was *"to prevent infection"*; now the statement is, *"use it to lessen the risk."* It is also said that condoms reduce the risk of contracting sexually transmitted diseases, such as AIDS. Do contraceptives reduce the risk of contracting a disease with a hundred percent mortality rate? This type of risk reduction is like shooting at oneself with a revolver that contains only one bullet; one has to be extremely stupid to allow himself to be fooled by that. Is this the only option that can intervene between us and death? And they call using condoms risk free? To reduce the risk is not to eliminate it. It is time to stop thinking this way.

The only absolutely safe protection against AIDS is God's 6th commandment, *thou shall not commit adultery.*

✠   ✠   ✠

The man who lives his sexuality as an animal is only half a man. He has abandoned all attempts to be a successful human being. He is a man who has resigned himself to failure and has put up his white flag of surrender.

---

[33] *Phil* 3:18-19.

People who have resigned themselves to failure will generally seek to drag others to their ruin, because they want to destroy in others what they cannot respect in themselves and will consider those who do not want to follow them as weak, naïve, unhappy, or foolish. They will even resort to lies asserting that purity is impossible, that it is a lie that there are heroic women and men who are living it, or, in any case, that it is unnatural or that it is only for the weak who allow themselves to be deceived by priests and ultimately, by Jesus Christ.

Men who promote animalistic ideas, do so in order to hide their own weakness and avoid acknowledging their own failures and their own humiliating surrender to their instincts. They do not want to fight; like toads they wallow in the dribble of their own impurities. They do not want to accept that there are young men and women who are much better than themselves because they have a clean gaze and pure heart. They do not want to confront the fact that there are many young people stronger than they are, who know how to hold out for true love and for life, who soar high like eagles.

Is he who lives according to reason weak? Is he who does not have courage to raise himself above animal sensations strong? Is he who recognizes his dignity and nobility weak? Is he who degrades himself strong? Are the victorious weak and the defeated strong? Is he who is lord of himself, weak and he who is slave to that which is inferior, strong? Is man weak and are animals strong?

Today, these lies are given credence by doctors who, in the name of science reinforce lies with perverse advice; the press and television promote and sponsor them.

The people who mistakenly accept this scientific agenda, fail to recognize the attacks against the integrity of their personhood.

They fail to realize that man is made for:

Triumph, not defeat,

Love, not egoism,

Heroism, not cowardice,

To be a lord, not a slave.

Man is: **lord**, because whoever triumphs over himself is stronger than one who conquers entire cities.

And so, my dear young friends let us not be daunted. It is true that victory is hard won. Many times society, our companions, or environments, work against us, but the word "impossible" should never come from your lips and a feeling that should never darken your hearts. You can never accept the word "impossible" if you want to follow Jesus Christ. A young person who follows Jesus Christ is, with Him, omnipotent and *with God nothing will be impossible.*[34]

The choice is in your hands: eagle or toad?

---

[34] *Lk* 1:37.

5.

TELE-ADDICTION

*"The mass-media cannot be subjected to
the criteria of special interests, sensationalism or instant success;
rather, taking into consideration the exigencies of ethics, they must
serve the constructing of 'a more human life.'"*

*Speech at UNESCO,
June 2, 1980.*[35]

There has never been a generation like the present one, in that, we live without real communication with our contemporaries, yet we have so many means of communication. Young people confirm this in their everyday lives when they think their parents are too distant, or when the parents confirm that their children are strangers.

Someone once said: "Now we have internet....to tell us what?"

Following is a common family scene:

A son comes back from high school or work. Perhaps his mother is there. If she is home, perhaps a crossing of questions and answers will take place between them:

Mother: "So....?"

Son: "Good"

Mother: "Any grades?"

---

[35] Editorial translation.

Son: "..."

Mother: "Do you want to eat?"

Son: "No, mom... I'm not hungry."

Psychologists agree that this is not "family dialogue," and we don't need to study psychology to know this.

Whether or not "mom" is home, the silence or the dialogue can be followed by a ritual repeated to the point of weariness, plugging himself into a walkman, turning on the TV, or turning the stereo volume on high to stun himself with FM radio. The point is just to escape, TO GO AWAY.

TV isolates

TV speaks but it does not listen. It runs by its own time, not ours and imposes ideas on us by addressing the masses, the anonymous youth, usually for its own interests. It is a medium that depersonalizes because it does not address you and does not know or care about you as a distinct person.

You may ask, "Then we should not watch television, Father?"

It is not correct to come to that conclusion. Yes, we can watch television. In fact, in a sense, it is necessary to watch it sometimes, but do so as little as possible and with a critical eye. If we cannot do that, then it is safer not to watch at all. If we do not let the TV screen master us, we will not be deceived and enslaved by it, as many are.

We are convinced that TV is a medium that if used well, can have great advantages. Certainly, it represents great human progress if it is used for good. But that does not change the fact that today TV is generally used by the transmitter and by the receiver as a school of counter-culture and, consequently, does cause harm. In Spain they call it *"tela-moron."* "You say that because you are old fashioned and against television." No. We are against the way this form of media is used, not the television itself. Television is something good: it is used in medicine, in universities, in high level cultural programs, etc.

Television produces addiction

To say that television produces addiction means that, although the one who watches it *knows* that it is not "the be all and end all" of life, it nevertheless generates in the viewer an anxious need, as if one day it would fulfill all his expectations, or as if it were impossible to live without it. Many people automatically turn on the television as soon as they get home.

Professor Jacques Piveteau proposes an experiment to identify "tele-addicts":

"Spend a previously determined period of time (maybe a week, fifteen days, a month) without any television. Afterwards, tell us what happened among the family members, such as the difficulties, quarrels or dialogues that came up. If we are not addicted this will not be difficult. But if it is hard, what should we conclude?"[36]

Television will be inoffensive when one can live without it, but many young people today know more about their television heroes than they know about their own family. TV idols form a parallel plane of existence that invades the house, but has nothing to do with the reality of the house. The logical consequence of this is to tend to a kind of schizophrenia. When an adolescent turns off the television set, living with those in his house can be strange for him.

Another addiction arising at the moment is the *addiction to surfing the Internet.*

Danger of the television

What makes TV dangerous for a young person? We will take a look at a list made by the French psychologist Mirielle Chalvon[37]:

---

[36] Cited by "*La tele-adicción,*" (Fundación Argentina del Mañana: Buenos Aires, 1994), 60. (Editorial translation).

[37] Cited by "*La tele-adicción,*" (Fundación Argentina del Mañana: Buenos Aires, 1994), 16 ff. (Editorial translation).

1. The excess of speed

Television is not a good learning tool because it prevents reflection, and the information that is presented cannot be well assimilated. Its method is not "to make us think"; but to "trap" us. When the spectator sits in front of the screen, the images anesthetize the discernment[38] filters in such a way that everything is received with indifference: violence-peace, love-hate, grudge-pardon, good-evil, truth-error...

2. It produces shortcomings in the capacity of expression.

After watching a movie, many people demonstrate problems summarizing the logical sequence of what they saw, beyond the main point of the movie.

3. It underrates the value of the ideas.

It does not so much matter the depth of what is said but the spectacular way in which it is presented. It is as if what we see with our eyes eclipses what we understand with our ears.

4. It does not give us true ideas.

A *language of images* –for TV is "sound in images." TV is directed more to feelings than to spirit, more to moving our sensibility than our reason. It does not seek to form.

For example, one would hardly try to talk about the virtue of purity, or "advertise" God. But, in advertisements for coffee, washing machines, cars, and other commodities, sex is often used to sell because sex sells. There are TV shows where anyone is invited to present anything in any way he likes, such as sociologists or psychologists who show in their programs how to use condoms.

---

[38] To explain simply, "discernment" means the capacity to recognize what is good or bad in relation to the end, in order to choose the good and reject the bad. It is no more than certain ability in the exercise of prudence. It is what we mean when we say that we need a critical spirit.

5. It does not respect the needs of youth.

TV does not respect you as a person. This is proven by what we have been saying all along regarding the disrespect shown towards virtues like purity, worthiness and the right way to live. Often TV will air "the five minutes of God," followed by the coarsest programs of low humor. Yes, the caricatures of God appear: astrologists, fortune tellers, mind readers, pseudo-psychologists. **You do not matter to television; what does matter is good ratings.** Those in the television media know that if they began to communicate reality to you across the screen, it would become more difficult for them to capture your attention, sell products, make money or to do business with you. You are being used to make this media so they can make thousands of dollars for every second of advertising.

6. It exhausts us and empowers the tendency toward evasion

This is another unquestionable point. The ambition to copy, or somehow *live* the sensationalized, fantastic and exciting life that television promotes, necessarily creates or reinforces the tendency to evade daily life, which involves serious commitments, and great responsibilities.

It plays with the passions and the feelings of the young people who are caught, thousands of innocent teenage girls who are permanently on the edge of their seats waiting for the soap opera heartthrob's decision about the two loves in his life. TV becomes so addictive because of the fantasies it engenders, that those who get caught up in it have difficulty turning it off, and become, in fact, enslaved.

Consequences

Some of the effects of television addiction are: functional illiteracy caused by reducing the spectrum of commonly used language; low performance in school caused by taking away the ability to think; isolation, and family division. With respect to this last one the Pope commented: "Even when television programs themselves are not morally objectionable, television can still have negative effects on the family. It can isolate family members in their private worlds, cutting them off from authentic interpersonal relations."[39]

It also takes away the lordship that the young person should have over himself and over his time by enslaving him.

It incrusts vices within him and extracts virtues.

Imperceptibly, TV configures your demeanor and your way of thinking. It brutally conditions your freedom. It gives you the patterns of life and the criteria to exercise your freedom. It sets up your head for you and then destroys it. It subjects you to those who bestow "sense" and you end up not thinking for yourself.

✠   ✠   ✠

Have you ever heard that Jesus Christ is God or that you have to save your soul, that hell exists or that you have to work to be virtuous on prime time television?

You will not find God on prime-time. Instead you will find a panel of frustrated old women defending abortion, transvestites defending their "rights" and their twisted ideas. Yes, you will find error equated to truth, and evil equated to good.

That is why the Pope declared emphatically: "The truth should be the source and the criteria of freedom, even in the media. Whoever considers what is true as false is not free; whoever affirms what is false, holding it up as truth, is not faithful. Respect for the truth lacks both when we affirm what is false, and when we say only one part of the truth, deliberately withholding the rest."[40]

The influence of television is evident in our society. Television is not interested in the truth. Terrible things occur when means of communication fall into the hands of people who are not

---

[39] JOHN PAUL II, *Message for 28th World Communications Day*, 1994.

[40] JOHN PAUL II, *Speech to Catholic Journalists*, OR 10-02-1989. (Editorial translation).

interested in truth or goodness, people whose only interest is money.

Not only does TV give false news by employing calumnies as a means of political pressure, it also promotes explicit propaganda for the culture of death, where lies are often indistinct from truth, false principles of action are introduced, and youth are given false criteria through "magic" words that are stereotyped and radically ambiguous.

The word "discriminate" is an ambiguous term in permanent use in all the programs of a certain level. It is used intentionally so as to interfere with a person's capacity to react appropriately to what is foul, terrible, and disastrous. Those who attempt to react appropriately are accused of discriminating or being "fundamentalist." This is nonsense. Those who perpetrate lies discriminate against the truth, against the good, against God.

Being a Christian means that we are commanded to hate the sin not the sinner and defend the truth. This is not discrimination. On the contrary, those who do not give us space to do this and do give space to error and lies are the ones who discriminate against us.

But it is not correct to take a position that mass media is absolutely perverse. This reasoning would not recognize or value human technical progress, which in itself is good. However, even wholesome programs are often coupled with bad advertisements or previews.

Remember that human progress must be moral with a clear understanding of human dignity, of its fundamental capacity of unconditional adhesion to the truth, and its fundamental capacity to responsibly exert freedom in the realm of the good.

Beware of the "*tele-moron*," it only makes people "*tele-morons*"!

6.
TAKING RISKS JUST BECAUSE?

*"The man of our time is so fascinated by the discoveries of
science and the exhilarating applications
that technology has achieved, frequently so absorbed
in his own works that he forgets the Creator."*

*Homily in Lucca, Italy,
September 23, 1989.*[41]

What is life? What is death?

Placing the correct value on life necessarily leads to placing
the correct value on death, the point at which life itself is
sacrificed for something that is worthwhile or, in all cases, the
moment of passage in which we find ourselves alone before Him
who knows us better than we know ourselves. Many can deceive
themselves; but nobody will be able to deceive Jesus Christ.

There are young people who don't know why they exist or
what to live for. They do not know what to die for.

In recent years, the increase of fatal traffic accidents involving
young people is remarkable. These victims are young people like
you.

Some few months ago on Ricchieri Avenue, which leads to
the Ezeiza Airport in Buenos Aires, a 16 year-old caused a car
crash that, thank God, miraculously did not have very serious
consequences. A "ladies man," he was accompanied by two girls.

---

[41] Editorial translation.

Do you think he realized what he had done? Apparently not, because when he was questioned by a journalist, he responded with an attack. The remarkable thing about this incident was that he "knew it all." He refused to admit fault, and told the journalists everything that came to his mind in order to show that "he could take even more."

Perhaps his nerves caused him to behave that way, but it does not explain why unnecessary risks to life, such as excessive speed, are taken in so many other cases.

I know an extremely imprudent 23-year-old. He never thought about his actions, and every time I spoke with him it was as if everything was off kilter. One time he was driving with his girlfriend on a highway in Buenos Aires. His driver's seat was a little bit loose and he was going pretty fast. All of the sudden he had to maneuver in order to avoid another vehicle and his seat slid backwards. He hit a parked truck, a tree and finally crashed against a wall. He was saved by a miracle. Do you think the accident changed him? No, it didn't.

When we seek explanations about why many things happen, usually all of them are reduced to one principal: the eclipse that is suffered in young people's consciences about the value of life, an eclipse that will not allow them to "rewind," to stop and "go back"... and to live according to the real meaning of life.

Another cause of the risk-taking is the characteristic desire of youth for adventure. It is not the desire itself, but rather that the desire is badly directed, or "out of focus." A desire for adventure that is motivated by the passions and dominated by inferior goals, such as pleasure, is disordered. A young man driving 90 mph feels omnipotent. The addiction to speed is also a path to nothing.

Motorcycles are even more dangerous. For, a young man who more or less drives well and likes it, will find that a motorcycle is easier to drive and handle. He will try to affirm that it is more secure, but it is not. This false confidence ends up being the cause of the most horrific accidents. A motorcycle has no other bumper than the driver himself.

Other causes of horrific traffic accidents are bets among gangs or friends, or simply wanting to look cool and excel at something. It is easy to forget that it is much better to excel in healthy ways, not with a head broken by a windshield.

We have already said it; but it is best to insist: car accidents are problems that mainly concern young people, who risk their lives in unnecessary ways, participating in clandestine races, only to lose the one race worth running: life. They do not understand the value of life or the final destiny that awaits us. They prefer the ephemeral to the lasting; the instantaneous to the permanent. This attitude illustrates that their lives are moving in the wrong direction. Sometimes, the best thing that could happen is a minor crash that would keep them from driving for a while, to give them time to think, so that their calling to be mourned on a dashboard doesn't become a reality.

Death caused by car accidents is called *"white death."*

There are young people who conduct their lives as carelessly as they drive their vehicles.

Perhaps the end of those lives in some cases can be called *"eternal death."*

7.
THE WILL TO POWER AS IRRATIONAL VIOLENCE

"Violence, in any form, is a denial of human dignity...
Society has a heavy responsibility. Everybody must be willing to
accept their part of this responsibility, including the media."

Denver, August 14, 1993.

And you will hear of wars and rumors of wars.[42] As Benedict XV accurately noted, war in our century has become a permanent institution. We can verify it daily by the slaughters in the ethnic-religious war in the ex-Yugoslavia, the millions of deaths in the recent civil war in Rwanda, the guerrilla insurgency that has plagued Latin America for decades, the provocation of international wars that put the world at the edge of self-annihilation merely for greedy economic interests like hegemonic dominion of the petroleum world, the racial segregation in South-Africa, Germany, France, and Spain... It is the century of the will to power...

The philosopher who spoke of the "will to power" was the German pessimist Nietzsche. Nietzsche once said "God is dead."

The will to power, according to Herman Hesse, a follower of Nietzsche, is like a mark worn by the strong, as he wrote in *Demian*. This mark is similar to the mark of Cain, who killed his brother: the mark of the stronger. This is the mark of the rebel

---

[42] *Mt* 24:6.

who wants to destroy what is good, beautiful, noble and fragile, just for the sake of it. This evil is beautifully described by the American poet Adelaide Crapsey[43] in her brief poem "Susanna and the Elders," the chaste woman who did not want to submit herself to the perverted old man who threatened her:

– "Why do
You thus devise
Evil against her?" "For that
she is beautiful, delicate;
therefore."[44]

Today we are witnessing a chaotic unfolding of what the will to power means: the translation of the will to power into the cornerstone of a culture is nothing more than the culture of death. And we cannot be silent witnesses. We must denounce error to defend the truth; we must crush death to defend life; we must destroy evil to promote good. Only by doing this can we replace the civilization of death and anti-life with the civilization of life and love.

A violent society

As the example of Cain demonstrates, violence is not exclusive to our time. However, its intensity is exclusive to our time. The violent acts of today cannot be compared with the violent acts of previous decades.

A couple of examples will suffice. The first one is the emergence of younger criminals, children who make Jack the Ripper look like a little baby. Children who are murderers! Children! Childhood is meant to be a time of innocence, eternal games, singing, laughing, and continual wonder. Four years ago in England, two children aged ten and twelve years old, murdered a

---

[43] Adelaide Crapsey, born in 1878, died 1914.

[44] ADELAIDE CRAPSEY, *The complete poems and collected letters of Adelaide Crapsey* (State University of N.Y. Press: New York, 1977), 72

two-year old child. Subsequently more cases have appeared involving even younger child criminals. Not long ago, also in England, a thirteen-year old girl was kicked to death and left on the street by another girl because of a fight that developed between two different girls' schools. A woman who witnessed the crime said that they looked like animals. She was right.

Other cases are even worse because of the malice they manifest. In addition to armed children and to theft perpetrated by children, there was a public case of violence that was frontal, direct, irrational, senseless, cold and voluntary. In the United States, a mother who was pregnant with twins, wanted to abort one of them! Her excuse was that she did not have enough money to support two babies. When the case was made public, pro-life organizations offered to provide what was needed to raise and educate the baby with dignity, citing the option of eventual adoption, but she did not listen to them. She coldly went ahead with the murder of her innocent baby with extreme cruelty.

Bill Clinton, the former president of the United States of America, approved one of the most inhumane forms of abortion: decapitation of babies *as they are coming out of their mother's womb*. Mr. Clinton might very much be "Mr. President," but he does not seem to be much of a human being.

To sum up, the presence of children and adolescents in armed and violent situations is a growing phenomenon, mostly since the fifties. We can also recall the presence of children and adolescents in armed movements: guerrillas, drug-terrorism, death squads, etc.

We live in a violent society that day by day exerts a more accentuated violence.

Environments and places of violence

Every day, we witness the existence of the will to power as a "passion for causing harm."

We can see this in the field of sports. It is incredible that human beings are capable of killing because of a soccer match. The fact that this kind of violence exists is partly due to the media, magazines and programs that "make novels" out of sports, among other things. An unreal world of statistics, possibilities and speculations is woven together, causing a person to go to the field with his expectation and imagination inflated and expectations are cultivated not really understanding that all that is really happening is that twenty-two human beings are running after a leather sphere with air in it. It is not wrong to like soccer or go to games, but what is wrong is to see more of a contest in sports than what is really there. Defending our team becomes a question of honor and people are capable of risking their lives to defend that honor: "My side is tougher." When River beat Boca 2-0, after 10 undefeated games, two River fans were killed. A young Boca fan said: "All right... 2 – 2."

Violence in everyday life is a direct result of the proliferation of violence in movies, as well as in cartoons for children that, no longer have the charming sweetness of Walt Disney. Today's violent teenagers are the children who years ago let the exhalations of the culture of death enter their imagination in the form of cartoons such as He-Man and Dragon Ball. These violent super heroes are the models that have "formatted" their imaginations after a few years of exposure to the brain washing effects that television exerts.

Another extremely important cause of violence is the increase of pornography. The reason for this is because our sensibility has two spheres of action: the concupiscible appetite, which is the tendency toward what produces pleasure; and the irascible appetite, which is the tendency to reject or attack that which prevents us from obtaining the pleasure that is desired. Both spheres operate as a whole. Therefore, in a society where unconditional primacy is given to the free use of sexuality, potentially violent individuals, who seek to destroy anything that prevents them from getting the pleasure that society tells them they must have, are being created. If a young man who may or may not be drunk or drugged rapes a girl who passes by, who cares as long as he does not get caught? If it is unlikely he will be arrested, why wouldn't he jump the guy, or guys, who walk by better dressed than him? Why not impose one's power on another if one is stronger?

There is a moment in which violence becomes pleasurable within the psychology of the aggressor. Those who are violent by occupation develop a certain passion for doing evil and making people feel bad.

✠　　✠　　✠

The Prophet says: *Your sins have kept good from you.*[45]

Our society has animalized itself by making a pact with depravity. What is high and majestic is rejected for what produces pleasure, and the direct consequence of this is hedonism and violence at all levels of society. It is true that there are more causes for societal ills, such as misery and hunger, but "irrational violence" is the primary result of the will to power. Social problems have their cause in the violence that those who are in power exert in some way.

Sin takes away peace and destroys the social order. Many who promote abortion, defend divorce and premarital relations, and make sex a supreme value are the same ones who complain about violence.

A young person that has a "will to power" over and against others is actually a weak, sick and twisted soul who, at heart, cannot bear himself. He fights with others because he does not have the courage to fight against his own defects. Instead of battling his passions and weaknesses, he foments them and becomes enslaved to them.

The true hero, the young man that truly has the "will to power" is he who is capable of conquering himself.

"Will to power" over himself: That is the formula for being how God wants us to be.

---

[45] *Jer* 5: 25.

8.

RELATIVISM: A TYPE OF
ADDICTION TO LIES

*"To be free means to bring about the fruits of truth, to act in
truth. To be free also means to know how to surrender,
to submit self to truth, and not the truth to self,
to our own vanities, and our own interests."*

Speech to University Students in Rome,
March 26, 1981. [46]

Man lives by a set of moral values, either ordered or
disordered according to what he has been taught. The more
ordered our set of values, the more respect for the real order of
things will develop within us.

It is easy to recognize that when someone wants to dominate
a people, the first thing attempted is to remove their supports.

Those who have disordered values and who attempt to
dominate or corrupt others or society at large, will start their
attack by creating confusion about what is true or untrue.

If I can see the enemy attacking me, I can defend myself; if
my enemy attacks me in darkness, I am at a disadvantage. If the
roots of society are targeted, the first line of attack will be to
obfuscate the light of truth.

---

[46] Editorial translation.

Attacks on the principles of a society are usually in the form of a "cultural revolution," often silent and stealthy, such as euthanasia. This "quiet" revolution is effective because people are led into becoming "moldable" material, people with principles and values that are ruled by situations and not by God.

It will turn them definitively into "the masses," as Ortega and Gasset said. Men who are easy to dominate, like marionettes, express the ideas of others, like puppets.

So, what principles will be targeted by relativists?

1. Belief in **God**. A man who does not cling to God is a man who does not have roots in eternity. A man who believes in nothing cannot differentiate between good and evil; his judgments are submitted to his time and history. This is a man for whom there is no destiny beyond this earth, and consequently, no law beyond that which he imposes himself. Why, then, be good, when it is so hard, if by being bad, one can have everything the world has to offer? Why not, then, be a drug dealer, if it is much easier to get rich that way?

2. **The Catholic Church.** This is an institution by which God sends salvation to mankind. Discrediting the Catholic Church, sects make the Church seem like just one religion among many. Campaigns will be organized to ridicule the Catholic faithful and their priests. It is noticeable how many TV shows highlight priests or seminarians with "problems," as if it were a common everyday thing, creating mistrust among the faithful in their pastors, and hindering the transcendent role these pastors must play. *I will strike the shepherd and the sheep of the flock will be scattered.*[47]

3. The Image of the **Homeland**. This is another area that is targeted so as to undermine societies. Encouraging populations to mimic foreign values and disown their own cultures creates contempt for themselves, their origins and their own land. For example: Folklore doesn't sell like rock does.

---

[47] *Mt* 26:31.

4. **The Family.** This is the basic unit of society and is attacked in multiple ways. Some examples are the voting records on divorce laws, and the anti-birth mentality that promotes the marketing of contraceptives, and many other elements.

5. **The School.** Children spend 6 hours daily at school and it becomes, in a real sense, their second home. Attacks on schools often take the form of another "cultural revolution," with *psychogenesis*. This is not an incidental attack, but is well studied and premeditated. It is not a new method, but a new orientation of the ends and objectives of education.

✠ ✠ ✠

Errors committed or attacks against the roots of society are the fruits of ideologies and ways of thinking that are not new. Young people must be well-educated in order not to be deceived, because these erroneous worldviews that drive public opinion are rampant in the mass media. For example, Karl Marx's dialectic and practical materialism used mass media to overturn culture with his revolution. Gramsci is one of these interpreters who wanted to overturn culture with the revolution that Marx proposed, using the means of mass media for this attack.

This deviation towards subjectivism that human thought has taken began with Rene Descartes and Immanuel Kant. Kant stated that it is not human knowledge that must correspond to reality but it is reality that must correspond to man. Stated this way, it shows itself to be something ridiculous and completely opposed to common sense, as anybody with a little sense would be able to see. Nevertheless, these philosophies are often taught explicitly or are underlying many things that are taught, not only at the university level, but also at the high school level. Every so often these same errors are thrown into the market of the cultural revolution and promoted as an original product. And it is very easy to find buyers who are ignorant or taken off guard, gullible people who believe they have invented the wheel. It is a wine that easily intoxicates and often ends up being the mandatory drink of teachers and academics who develop theories of education. This is terrible because it is these people who shape society, for they have the responsibility of providing young people with the criteria of action and the principles for what they do. These are bad starting points and worse ending points.

There are two concrete examples that will allow us to present what we could call the "anthropocentric revolution" of culture: psychogenesis and *mass media*. First we will discuss psychogenesis.

What is *psychogenesis*? Where does it come from and what does it do?

The technical base of this concept is made up of some of Jean Piaget's[48] hypotheses, whose errors, caused by an exclusively biological-evolutionary conception of man, have serious consequences when applied to education.

The development of a child's personality and knowledge has a natural and progressive character. It begins with sensible knowledge that is provided by the external senses—until it reaches the intellect. In this progression, reality is "built" by the child from within himself: there are no objective truths, no established imperative morals to which the subject must accommodate himself. What the subject decides as true is true; what the subject decides as good is good.

Because the objectivity of moral norms is nonexistent, the educative act that should be moral becomes merely a practicing autonomy, creating pure moral anarchy. These theories are supported by a false interpretation of creativity, confusing true creativity— wherein man transforms nature and fulfills his essence of "being an image of God," with gross arbitrariness concerning what is true and good. Furthermore, they will seek to create a false capacity for "critical" judgment, making children and young people accustomed to question everything received from their parents and their traditions without due reason. Using the excuse of opposing authoritarianism, the true authority of

---

[48] JEAN PIAGET was born in Neuchâtel (Switzerland), August 9, 1896 and died in Ginebra September 16, 1980. He was professor of Psychology in the Universities of Ginebra and Paris.

parents will be destroyed, creating a false dialectic and making children and youth mistrust those who gave them life and who are primarily responsible for their education.

What do the defenders of psychogenesis say?

Its defenders say that it is a change of attitude. They present it as a new relationship between student and teacher, where the child feels understood rather than rejected and consequently is no longer sad, or bored, and does not destroy everything.

In fact it is a true educative REFORMATION or REVOLUTION. It is true that we must improve many things about education. That is an incontestable truth. But this improvement must be oriented to actually carrying out the essential plan of all education, the perfection of man as a person, and his commitment to goodness and truth.

The re-inventors of the wheel have changed the ends of education, emptying them of content. The educators of all times agreed that the professor knew more and the student knew less; teacher taught and student learned. Since the student knew less, he did not know what was important for him to learn and, for that reason, the teacher administered different doses of teaching according to the student's capacity and progress in assimilation. That model has changed to one that expects children to construct their own learning. They tell the teacher what he should be taught. Thus, primacy is given to personal experience rather than to what can be learned from others.

A teacher, for example, would not be able to tell a child: "This is a knife. Be careful because it cuts." Rather, he would have to give the child a knife so that he learns from experience that it cuts.

The false principle is that we must experience everything and that we only know well what we have personally experienced. I do not need to **experience** suicide to see that it actually ends my life. I do not have to murder someone to know that it is a bad thing. I do not have to use drugs to know that it will take me to my death.

87

Furthermore, there is a false understanding of freedom: the child can do whatever he wants, however he wants, and the teacher cannot reprimand him. As we have seen, that false understanding of freedom will translate into a false autonomy with respect to truth and goodness. The child will be judge, teacher, self-evaluator...

So, the teacher will only have the function of promoting and channeling the child's spontaneous initiatives: if he wants to talk about flowers and birds in Spanish class, we would have to let him. If the child wants to stand on his desk, then we would have to let him, because "we cannot impose anything on him." Language is seen as only a means of expression and not as a reflection of things. Therefore, if a child wants to call the blackboard "ball," he could because "it comes from within"... The role of the teacher completely disappears. The teacher must bring himself to the student's level and limit himself to suggesting, motivating, guiding, creating situations; he will never have to correct an erroneous student, because errors do not exist, and that would be a way of inhibiting or coercing the child. The teacher will no longer be a role model nor a source of truth.

The consequences of this educative system are horrifying and we have lamentable results. These ideas were applied in Europe (England, France, etc.) in 1950. That 35-45 year-old generation today is in serious existential crises. The lack of social integration and respect for authority, and the inability to adapt to the norms of coexistence, has brought about tendencies to avoid reality through drugs and alcohol addictions.

Above us there is a natural and supernatural order that is **prior** to us and is given to us; we are not its creators. It is **superior** to us in that we cannot manipulate it, **intangible** in that its laws are unchanging, and **transcendent** in that it will continue when we no longer exist.

We may conclude that relativism is a path to nothing.

☩   ☩   ☩

As we have discussed, we can identify two fundamental purposes of psychogenesis:

a) To form people who create new things, without repeating those of past generations;

b) To form intellects that rebel against authority and do not accept anything that has been given to them.

These two purposes go completely against human nature. Every soul needs the splendor of truth, which it knows with its intellect; needs the conquest of good, which it desires with its will; and the brilliance of beauty, which makes him enjoy what he knows. Therefore, to introduce this change at the very beginnings of education is a serious attack against human dignity, leading away from truth, goodness and beauty.

The intention of implementing this type of education consists in the creation of a new model of human being, with moral and intellectual autonomy from established values. The result would be a person whose world, principles and language are self-focused and therefore without true and beautiful values; he will be a person easy to manipulate.

Pius XI warned: "All model of education is erroneous if it is partly or fully based on the negation or forgetfulness of original sin, grace and, therefore, of the single forces of the human nature. Such are the present systems of diverse names that appeal to a limitless autonomy and freedom of the child, and that diminish or even suppress the authority or the work of the educator, attributing to the child an exclusive preeminence of all natural and divine superior law in the work of education."[49]

Education has a determining role in the construction of a personality. Special care must be taken to ensure the effective transmission of essential values that must qualify the life of a being made in the image of God.

---

[49] Editorial translation.

"Education is the proposal and assimilation of *values*, which are the foundation of the identity, dignity, vocation and responsibility of man as a person and member of society."[50]

Among these values, moral values have an undisputed primacy:

"The formation of man consists in the development of his own capacities, in the formation of his own freedom, through which he decides about himself."[51]

"It is also necessary to promote the maturation of the person, helping him to develop his socio-cultural, moral and religious dimensions through the right use of freedom. The individual formation of the human personality cannot but tend towards the integral growth of relations with others, the world, and, primarily, God. *One there is who is good*.[52] As St. Thomas reminds us, this implies, above all, ethical formation, which has the primacy in the integral formation of the person."[53]

Relativism is a lie. It does not liberate man, but enslaves him. Freedom can only be fulfilled in adhesion to the truth. "Free is the man who is capable of deciding according to the greatest values and goals: *The truth will make you free*.[54] The man who finds the truth at the same time discovers the base of his perfection and autonomy."[55]

Be free. That is to say, love the truth.

---

[50] *Letter to the Director-General of UNESCO, on the occasion of the World Congress on Youth (July 1, 1985)* Quoted in OR 7/1/1985. (Editorial translation).

[51] Cf. SAINT THOMAS AQUINAS, *Quaestiones disputatae, 11.* (Editorial translation).

[52] *Mt* 19:17.

[53] *Discourse at the St Thomas Aquinas Pontifical University (Angelicum) of Rome* 11/24/1994.

[54] *Jn* 8:32.

[55] *Discourse to representatives of the world of culture* (June 13, 1984). (Editorial translation).

9.
THE SECTS' INVASION

"As you well know, only Jesus can answer fully and
definitively the crucial questions of existence.
Only the church, the Mystical Body of the Redeemer,
Totally possesses the word that saves
and renews the human being."

Speech to the assembly
of the Movement for a better world,
May 25, 1991.

Jesus Christ said that one day others would come saying *I am he*,[56] but they are wolves in sheep's skin, who would come to destroy the flock.

The prophesy has been realized in the invasion of sects. Today we are plagued with false shepherds.

The lack of true shepherds leads people to seek out false shepherds. The lack of priestly and religious vocations is one of the factors that has brought us to witness what in Puebla was called: **"Invasion of sects."**[57] It is a fact that nature abhors a void; it is also a fact that if men and women do not fill their souls with the true religion, they will try to fill the void with a substitute or a caricature of religion, or the religion of irreligion. More than a century ago, The Holy Curé d' Ars said that if a people were left without priests, in ten years they would become beasts. If there is no one to preach the truth, people will live in ignorance and fall

---

[56] *Lk* 21:8.
[57] *Documento de Puebla*, 419. (Editorial translation).

into error. The good shepherd brings his flock to good pastures; the bad one will bring it to poisonous pastures. The good shepherds bring us to Jesus Christ, the Highest Good Shepherd. And so, we must pray to God to send workers to His harvest and ask that we might be docile legitimate pastors.

Characteristics of the good shepherd

- He works in daylight, and is not hidden: *enters by the door.*[58]

- He knows his flock well: *He calls his own sheep by name.*[59]

- He is an example for his flock and takes risks for them: *he goes before them... [he] lays down his life for the sheep.*[60]

- The flock follows him and recognizes his voice: *and the sheep follow him, for they know his voice.*[61]

- They do not follow the bad pastors because they do not recognize his voice: *A stranger they will not follow, but they will flee from him, for they do not know the voice of strangers.*[62]

- They do not follow one who is not a true pastor, but mercenary, who comes only to steal, kill and destroy...[he] *sees the wolf coming and leaves the sheep and flees...and cares nothing for the sheep.*[63]

- The Good Pastor comes: *so that they may have life, and have it abundantly.*[64]

---

[58] *Jn* 10:2.
[59] *Jn* 10:3.
[60] *Jn* 10:4, 11.
[61] *Jn* 10:4.
[62] *Jn* 10:5.
[63] *Jn* 10:10, 12, 13.
[64] *Jn* 10:10.

Not all the protestant denominations are sects

"National churches," such as the Lutheran Church, the Reformed (or Calvinist) Church and the Anglican Church are not sects.

Properly speaking, the Free Churches such as the Presbyterian, the Congregationalist, the Baptist, the Methodist, etc., are not sects either.

With these denominations, we try to make progress in ecumenical work.

Which churches are sects?

There are 5 different types of sects with whom, properly speaking, there is no ecumenism:

1°: Satanic sects such as the ophites or Neshanic, cainites, luciferians, patarinos, etc.

2°: Sects of Christian origin: the New Apostolic, The Pentecostals, Electronic Church, 700 Club, pastor Gimenez, Carlos Anacondia; some Baptists; Quakers; Holy Laughter, etc.

3°: Sects of Pseudo-Christian origin such as Adventists, Jehovah's Witnesses, Mormons, the Unified Church of Moon, God's Children, Eight Queens, The Friends of Men, etc.

4°: Sects of oriental origin such as Hare Krishna (International Society of the Conscience of Krishna), Sai Baba, the Gurus such as Bhagwan Shree Rajneesh (with his personal fleet of twenty-five Rolls Royces), Mission of Divine Light (Guru Maharajah Ji), Fe Bahai, etc.

5°: Sects of syncretistic origin such as the Rosicrucian Order, the Gnostic sects, theosophical, spiritualism, Afro-Brazilian (umbanda, macumba, candombé), pseudo-scientific (alchemy, dianetics, etc.).

And there are many more since they reproduce like viruses. In France, more than two hundred fifty new sects have been detected. And everywhere sects appear such as the "Superior Universal Lineament" (Valentin de Andrade), Ágora, Alfa-Omega, Amanda Marl, Rainbow, Esoteric Center, Transcendental Meditation, the New Acropolis, the Patriarch (Engelmajer Foundation), etc.

There are also some sects that are highly dangerous, such as Jim Jones' sect where, his followers were convinced to poison themselves, and almost a thousand people died in Guyana in 1979; or David Koresh, who led all of his followers to their deaths in Waco, Texas (USA) after many days of siege by the FBI; or "the Children of the Sun" who were burned in Switzerland and France, etc.

Warning

Many drifting young people are looking for a place to belong and it behooves us to teach them to defend themselves against these forms of aggression. In Spain, 13% of young people are potential victims of sects according to a study done by the Ministry of Social Matters published in "ABC."[65] Whenever the social fabric is broken there is a proliferation of sects.

The only "vaccine" against these dangers is to follow the Good Shepherd who gave His life for us: Jesus Christ, so that we may not be deceived by the false pastors who come saying *'I am the Christ,' and they will lead many astray,*[66] and, *Then if anyone says to you, 'Behold, here is the Christ! or There he is!' do not believe it. For false Christs and false prophets will arise....*[67] Jesus told His apostles and their successors, the Pope, and the Bishops: *He who hears you hears me, and he who rejects you rejects me,*[68] leaving us the golden rule so we may be sure that we are truly following Him. We will never be led astray if we are faithful to the Hierarchical Church. When we are confronted with stories of apparitions, visions, revelations,

---

[65] *Iglesia y Mundo actual,* n° 494-495, Mayo, 1994. (Editorial translation).
[66] *Mt* 24:5.
[67] *Mt* 24: 23-24.
[68] *Lk* 10:16.

messages, and prophecies, the first question that we must ask ourselves is: what does the Hierarchical Church say about it? The Church can never be wrong because of the promise of the Good Shepherd: *the gates of Hades will not prevail against it*,[69] founded on Peter and his successors.

Dear young people:

Be apostles to other young people. There are many who are adrift and perhaps by our own fault of not giving clear testimony of Jesus Christ, they end up attaching themselves to sects.

The remedy consists in giving an enthusiastic answer to their questions, in three specific fields·[70]:

1° We must know how to present a living liturgy;

2° We must live as true brothers to each other in our communities;

3° Our community must be characterized by an active missionary participation.

Therefore, we must satisfy the "desire for community, for participation, for the liturgy that is lived,"[71] of many of our brothers.

May we always be reflections of the Good Shepherd! May we always be transparent people, so that the Good Shepherd can be seen through us! We ask this of the Blessed Virgin Mary.

---

[69] *Mt* 16:18.
[70] *Documento de Puebla*, 1122. (Editorial translation).
[71] *Documento de Puebla*, 1109. (Editorial translation).

10.

ADDICTION TO THE ESOTERIC, TO THE OCCULT

"People today need to turn to Christ once again in order to receive from him the answer to their questions about what is good and what is evil. Christ is the Teacher, the Risen One who has life in himself and who is always present in his Church and in the world. It is he who opens up to the faithful the book of the Scriptures"

Veritatis Splendor, 8.

Man has an innate tendency to believe in something beyond everyday life and beyond visible, tangible, and sensible reality. Through this tendency, we realize that the life of man is not exhausted in the natural order, that man has another order: the supernatural one, which is most important.

There is a hierarchy in existing beings; and man is on the highest level of this hierarchy. To deny this is to put him on the same level as the other animals. A tree is superior to a rock because it has life; an animal is superior to a tree because it has sensibility, a man is superior to an animal because, in addition to life and sensitivity; he has a soul similar to God, by grace. From this comes the tendency to believe in things that surpass us. Religiosity is written in the very essence of a human being. The tendency to believe in something that transcends natural things is seen in diverse cultures throughout history.

Man has placed his god in different things: in the sea, the sun, the moon, etc., and he has adored and worshiped these objects. The Greeks, Romans, Etruscans and Persians, among others, practiced this type of religion. Those who were less advanced in their thinking based their religions on superstitions, oracles, sometimes in orgies, human sacrifices, and even in material objects, made by human hands. The Aztecs, for example, worshipped an idol to which they offered human sacrifices whose blood was given by means of a canal.

Over time, some men began to see the feebleness of their deities. Their gods did not fill man's need for the infinite. And so some, the most developed, were able to grasp the idea that there must be only one God, the eternal principle of all things. Examples of such men are Plato, Aristotle, etc.

Today, in spite of the scientific-technological advances of some countries in the world, there are great numbers of false religions, superstitions and an invasion of esoteric magic. This development not only appears in underdeveloped countries, but in countries that seem to have a high level of intellectual sophistication.

A clear example of this is a sect called Children of God, led by David Berg, better known as the prophet Moses David. He started his sect in the United States in the '70s, during the era of hippies. This sect has caused much damage, even in Argentina, by promoting a god that saves by using sexuality, prostituting its female followers, violating young boys and girls and kidnapping their faithful to brainwash them.[72] Another sect concerns the revolutionaries of "Supreme Truth" founded by Shoko Ashara, a self-proclaimed deity who caused a massive poisoning in Yokohama, Japan.[73] In Switzerland, the leader of a sect called "Solar Temple" killed his followers point-blank because they did not want to submit to him. In Waco, Texas, a sect led by David Koresh, who thought he was Jesus, massacred eighty-four people.[74]

---

[72] Cf. *Revista Gente*, September 9, 1993, 6-11; Diario *La Nación,* June 9, 1993. 13.

[73] Cf. Diario *La Nación*, April 23, 1995, 4.

[74] Cf. *Revista Gente*, April 11, 1993. 28-30.

Others, who make faith a belief in anything, expose themselves to being swindled by opportunists, as in the case of Mrs. Alcadia González. She was tricked and robbed by pseudo-psychic, Professor Gimenez. According to the pseudo-psychologist, her money was cursed and must be burned; of course, the psychic did not burn the money but only made it look like he did.[75] Another woman ended up with a serious health condition after being "operated" on by a "healer," according to *La Nacion* newspaper. The well-known Pastor Gimenez's wife, after divorcing him because of infidelity, founded another sect and declared on live TV that the religion of her husband was a fraud.

Fortune-tellers, astrologers, and others of their kind, aim to take money from naïve people by telling them that they can see and predict the future, a blatant falsehood. The future is contingent and free, something impossible to know because it has not happened yet. Only God knows the contingent and free future, and in exceptional cases, those whom He allows to know it. They cannot see the contingent and free future in its causes, as is the case for the necessary future, so if they cannot see the future, they cannot predict it.

– "Father, What's your sign?

– "The sign of the cross."

There are people who wake up in the morning and instead of praying, they read their horoscope!

There are some things that can be reasonably predicted because it is certain they will happen. For example, we can predict with total assurance that night will come. We can predict what is necessarily going to happen because the causes that make it happen are known. In general, this applies to physical things. These are the necessary futures, for example, "Every time it rains, it will eventually stop raining."

---

[75] Cf. *Revista Gente*, "Le falló el horóscopo," 18-11-1993, pp. 40-42.

Spiritual things, which depend on personal freedom and properly constitute the future of our existence, can never be predicted, because the causes are free: God's freedom and man's freedom. Only God can know a person's future and only those to whom He reveals the future can predict it, as in the case of authentic prophets. Astrologers, psychics, or "fortune-tellers" do not know the contingent and free future and their aim is to merely make money off the gullibility of simple people.

Recently there has been an increase in satanic sects in Italy, for example. A Bishop of the United States not long ago declared in a television interview that there are a large number of diabolic possessions because of popular satanic religions. Many people involved in these sects used to adore God, but now worship the Devil. Satanic possession, which is defined as a state where the devil has dominion over the body, begin with a relationship consciously established by the person, such as experimentation with a Ouija board, or the famous "game of the cups." We must be careful about what we play with. Diabolic possession, however, is not as pernicious as mortal sin, through which the devil possesses the soul of a person.

We need God. He is not found in occultism, or other sects that are founded on myths and legends. The true religion is not comprised of a group of naive people or swindlers who look to take money from gullible people, nor does it harm the human condition, bringing it down to a den of terrorism or sex.

We must seek God. But we must look for Him where He manifests Himself; we have to search for the true God and the religion that comes from Him. Almost two thousand years ago, Jesus Christ, true God and true Man, said: *I am the Way, the Truth and the Life, no-one comes to the Father but by me.*[76] This Jesus founded only one religion and one church, the Catholic Church, the church that consistently repeats to us His words: *I am the Way, the Truth and the Life,* under the crosier of His Supreme visible

---

[76] *Jn* 14:6.

Shepherd, the Pope: *You are Peter, and on this rock I will build my Church.*[77]

---

[77] *Mt* 16:18.

CHAPTER 3

Consequence of Addictions

"Whoever does not love remains in death" (1Jn 3:14)

"Faced with a situation that could sow discouragement and hopelessness even in strong spirits, I say to you: Youth, Christ, his message of love, is the answer to the evils of our time!... Only He is able to fulfill the longing for the infinite that nests deep in your hearts. Only He can satiate the thirst for happiness that you carry within yourselves, because He is the Way, the Truth and the Life.[78] In Him are all the answers to the deepest and most unsettling questions of every man and of history itself."[79]

Speeches in Lima, Peru, May 6, 1988.

---

[78] Cf. *Jn* 14:16.
[79] Editorial translation.

1.
"LIGHT" OR RESURRECTED?

"Precisely here ... we are faced with the bitter
experience...that man can build a world without God,
but this world will end by turning against him."

Reconciliatio et Poenitentia, *18b.*

Today we find ourselves as the protagonists of history, engulfed in a pitiless battle, a bloody battle between the forces of darkness and the forces of light, between the forces of death and the forces of life. Though men do not understand it, this battle is between the power of the Antichrist and the power of the Christ-God.

1. The "Light"-Man

I would like to discuss an aspect of our "**light** culture" [that is "lite" culture], which has acquired planetary dimensions in our times. We are living in a **light** culture, and lamentably, there are also "**light** priests" and "**light** religious," who, in the confusion of these times, believe that being "**light**" is similar to living as resurrected people. But this is not so. It is a very different thing *to be or to live* as "**light**" men, than to live as **resurrected** men, that is, to live according to all of the consequences of the resurrection of Our Lord Jesus Christ.

What is "**light** culture"? One of the definitions of the word "light," as it refers to culture, means that which is without weight, not serious, frivolous. As that definition applies to marriage, men and women who are not faithful to one another are practicing a "light" marriage. "Light" also means "superficial" and "noncommittal." This is what we refer to as "light" reading, or "light" industry. The "**light** culture" is made up of things that

105

have sparkle, but are without substance, one of the hallmarks of a civilization centered on images.

What is the "**light** man"? Other generations have called him a "flake," a man without substance. He is the human being who does not cultivate the higher potencies of his spirit: the intelligence, by seeking to know; the will, by striving to want and to love, to ensure that his passage through this world would leave it more enriched, and that new generations would be better off by his contribution. Furthermore, the "light" man does not use his intelligence to come to know the fundamental truths that give sense to human life and make it worth living. He is a man who does not wonder about the first and ultimate causes, who does not seek to discover the Supreme Being, give Him worship, and raise his intelligence and his will to Him.

Just as we have beer without alcohol, coffee without caffeine, cigarettes without nicotine, and sugar without glucose, *there are men without humanity*. The **light** man is a man without humanity.

This can be seen in the different manifestations of man: *high schools* where you do not study; *seminaries* without prayer, studies, discipline or love for souls, i.e., **light** seminaries. *There are priests* without humanity, *without priesthood*. What is a **light** priest? He is a priest without substance. His word has no weight, his life has no importance, his apostolate is ephemeral, and the effects of his actions are superficial. His sermons do not produce fruit, his parishioners are fewer every day—because of his many inhuman rules, his teachings ring of the choruses repeated by the ancient Pharisees, his testimonies are **anti-prophetic**.

But there are also men and women religious who, having promised to give themselves to God in body and soul, are faithful neither to their vows nor to their foundational charism; they do not live as consecrated people.

We are talking about empty, hollow people, people without a moral compass to distinguish between good and evil. In the end, they are moral relativists who have no immutable truths, and even their relativism is relative. Therefore they live in relativism. These are men and women who walk without direction: they are in the world and they do not know why, they walk without knowing where they are going. They believe that they are in the very essence of tradition or in the most daring advance of progress, when they are actually the guardians of museum antiques or the vendors of absurd utopias. These are the people who, when occasionally deciding to read, choose "**Kleenex** literature" (disposable like tissues), because they resort to books that are summaries of emptiness, designed to kill time, instead of being food for the soul and occasion for their own improvement.

2. The resurrected man

The Christian, the true man who lives as one resurrected, is very different. He lives the fullness of human nature and develops his spiritual potencies to the maximum. He has enough strength not to fold before the disordered inclinations of sin. He knows where north is and what must be done to reach it. He knows the path and he knows the goal.

The new man applies to his life all of the consequences of the resurrection of Christ. He is the new man who has substance and character and lives a joyful life. He is a man who knows what he lives for and knows how to live. He has been healed by grace and is elevated, perfected and dignified by it. He uses his superior potencies, his intelligence and his will, elevating these potencies by illuminating them with faith, and informing them with hope and above all with charity. He dives into the great mysteries: Trinity, Incarnation, Church, Eucharist, Eternal Life. If he is a priest, he preaches with authority and builds up the faithful. He adds and does not subtract; he has zeal for the House of the Lord. He gives his life to win over the sheep outside the flock and he does not trample the ones inside. He knows he will have to suffer in this world and carry his cross (who doesn't?), but he is convinced and has the assurance that comes from faith that suffering is necessary to arrive at the light. Suffering is necessary in this world, which will never cease to be a valley of tears. It is necessary to suffer so that one day, by the grace of God, eternal happiness will be his.

This is why, in spite of our limitations and weaknesses, we are determined to create schools that are not **light** schools. It is crazy to even think of building a high school in Argentina, even more in San Rafael, a school like the *Bachillerato Humanista*.[80] If we do not form men and women who can identify with the great Greco-Roman-Western culture, we will give diplomas, but we will have **light** men and women, "flakes." We do not want to do that.

As the mystery of the resurrection of our Lord instructs us, we are determined to clearly proclaim the Gospel of family and to teach young people and all people this Gospel. This proclamation of the Gospel must start with the right teaching of Catholic marriage, where a man unites himself to one woman and is faithful to and lives with her indissolubly until death separates them. (In cases of serious problems, there can be separation from cohabitation, but for a Christian who believes in the Gospel, a subsequent union is not permissible).

We need women religious who are true spouses of Jesus, not "widows of Christ." We need women who have their hearts full of love for God, the only Lord who deserves to be served; women with virgin hearts, undivided hearts, living totally for the Lord.

We must form priests who are convinced of the truth they teach, priests who are ready to proclaim the truth of Christ, with all its integrity, to all mankind. We need men of God who believe in the resurrection and are not afraid of anything or anyone. We need men who believe in the power of Easter and the strength and the power of the Spirit; men who believe that there is no greater power on the face of the earth that could surpass, or be compared to, the infinite power of Jesus Christ, King of kings and Lord of lords, the unconquerable victor over death and evil. We need priests who are not like the **light** man, who seems new because he is empty; but rather men who are truly new because they are a manifestation of the *Pleroma* [or fullness] of Christ, because they participate fully in the Paschal mystery of the Lord.

---

[80] The *Bachillerato Humanista* is a magnet school in classical education run by the Institute of the Incarnate Word.

This is why Christ has not asked us to be **light** people. The proposal is to live as **resurrected** people, who live to the fullest, according to our human nature elevated by Baptism to the dignity of adopted children of God.

And so, let us be aware, dear young people, that fleeting fashions will not give consistency and happiness to our lives. Fashions come and go. How many fashion trends we have seen go by! Do you remember? What will truly give consistency to our lives is the assurance that it is Christ who died and rose again for us, to save us from our sins and to bring us to the eternal life of heaven. What remains always firm, and will remain firm until the end of time, is the Truth of Jesus who is the same yesterday, today and forever. Only Jesus has words of Eternal Life, and He is the one who teaches the disoriented man of this millennium the meaning of the Way, the Truth, and the Life.

Let us ask our Mother, the Blessed Virgin, for the grace to give witness to this **New Man**, to this resurrected man, so that we might be apostles of Jesus Christ, knowing how to give our brothers the most important thing we can give them: the meaning of life, the way that leads to Eternal Life, which is to live in plenitude as children of God.

2.

ABORTION

"We cannot suppress life. We cannot reject life,
a gift from God. And I, as the vicar of Him
who is the life of the world, raise my humble voice in defense
of those who do not, nor ever will, have a voice.
We cannot suppress life in the womb of a mother."

Homily in Aquila, Italy,
August 30, 1980.[81]

In Cana of Galilee, the Virgin Mary left us as a testimony the following words: *Do whatever he tells you (Jn 2. 5)*. This is the message of Mary, the fruitful Virgin-Mother, the Mother of God.

What does God tell us? *Thou shall not kill...*[82]

Today, the world, in general, does not do what God says, but instead acts as an enemy of life, of God. By using a thousand fallacies and lies, the world reveals its enmity to life by trying to make a law to legalize abortion.

The false reasons

Let us take a look at some pseudo-reasons that the pro-abortionists give:

1. Defenseless young women who are **raped** by a stranger.

---

[81] Editorial translation.
[82] *Ex* 20:13.

Pregnancy by rape is extremely rare. In St. Paul (Minneapolis) during a period of 10 years, there were 3,500 rape cases; 0 resulting in pregnancies.

Using this reason to support abortion is often a pretext to open the doors to permit abortion for any other reason. And sometimes it is not easy to prove that a pregnancy is actually the consequence of a rape. A woman whose lover has left her can easily accuse him of this crime

The homicide of an innocent baby cannot be legally tolerated. The trauma that a mother suffers from abortion is more serious than the rape itself. The past cannot be remedied, but we can prevent what can happen in the future.

What erroneous logic allows an innocent baby to be sentenced to death as punishment for the crime!

2. There are cases where abortion should be done **"for mental health reasons."**

After a great decline in the number of "therapeutic" abortions (Cincinnati University Hospital did not do a single one in 15 years), all types of abortions were justified for the reason of "mental health." We can affirm with total certainty that no known mental disease can be cured by an abortion on demand.

Instead of destroying a person, the best thing is to use modern therapeutic methods.

3. What about the women who **threaten to commit suicide?**

In Minnesota, in 15 years, of the 93,000 pregnancies, only four women committed suicide while they were pregnant. The fetus in the uterus is a "protective mechanism" for the mother. None of these women had received psychiatric treatment.

However, we *can* affirm that mental damage normally appears in the women who have an abortion: irresolvable guilt, continuous self-reproach and depression. It is easier to take a baby out of his mother's womb than to take him out of her head.

Sometimes, a mother can have suicidal thoughts in the first months of an unwanted pregnancy, but what the mother feels in the last three months is very different. If all mothers who did not want their baby in the first three months of pregnancy had an abortion, at least *one third* of you all would not be living now.

4. A **woman has the right** to do what she wants to with **her own body.**

The right to life of the baby exceeds any right that a woman can have on her own body.

The fertilized egg or the embryo that is developing within a maternal uterus cannot be considered part of her body. It has a genetic code totally different from the cells of the body of the mother. It is the body of another person, of the child she carries within herself.

What's more, any type of abortion, in any stage of the pregnancy, is at least twice as risky for the life of the mother then childbirth itself.

Here is a list of disorders in women who have abortions:

9 % sterility

14 % habitual spontaneous abortion

40 % extra-uterine pregnancies

17 % irregularities in menstruation

20 to 30 % abdominal pain, dizziness, migraines, etc.

5. Others say that abortion vindicates the **rights and dignity of women.**

This is a remarkable statement from the people who always talk about the "fetus." How about if it is a "female fetus"? What if, instead of a boy, it is a girl? Where are rights of this little woman?

6. Other pro-abortionists say: legalizing abortion would **reduce the number of clandestine abortions.**

Legalizing abortion, does not reduce, has not reduced, nor will reduce the number of clandestine abortions in: Sweden, Japan, Germany, Switzerland, Russia, England, the U.S.A., or in any other country. Why? There can be several reasons why people opt for secret abortions:

– The husband wants the child, the wife doesn't.

– A woman conceives with a man who is not her husband.

– A single daughter who provokes scandal.

– A poor woman left by her husband... there is a long waiting list at the hospital.

Even if "legal" abortion is facilitated there will always be a great number of women who abort in secrecy. There will always be the fear of being discovered. "Legality" will never respect the privacy of the individual.

Legalized abortion tends to expand the practice of abortions, and it is impossible to limit what will not accept limitation. It is not only the children who are murdered, but our consciences, that cry out to us "do not kill," are also murdered. The death of the conscience of the guilty is of greater consequence than the life of the innocent.

7. Birth Control.

"The more people there are, the more hunger there will be in the world. If the number of people decreases, we will be able to better take advantage of resources."

This statement was one of the main arguments wielded in the Cairo Conference. It is based on the erroneous Malthusian Theory that the global population increases geometrically while resources increase mathematically, meaning resources will become increasingly insufficient. In fact, there are more than enough global resources. Given the enormous scientific advances in the recent decades, we can take advantage of everything that is produced in the following sectors: agriculture, livestock, oil, etc. There is more than enough food for the current world population and for the future generations for hundreds of years. If resources do not reach everyone it is because of the pride and avarice of rich nations. There is no reason to decrease the number of companions at the table; rather we should multiply the bread on the table.

8. The **decrease or elimination of poverty** was also used as an argument in Cairo.

This is a false argument because it is a universal truth that a nation can take better advantage of its natural resources when it has a high population and, conversely, when population decreases, poverty increases.

It would be absurd to adopt this argument which seeks to eliminate people because there is not enough money. Why don't we start by eliminating older children, say twelve years old or older, who cost more to maintain than a baby?

This becomes more ridiculous when the one making this argument is a person, a family or a country with economic power. Instead of redistributing wealth to eliminate poverty, they want to eliminate the lives of the poor.

9. **Serious complications in the health** of the pregnant woman at the time of childbirth or before.

"When a pregnant woman has a condition that threatens her life, she should abort, because it is preferable to save the mother's life, even if it means sacrificing the child."

Seldom does a pregnancy put a mother's life at risk. Consequently, legalizing abortion across the board because of these rare situations is not justified. In any case, nothing justifies a murder, especially of an innocent baby. Therefore, the normal evolution of the pregnancy and delivery must be allowed to continue without threatening the life of the baby. From the medical point of view, the baby's death does not in any way improve the prognosis of the woman. The prognosis depends on the condition the woman has and not on the presence or absence of the child in her uterus.

✠   ✠   ✠

To all this we can add the serious responsibility held by all who propose diverse artificial contraceptives as an alternative, contraceptives that can have horrible consequences for the woman as well as for the baby, in the case that they fail. In fact, they are not infallible.

Some facts that can help you:

Contraceptives have several "points of impact," that can vary with each contraceptive, sometimes operating in a successive chain, so that when one effect fails, another follows, and so on. They intervene in all the steps of the process of fertilization: from the entrance of the spermatozoid (spermicide) and ovulation (anovulatory), to the implantation of the egg in the uterus (IUD, RU 486). Those methods that act in these last two steps cause the elimination and death of the product of gestation, the already formed human person. For this reason they should be called **abortive**.

There is the tendency in the press and even in medical literature to present contraceptives as innocuous for women, when, in truth, all are harmful to some extent. Some of their effects include sterility, cardiopathies, extra-uterine pregnancies, dilated veins, inflammation of the pelvis, fallopian tubes and ovaries, breast cancer, endometrial cancer, ovarian cancer, etc....

We have to stand for life

Abortionists and pro-abortionists are against life, family, matrimonial ethics and societal peace.

Mother Teresa of Calcutta unforgettably said: "If a mother can kill her own child in her own body, why should we not kill each other!"

And John Paul II said: "If the right of citizenship is granted to the killer of a man when he is still in the mother's womb, then for that very reason a start is made down a slope of incalculable consequences of a moral nature...would we succeed, subsequently, in defending man's right to life in every other situation?"[83]

Abortion is protected by the lack of understanding of the value of human life, the dignity of man; abortion is supported by the primacy given to technology over ethics, things over people, matter over spirit.

For example, the former president of the U.S.A., Bill Clinton, is known for his favorable position towards abortion. He allowed the commercialization of the French abortion drug RU 486. He prohibited educational counseling in abortion clinics, and allowed the continuation of research on fetal tissue that was later used for commercial purposes.[84] Mother Teresa said to him: "Please, do not kill the child; we will take care of him... Please, give me your children. With great pleasure I accept all the babies who would die because of abortion."

A true testimony of life is the case of Gianna Jessen. She is only fourteen years old. Her mother attempted to abort her when she was between 24 and 30 weeks of pregnancy, but she survived. While in the maternal womb, Gianna swallowed the saline solution injected into the uterus. Usually, the solution kills quickly, but in her case, it caused a cerebral paralysis. She was saved when a clinic employee placed her in an incubator. Later she was adopted. Gianna also has *Spina bifida*. The doctors thought she would never walk, but in spite of predictions, she walks now. Moreover, she sings very well. Gianna gave her testimony at the Human Life International Congress, a Catholic organization that fights abortion.

We have to stand up for life like St. Gianna Beretta Molla, who preferred losing her own life to destroying the life of the child she carried in her womb. She died as a fruitful mother, as an example of love for life and love for Love. Let us love life.

---

[83] Angelus Message April 5, 1981.
[84] Cf. Diario *UNO*, Mendoza, 08-14-1993.

Let us fight so that this plague does not spread!

Behind the contraceptive and anti-birth mentality, natural as well as supernatural, there is a logic and a root: **the logic of anti-life and the root of the rejection of God as God.**[85]

---

[85] Discourse, 03-14-1988. (Editorial translation).

3.
SWEET DEATH:
THE MASTERS OF ANESTHESIA

> *"A legislation that contradicts essential moral truths with*
> *respect to the supreme gift of life opens the way for new forms*
> *of totalitarianism which, by the negation*
> *of transcendent truth, destroys authentic dignity."*

> *Speech to the Bishops of Canada*
> *in the visit ad Limina,*
> *November 19, 1993.*

Homicide and suicide are as old as the existence of man, beginning with Abel's murder (Cf. *Gen* 4:8) to the present time. And through all the wars that have been fought, the World Wars are the events that stand out the most. It would seem that the 5th commandment has been violated at some point…

Many ideologies that cultivate death have contributed on the theoretical plane, by trying to provide "philosophical" support and sustenance to the death of man at the hands of man. I am thinking of Hegel, Marx, Nietzsche, Heidegger, Sartre, etc…

Not even medicine has been spared from manhandling by the anti-life mentality.

In the middle of the 21st century, the same thing that happened in Sparta more than 2,500 years ago is being repeated. Our society, like the Spartan, demands well made products that are perfect and have a guarantee. If quality control finds a defective baby, it will be rejected and returned with its original receipt, to wit: **Abortion.** And if a person is failing, there is another prescription: **Euthanasia.** If it is determined that some people are no longer useful to society, they will belong to the tragic group of those *destined to die a sweet death.*

Why? Because their existence no longer has meaning, they are not useful.

Who says their existence no longer has meaning? Do they say it? *NO.* Others say it.

Let the others kill themselves: the great doctors who practice euthanasia on others. Some of them are doctors of medicine or psychology who openly sponsor and defend abortion and euthanasia. They are philosophers of death and legislators who make laws for their own good against the good of others.

These people seem to believe they can dominate the world, that they themselves will never be old, and that they are exempt from the laws of nature. They do not know about the "boomerang effect": *Put your sword back into its place; for all who take the sword will perish by the sword.*[86]

Their life mentality is only read in the key of commercialism; their codes for reading things are limited to only two aspects: utility or uselessness. They understand life as being one more product of the consumerist society, where its value is exactly correlative to its productive utility.

They write and philosophize about the great good that the death of the "useless" old people will be to society, seated at their comfortable desks in front of their PCs.

The deformation of consciences

In order to bring about their aim to condition society to euthanasia, a good campaign is indispensable. It is about creating the idea that there are increasing numbers of people who want help to die. Examples of those who declare that they have helped many die to free them from a life no longer worth living are

---

[86] *Mt* 26:52.

publicized and therefore made to seem somehow "normal." Besides the arguments, the underlying purpose is to make the idea of euthanasia something "normal" and common, to allow it to be present, floating in the atmosphere. Here we refer to euthanasia as "death without pain."

What we currently see in society is that the judgments people held about abortion, divorce, and euthanasia are diminishing in vigor. Initially, the response was a resounding "NO." Then "maybe" was incorporated, followed by "it depends." This sequence occurred in Argentina with the divorce law which began with a "no" and ended with a "yes." It makes me think of graffiti that said: "Before, homosexuality was prohibited; now it's allowed... I'm leaving before it's obligatory."

Do not be naïve. Do not let yourself be deceived.

"Euthanasia" comes from Greek, meaning "good death," a term that has been intentionally distorted. A good death is a death in the grace of God, that is to say, the death of one who, when his time arrives, has entered into a strong friendship with God during his earthly existence, which will eternally fill him with joy. Any other death is not a good death. If someone beheads you while you are sleeping, you will hardly notice... But are you prepared?

The anti-life mentality will seek, at all costs, to create the impression that what has always been black is actually white, and that what the "cavemen" and the "medieval" retrogrades always said was bad is actually good.

The necessity of transcendence

Temporal life is only fully understood in relation to eternity; to think otherwise is to relegate the gift of life as meaningless, empty, or as Sartre said, a useless passion.

When there is no knowledge or recognition of life after death, that we will be judged, that there will be rewards and punishments, that some of us will be saved and others condemned, then it is logical to ask: Why prolong a life that is painful or full of anguish?

The preservation instinct that is present in every creature is part of the natural law and that alone should squelch the argument for euthanasia. For example, it would be enough to see a man who touches a hot iron with his hand. Quickly the other members of the body come to his aid... their goal: preservation.

However, there are various aspects about euthanasia that we must consider. For example, euthanasia is referred to as eugenic when, for false social or economic reasons, it is presented as a way to liberate society from disabled or handicapped people, patients with chronic diseases, people who consume without producing and are consequently considered a burden on society. When the intention is to alleviate pain, it is called mercy killing, the act of homicide to avoid suffering.

There is another interesting division: euthanasia is voluntary when the patient requests it, by word or by written consent through a will; involuntary euthanasia is applied to patients without their consent, or with imprecise or ambiguous information. This was Hitler's method for eliminating from his country all the handicapped.

The excuses

Those who propagate death make up many excuses. They cite situations where all ordinary and extraordinary means have been exhausted, or that the life expectancy is very short; situations concerning people who cannot care for themselves, or do not respond to stimuli and appear to be unaware of their surroundings. They talk about organic insufficiency in at least two systems or the verified and reiterated inefficiency of treatments, lack of treatment options, irreversible complications, etc. These "logical" statements are really about an attempt to trample on the dominion of God over human life.

The meaning of suffering and death

All men go through the experience of physical or moral suffering during life, in a greater or smaller degree. Everybody is going to die some day, but suffering and death do not have an integral and complete explanation apart from the light of faith and transcendence.

It is true that there are consequences of original sin: *Sin came into the world through one man and death through sin.* It is even a greater truth that our sins have been assumed by Jesus Christ who by becoming man, has desired to suffer and desired to die. He underwent all of our sufferings on the cross. He died all our deaths.

That means that because God died in Jesus Christ, and because the God-made-man, suffered like man, human suffering and death have acquired a divine dimension. Even in our sufferings and death we must imitate God.

Before God, the weak, handicapped and sick are loved greatly. In some ways, the part of our human nature that shrinks before pain and death and tries to avoid them at all costs, is understandable because it is a natural and spontaneous reaction. Many who allow themselves to be overcome by fear when faced with pain, lose the true meaning of suffering.

A society which helps patients to bear their pain, and helps the weak to continue their arduous journey is a generous society. A society that knows how to take care of the needs of those who are not able to care for themselves is a society of men who in loving their brother, whom they see, love God, whom they do not see.[87] It is a truly human society.

Man does not have the right to procure death for himself or others. His very existence is the unwavering testimony that man's primary vocation is to live. Man is the being called to Life.

Euthanasia is considered a crime everywhere in the world, except in Holland. The law in the penal code in Norway, Switzerland, Denmark, and others is already relaxed, but in Holland, euthanasia and suicide are socially accepted. It is a cowardly attitude to take before the decline of temporal life.

---

[87] Cf. 1 *Jn* 4:20.

In dealing with a patient who has a terminal illness there is no place for a passive attitude, shrugging the shoulders in discouragement and waiting for death to come. We must have an active, dynamic, and human attitude, directed to the patient and to the family that surrounds him.

Not to accept life as a gift, even in the most difficult cases, is a rebellion against God who is the Author of life.

We must be aware of the true value of life to know how to "live" our own death. We must not deny minimum care to anyone, be it a child, a deformed, disabled, or dying person. To do so is to be complicit with a society whose businesses do not leave time to tend to those who cannot be productive in the marketplace.

Young people must discover the value of suffering and of Christian death. Live your life as a gift and as a vocation! We are responsible before God who said of himself: *I am the Way, the Truth and the Life.*[88]

---

[88] *Jn* 14:6.

4.

AIDS

It is not far from the truth to affirm that parallel to the diffusion of AIDS we have seen a sort of immunodeficiency on the plane of existential values which cannot help but be recognized as a true pathology of the spirit.

Speech to the Fourth International Conference for Healthcare Agents, November 15, 1989.[89]

A.I.D.S.- Acquired Immune Deficiency Syndrome

-Acquired: It is a virus that comes from without and makes itself inherent to an organism in a chronic way.

-Immune: It means defense. The defense system of the human body, made up in part, by white blood cells.

-Deficiency: A severe diminishing of proper functioning with the absolute incapacity to react when faced with pathogenic organisms.

-Syndrome: A collection of signs and symptoms that lead to the diagnosis of a disease.

AIDS is one of the saddest and most destructive sicknesses that preys upon our time. Even more serious than AIDS is what

---

[89] Editorial translation.

125

I call **MAIDS**. Before all else it is a moral problem. **MAIDS:** *Moral Acquired Immune Deficiency Syndrome.*

What is AIDS?

It is a condition caused by a virus called HIV (Human Immune deficiency Virus).

The first cases of AIDS were purportedly analyzed in Los Angeles around 1981. The patients were homosexual men affected by a serious lung infection and a cancer called Kaposi's sarcoma. But the most noteworthy characteristic was the complete shutdown of the entire defense system in addition to their anatomical destruction. As it was improbable that these symptoms would be caused by known bacteria, fungi, or parasites, the etiological agency orientated their search toward viruses. In 1983, scientists in Paris' Pasteur Institute discovered it and named it: LAV (Lymphadenopathy associated to a virus). In 1984 and 1985, two similar viruses that produced AIDS were discovered in the U.S. and Africa. They are called HTLV-III (human T-cell leukemia virus) and LAV-II.

These two viruses belong to the retrovirus family, so called because of their own code of viral proteins (ribonucleic acid-RNA) can be transformed into the protein code of human cells (Deoxyribonucleic acid-DNA) by the inverse transcription. Once transformed into DNA it joins to the DNA of the host cell, changes its information, and eventually destroys it. The altered DNA then reproduces and finally both the original virus and its copies abandon the cell to find other cells where the same process takes place. It is something like a fifth column, as if there were a regiment of the enemy army marching among our own, ready to betray at any moment.

The danger of the virus comes from its special affinity for human defense cells. Once it has entered an organism it is detected by T4 lymphocytes, or helper cells, which stimulate the production of white blood cells and the virus is absorbed. After infecting the cell, the virus renders it completely ineffective. So the organism as a whole is left without defense (immune deficiency) against any pathogenic microorganism (new viruses, bacteria, fungi, parasites). It is present in all bodily fluids, but only reaches a concentration capable of infecting others in blood, semen, and to a lesser degree in breast milk and in vaginal secretions, which are the forms of contagion.

The process by which the disease advances can by studied in different stages[90]:

a) *The early or acute phase.* The individual possesses the virus in his organism; but does not show symptoms. Nevertheless, he can infect others. This is called the "asymptomatic period" which lasts for weeks.

b) *The intermediate or chronic phase.* The individual begins to show the first symptoms and can continue to infect others because the virus multiplies quickly. It is called the "period of complex related to AIDS" (CRA) which can last for months or years. Among the best known symptoms are: weight loss of over 10% of total body weight, fever from an unknown cause, persistent diarrhea for more than thirty days (intermittent or constant), and severe and constant fatigue.

c) *Final or crisis phase.* Once this phase begins, the prognosis is irreversible: the person will die in weeks, months or years. This phase is of variable duration and presents all of the symptoms that correspond to the different sicknesses that make up AIDS (pneumonia, cancer, systematic mycosis, gastrointestinal infections, disorders of the central nervous system that can lead to dementia, etc.).

AIDS is highly contagious from its inception and there are three mechanisms of contagion[91]:

---

[90] Cf. DR. JOSEPH M. GATELL ARTIGAS Y COLABORADORES. *Guía práctica del SIDA, Clínica, diagnóstico y tratamiento.* Ed. Científicas y técnicas, S.A.: Masson-Salvat Medicina, cap. 3, p. 16, 1992.

[91] Cf. DR. JOSEPH M. GATELL ARTIGAS Y COLABORADORES. *Guía práctica del SIDA, Clínica, diagnóstico y tratamiento.* Ed. Científicas y técnicas, S.A.: Masson-Salvat Medicina, cap. 2, 1992.

1) Parenteral Transmission:

-Drug addiction, intravenously;

-Blood transfusion or related issues;

-Organ or tissue transplant;

-Mucosal exposure, or accidental parenteral exposure.

2) Sexual Transmission:

-Homosexual relations;

-Heterosexual relations.

3) Vertical Transmission

-child infected from his mother;

-intrauterine infection;

-infection during delivery;

-infection during breast feeding.

However, it is *not* transmitted by:

-the use of telephones or sanitary or hygienic instruments (it can be transmitted by common use of blades for shaving, toothbrushes, razors, scissors or other pointed objects);

-coughs, sneezes, saliva;

-food, water, drinking straws;

-displays of affections, kisses, hugs, caresses;

-sharing a room, means of transportation, pools, towels, clothes;

-family, school, work, or athletic relationships;

-insects or animals (cats, dogs, birds, etc.).

Statistics have been published that show that the number of people infected is constantly rising. To give us an idea of the spread of AIDS, between 1981 and 1988, 119,818 cases of the disease were reported worldwide. In 1991, 500,000 were recorded, but because there are cases that are not recorded, it is estimated that the real number is 1,200,000 infected. The number of asymptomatic carriers is much more alarming: it is calculated to be from 50 to 100 times the number of those who are sick, which would total 60 to 120 million asymptomatic carriers.[92] This means that one out of every 80 to 90 individuals is a carrier and every carrier is also a transmitter.

This plague can be found among all the continents of the world:

-In the American continents, the most affected country is the United States, having 60% of the total cases, followed by Brazil, Mexico, Canada, Haiti, Argentina and Venezuela.

-In Western Europe, AIDS has spread to all countries, beginning in France and then moving to Italy, Spain and Germany.

-In the African and Asian continents, the virus spreads at a high velocity. (It is believed that HIV is a mutation of the green monkey virus. The green monkey is a domestic monkey that is used in some foods. It probably spread to humans in processing).

✠   ✠   ✠

These are the "technical aspects" of AIDS, but these are not the most important aspect.

Earlier, we mentioned **MAIDS**. The gravity of AIDS is, above all, in what it signifies. Why?

AIDS is, in the end, the result of abuses committed against nature. Take a look, dear young people, at any book that

---

[92] Folletos "Nueva Cristiandad," (Institución Social Católica). "Léame, yo soy el SIDA." "El SIDA y los preservativos".

impartially speaks about the topic. You will find that the behaviors that most often tend toward the spreading of the virus are, among others, prostitution,[93] sexual promiscuity, homosexuality, marital infidelity, drug addiction and use of condoms. These behaviors are held up as normal in a society whose supreme values are regulated by hedonist criteria and moral relativism.

There are people who propose condoms as "therapy." This is truly ridiculous. We have often seen graffiti that says: "AIDS. Please use protection." It is unbelievable. It is just as unbelievable as if a lover were to say to his loved one: "They're attacking us. For goodness sake, let us play Russian roulette." And this is truly the case, because condom use contributes to the spreading of AIDS in two ways:

-By its absolute inability to prevent the infection (that the virus would pass through the pores of the latex is very probable, since the virus is .1 microns in size and the pore is .09 microns in size. In fact, it has been proven that sperm that are thirty times the size of the virus have passed through the pores.)

-The percentage of failures in the use of condoms is very high, around 40 to 50%. This amounts to a failure rate of one in every two or three uses.

However, let's suppose for a moment that an **ultra-safe condom** were to be invented (something that is absolutely improbable in practice) that would prevent even a single virus to pass through it, this would be worst of all because it would give a false sense of security. Instead of solving the root problem of genital addiction, it would make it worse by encouraging the behavior.

---

[93] A young woman who worked as a prostitute in an Argentine province felt sick and when she was examined it was confirmed that she had AIDS. Later she revealed that she usually did about ten jobs a night. Just think of the number of people who would have contracted the virus. Possible cases of infidelity later become a source of death for one's own loved ones.

Those who propose the use of condoms as a solution are those who do not want to destroy evil at its source, because they do not want to change their life style and the inversion of values that directs their path through life. Even on a technical level, it is a false solution.

That is why I say that moral immunodeficiency is even graver than physical immunodeficiency. A large part of humanity is submitted to this moral immunodeficiency in this eclipse of the moral conscience, in this ethical night that seems to have fallen over the world.

Man is not made simply to enjoy himself. Sex also has the purpose of transmitting life. When used incorrectly, submitted to the capricious decisions of human beings without principles, it becomes the seed of death. And so, AIDS is a warning from nature. If I throw myself out of the twenty-eighth story of a building I can repent in the air and God will forgive me—but nature will not forgive me because it has its laws and these laws do not operate according to my personal decision. If I use my sexuality in an unlawful way, instead of rationally as a true human being, the laws of nature will have their way.

And so, dear youth, the "latex vaccines" are worthless as are the campaigns that promote them. What is important and worth the effort is getting to the root of the problem.

What is the root of the problem?

Man was not made for pleasure, but to truly love. The solution then is to put all bets on love, on true love.

God suggested the most effective solution to the problem of AIDS on Mount Sinai when he told mankind: *Do not fornicate!*

5.

RESENTMENT

"It sometimes happens that under the weight of acute, unbearable pain someone directs a reproach at God, accusing him of injustice; but the lament dies on the lips of whoever contemplates the Crucified One suffering 'voluntarily' and 'innocently.' [94]

We cannot reproach a God uniting himself to human sufferings!"

Message for the Second World Day for the Sick, December 8, 1993.

I

Imagine there are a hundred little windows in the soul or in the heart. You could have ninety-nine of them closed, but if one is left open, smoke could enter, and allow the entire heart and soul to be filled with smoke. Once this happens the soul is in darkness. It cannot see where to walk and it leaves the path, loses itself, and doesn't reach the end. This little window is called resentment.

Today it is common to meet resentful people.

II

Who are resentful people? Resentful people are those who have resentment or anger, which is a disagreeable and disdainful impression that causes different emotions to arise in the spirit. Sometimes they feel mistreated by society or by life in general.

---

[94] *Salvifici Doloris,* n. 18

What is resentment? It is the action and the effect of resenting something, of beginning to lose strength; of feeling offended, of being angry or grieved about something.

III

How does the *resentful person* act? It seems to me that there are two principal behavioral characteristics of the resentful person.

The first characteristic of a resentful person is that he lets himself be controlled by his disagreeable feelings, his displeasure and annoyance, instead of fighting to come out ahead. He is very inclined toward disgust, distastefulness, tedium, anger. It is as if he were "poisoned" and were seeking to poison others by his depression and pessimism.

Feelings of resentment can have many causes:

-the perception that his intelligence is less than others;

-lack of the physical beauty she would like to have, or the physical strength he would like to have;

-lack of enough money;

-obligation to study;

-lack of a job, a boyfriend, or something else.

IV

The second characteristic of a resentful person is the unwillingness to take responsibility for oneself. Others are always at fault, never the individual himself.

Who are the "others"?

-They could be his parents: because they were poor, uneducated, didn't give him what he thought was their obligation to give him; they were separated.

-They could be his friends or companions: because they are lucky or successful, because they have more gifts or talents, because they are better or happier.

-"They" could be society in general: it doesn't understand him, it mistreats him by not giving him opportunities...and therefore, these are the people who usually damage road signs, break street lights, deface or destroy statues and monuments in plazas, vandalize public telephones, bathrooms or schools... They end up becoming maladjusted.

Ꭹ

The last option, which is the most serious, is that resentful people blame God for what happens to them.

Their reasoning would be as follows:

-I had an accident driving at high speeds: it's God's fault!

-I'm not as pretty as I should be: it's God's fault!

-My parents separated and abandoned me: it's God's fault!

-I can't find work: it's God's fault!

-My studies are going badly: it's God's fault!

-I don't have money; I can't get a girlfriend: it's God's fault!

-I'm unhappy and unlucky: it's God's fault!

-Society mistreats me: it's God's fault!

Now, God doesn't want evil, doesn't cause or create evil, but He permits it for two reasons: He respects our freedom to choose; and He is capable of drawing good from evil.

Who had their foot on the gas in the accident? God?

Who decided that your parents would separate? God?

Whose fault is it that you don't study? God's?

Whose fault is it that because of your bad character you can't find a boyfriend? God's?

You don't have faith in God, nor hope in His promises, nor do you love Him as you should, and you are unhappy and unlucky. Whose fault is it? God's?

Society doesn't treat you well, but what do you do for society? Is it God's fault?

VI

We should not let ourselves be carried away by resentment. On the contrary, we must try to see the good that comes from the evil around us.

-You had an accident, and you are alive: give thanks to God for that! Don't speed so much from now on; be more prudent.

-You don't have a beautiful face? Don't worry because some beautiful women are empty inside. On the contrary, those who aren't very pretty are those who have a beautiful spirit, which is worth more; in the end this is all that counts.

-Your parents have separated, maybe? Forgive them. Perhaps they got engaged very young and got married without knowing each other very well; maybe they didn't think they were really meant for each other, or because God was the third wheel in the family.

-Know well the one who will be the mother of your children. Ask for advice from prudent people about what Christian marriage is. It's not rose colored as often portrayed in the soap operas. The honey moon phase passes very quickly; the honey goes and they are left with the moon. Start praying now for your future husband or wife, for your future children, and God will bless you.

-Apply yourself to studying seriously and stop living in the clouds.

-Change your sour temper. Be docile to the Holy Spirit and you will obtain one of His fruits: joy. Live according to Christian charity and you will reach one of its effects: joy. And if you are authentically joyful, you will find good and lasting relationships because people will seek out your company and you will be able to choose well.

-Believe in God and have hope in His promises: He never fails! Love Him above all things and even in this valley of tears you will be happy.

-Instead of complaining about others, offer a hand. Build them up! Edify them! Don't let yourself be ruled by your "depression or pessimism" or by those of others!

6.

SOLITUDE

"Man cannot live without love. He remains a being that is incomprehensible for himself, his life is senseless, if love is not revealed to him, if he does not encounter love, if he does not experience it and make it his own, if he does not participate intimately in it. This, as has already been said, is why Christ the Redeemer 'fully reveals man to himself.'"

Redemptor Hominis, 10.

We live in a world of loners, one of the many contradictions that we see today. The world preaches that humanity should be one great family and boasts of seeking peace and union between nations, but its slogans and principles do nothing except create loneliness: lonely people who live without worrying about others, who look out for their own interests, who don't dialogue, who close themselves with seven keys in the chest of their egoism.

Solitude destroys people. By nature, man is a sociable being who can and should communicate.

Types of solitude

There are several forms of solitude.

There is the solitude that is freely sought—except in the case of sickness—by those who can't stand the company of others.

This is the behavior of those who live beneath the common human condition. It is the behavior of beasts.[95]

There is the solitude of hermits who freely choose to give themselves to God, a choice that elevates them above the normal human condition. This is a special solitude that is not in opposition to human nature, rather it raises it up; it is *supernatural.* For example, Saint Paul the Hermit, Saint Anthony the Abbot, Saint Pelagia, Saint Simeon the Stylite—so called because he lived on top of a column—Saint Benedict in Subiaco, Saint Francis of Assisi in the Holy Valley, and Don Orione at Mount Sorate were all hermits, but not all are called to this kind of solitude.

Aristotle said 25 centuries ago: "he who associates not with others is either a beast or a god,' i.e. a godly man."[96]

There is another type of solitude in between these two groups that affects us as members of this "modern culture." An example of this is the philosophy of existentialism, which "finds the absolute only within the most interior nucleus of one's own soul, only in the most *hopeless isolation and seclusion* from others... (thus one lives) the most vexing spiritual existence of abandonment."[97] Man becomes closed in upon himself, without external reference points that help him to transcend.

This solitude often results in another type of solitude, **immitigable** solitude that produces the consumer society. This is the solitude of those who, whether they live in the company of others or not, **wander about with their isolation over their shoulders**, even if they are in close quarters on a bus or in the

---

[95] Cf. ST THOMAS AQUINAS. *Summa Theologica* II-II, 188, 8. *"...hoc est bestiale...".*

[96] Cf. ST THOMAS AQUINAS. *Summa Theologica* II-II, 188, 8. *"...hoc est bestiale...".*

[97] BOLLNOW, OTTO FRIEDRICH. *Filosofía de la esperanza,* (Cía. Gral. Fabril Editora: Buenos Aires, 1962), pp. 22-23. (Editorial translation).

stands at a soccer game.[98] This type of isolated person can be a successful business man, an athlete, a charismatic politician, or an adolescent who, longing for the childhood he left behind, begins to observe with anguish the world of adults that he must enter.

Those who experience this intense isolation usually have these common characteristics:

-withdrawal,

-difficulty initiating new friendships,

-timidity,

-very low self esteem,

-the belief that their success depends on others and their failures belong only to them; this leads to a dysfunction in their identity.

There are multiple factors that push people into immitigable solitude. Unemployment, economic or psychological insecurity, violence, uncertainty about the future, or the pressures that come from everyday living are all contributing causes. It can be the lack of peace that surrounds some people and prevents them from seeking true friendships because of past failures. Or it can be intolerance for others and the inability to overlook the defects of others that create isolation. These factors cause isolation and hatred of the human race. Jean Paul Sartre, who as an existentialist, said that **hell is other people**.

Because solitude is totally contrary and opposed to human nature and engenders disgust for life, it can bring death. There can be nothing more terrible than not loving life. This attitude usually leads to the following problems that are diametrically opposed to the love of life:

---

[98] Here we follow the research of Jorge Palomar in his interview of Professor Héctor Fernández Álvarez, published in *La Nación* Magazine, pp. 55-56.

Addictions: not only drug or alcohol addictions, but all kinds of vices, such as violence, addiction to television, which symptomatically manifests the isolation that people suffer today, unrestrained sex, etc.

Depression: a symptom of despair that, in the end, can lead to suicide.

Suicide: a problem that has increased and is a sad phenomenon of our times, especially among youth.

Tragically, adolescents are often most vulnerable because they tend to develop idealistic expectations that cause them to dwell on the differences between what they have and what they would like to have, and between what they do and what they would like to do. What's more, there is a very high correlation between the solitude that parents suffer and the solitude their children suffer. Lack of parental and familial affection towards children and adolescents creates loneliness.

Paradoxically, an enormous proportion of people, especially youth, feel most alone in big cities.

The question is, "What is the ultimate root of solitude that is contrary to human nature?" The answer is the solitude of the atheist.

Atheism is the most pernicious and destructive kind of solitude. When it gains power over a person, it destroys without mercy.

The other kinds of solitude are nothing more than manifestations of atheism, at least on a social level.

Man needs others to reach his end. He depends on others to reach his natural goals: education, the development of his life, the education of his children, etc. But, in order to be happy, God, who is the very source of happiness, cannot be pushed aside. His grace alone can help man.

The world today has broken off from God. It has put man as the center of the universe instead of God. Its desire to build enormous societies without God is impossible because a world without God at its center is empty and man without God is not man. And so, the world has sunk into chaos. Man without God is a stranger in the universe with nowhere to go and no origin. His own existence becomes an insupportable torture: Why is there suffering? Why are there pleasures and joy?

There are two types of atheism: theoretical and practical. Theoretical atheism denies with the intellect that God exists or that God can be known. Practical atheism, while affirming the existence of God, marginalizes Him and makes Him disappear from the horizon of personal existence. Practical atheists do not deny God but they live like atheists because they love sin. They know that God exists, but they cannot stand the company of God nor of good people, because this company continually accuses them.

At the end of the 20th century, a wave of immorality and sin has come upon us. Evil has always been in the world, but never so much that it threatens to drown the good. For this reason Pope John Paul II called this culture the "culture of death" or the "culture of sin," two things that go together. Sin is an aversion to God and the man of today has turned his back on his Creator, he has rejected God, and this is why he suffers deep solitude. Because, as the Pope says, when man sins, he turns his back on God, and a deep rupture swells up in him, which descends through three levels into solitude itself.

1. Rupture from God: In a sense, this is an act of suicide, because it is a breaking off from the source of life. The consequences are: depression, despair, deep sadness, seeing life as a tragedy, or laziness in fulfilling the purpose of our lives. Paradoxically, laziness sometimes manifests itself as hyperactivity, that multitude of secondary activities that flood people's lives and in which they seek to hide their solitude. They are busy doing many things, but not the most important thing, which is to use the necessary means to reach the ultimate goal, and to live life according to its true meaning.

2. Rupture with others: The rupture from God who is life will extend to other relationships. Incapacity for friendship, lack of solidarity, and egoism are the consequences of this rupture.

3. Rupture with oneself: When man breaks with himself, he suffers the deepest and most painful kind of solitude, a rupture from his own self. He no longer knows what is best for him, but seeks to escape, at any cost, from the pit in which he finds himself, even if it means taking his own life. The emptiness and resentment he feels toward himself feed his resentment against God, and vice versa. It becomes a truly demonic attitude. It is not for nothing that the Gospel speaks of a "mute" demon: closed completely in on himself, living in total solitude that impedes his communication. Man cannot live in absolute solitude but will seek replacements by looking for company in things that cannot satisfy his solitude. And when those replacements fail, he seeks to end his own life.

✠   ✠   ✠

What do we have to do to avoid the trap of isolation?

Jesus Christ. He is God made man. God became one of us to join us in our pilgrimage on this earth. He redeemed all of the sins and evils of men; he also redeemed our solitudes...

The great solution to loneliness, then, is to live the Christian life to its fullness by fulfilling the first and most essential commandment: *Love the Lord your God and your neighbor as yourself.*[99] The authentic Christian is never alone because he enjoys the intimate company of God and the Lord Jesus: *If a man loves me, he will keep my word, and my Father will love him, and we will come to him and make our home with him.*[100] Christians raise their minds and their hearts to God in prayer several times a day, and so they never consider themselves alone. They say to Jesus time and again: *Stay with us.*[101]

Christians who live the great commandment of love of neighbor will never be alone because they see Christ in the poor,

---

[99] Cf. *Mt* 22:37-39.
[100] *Jn* 14:23.
[101] *Lk* 24:29.

the sick, and the needy, and "through a sincere gift of himself,"[102] reach their own plenitude.

And the Lord who promises: *I am with you always, to the close of the age,*[103] will stay with us and will be our great friend and companion on the journey.

And so, with renewed confidence we ask him: "**Stay with us Lord!**"

---

[102] *Gaudium et Spes*, 24.
[103] *Mt* 28:20.

7.

SUICIDE

*"Coming into the world, man already brings
with him the announcement of his own death.
A certain trend in contemporary philosophy
interprets existence as a life intrinsically
focused on death.
But man cannot be fulfilled in death.
He reaches his own fulfillment
only with a full and decisive life."*

Homily, January 1, 1995.

Death, which is normally considered "outrageous" when it comes as a sudden interruption of a life full of hopes, has become for many a "vindicated liberation." Existence is considered nowadays as meaningless because it is submerged in pain and relentlessly condemned to ever greater suffering. This suffering, having been foreseen, makes the present moment intolerable.

We must value the gift of life

Modern man has proclaimed himself the king of his life and, paradoxically, reaching the throne of pride, has decreed his own death.

What is life? It is the fundamental gift of existence itself. We can consider it as correlative to our very being. Our being is something that we have received; and so is our life. It is a gift which ultimately comes from the source of life, God. If man were the cause of his own life we would be immortal. But life escapes our power. There is a superior being who has perfection at the highest level, and who gives it to others by participation: God.

147

Chesterton says that men in general are usually very appreciative of someone who gives them a new pair of shoes; but they are indifferent to the gift of being that enables them to put them on every day. That gift, life, is the gift without which other gifts have no occasion, since no one can give something to nothing.

While God gave animals the capacity to "grow and multiply" when he created them, the activation of this capacity in man goes along with a special intervention from God: the creation of each spiritual soul at the moment of conception. This new being is lovingly welcomed in the family and then, in turn, inserted into a community with established rights and duties.

So, when a man makes use of his life, he has to give an account of it before three "tribunals":

1. The personal tribunal: *Conscience,* which can become obscured by a deviant will and un-dominated passions, always, in one way or another, makes an appearance.

2. The communal tribunal: *Civil justice,* which, being human, is imperfect, but won't fail if it is guided by right natural reason.

3. God: Divine justice, which says, I kill and *I make alive.*[104]

A suicidal person then is a person who, for multiple reasons, fails to appreciate the gift of existence. He doesn't know what life is worth! He has conducted himself according to a scale of values that deceived him, and failed to live up to its promises, leading, in the end, to loneliness, tiredness, and sadness.

Testimony of a suicidal person

A suicidal man, before killing himself, wrote:

"It has been many years since I have felt any emotion. I feel guilty beyond words about these things: for example, when we're backstage and the lights go out and the roar of the crowd begins,

---

[104] *Dt* 32:39.

it doesn't affect me. The truth is that I can no longer lie to you or myself, nor anyone else. I cannot deceive the people, pretending that I am having fun 100%. The worst crime is to deceive. Sometimes I feel that I punch in the time clock before I walk out on stage.

"I have lost the joy of living...It is better to go all at once than to die day by day. I need to be slightly numb in order to regain the enthusiasm I once had as a child...For many years I have had a burning, nauseous stomach. It has been years since I have tried anything. I have lost all enthusiasm, even my music is no longer sincere and everyone has noticed."[105]

This was written by Kurt Cobain, from the rock group "Nirvana." From the analysis of these lines, we can see the gravity of the problem and the principles for a solution.

First of all, he presents the solution for his problems: "It is better to go all at once."

This is a serious error. Usually a young person who wants to kill himself wants to do it because he is tired of life. But is it a true life he is living? Would he, perhaps, be tired of going down the wrong paths? Would he actually be tired of his errors, namely sin, rather than life?

Experts say that suicidal people, before the fatal act, often send out an S.O.S. to the people around them, at least cryptically. A consummated suicide, on many occasions, is a response to deep indifference to the call for attention. For this reason, there should be someone who knows and wants to explain to them that life is the most precious good that we have and to lose it is the worst evil that can come about. One evil can never be the solution to another evil, even the most insupportable one. If we see a person trying to jump off of a building, we should seriously attempt to show him that the street will be invariably harder than life.

---

[105] Editorial translation.

✠ ✠ ✠

Elton John, the celebrated English singer, explains in these words his recovery from two attempted suicides:

"One day I was finally able to pronounce the three magic words: I need help."

That was when he received an effective remedy:

"Doing things for yourself is the best therapy. Vacuuming, washing, ironing, all ended up being a fascinating experience that helped me get my feet on the ground."

Faced with the interior isolation of an individual, the best solution is work. But work should raise him up to a superior end because if not, the opposite happens. As Cobain said: "Sometimes I feel that I punch in the time clock."[106]

For Elton John:

"The catalyst was the case of Ryan White, an adolescent who contracted AIDS by a transfusion. Ryan wasn't allowed to go to school anymore and someone put a bomb in his house. I approached him and his family and I helped them move out of the city because people treated them as if they had the plague."

Considering the pain of others awakens compassion and, with it, the soul becomes open to mercy. Personal problems, seen in comparison to others, are inferior.

"I went with them to the hospital," he continues, "the last week of Ryan's life. There I was with that unconscious boy, watching how his mother forgave those who had been cruel to them and now asked for pardon....And I would complain about everything! If I had any doubt, during those days I confirmed that my life and my priorities were wrong."

---

[106] Editorial translation.

Above all we should profit from that last sentence. Whatever the personal reorganization of the priorities of this man might have occurred afterwards, the astuteness of the observation is notable. It is necessary to change our priorities and our system of values for the good of our spiritual health.

A young person who is not moved by the intellect, but rather by the passions, does not possess the firm principles on which to construct his existence. He is like a leaf in the winter, separated from the branches and blown by the wind wherever it goes. A young person without noble ideals is easily swayed by the majority; he tends to avoid difficult or high things, and chooses easy and low things. This person is a perfect candidate for depression, loneliness, resentment, tedium with life, and suicide.

Fulton Sheen always said that just as the absence of game makes a hunter tire of his sport, absence of direction makes the mind tire of life.

Sin and suicide

Finally, there is something else of importance in the declaration of Cobain: He said, "I feel guilty."

The problem at the root of suicide and also of our society has only one cause: sin. Seeking happiness where it cannot be found generates an existential vacuum that drives man to despair of ever reaching happiness. There is only one definitive cure: drawing near to the source of happiness which is God through His sacraments of frequent Confession and Communion. They are the only balm for our sufferings, our anguish and despairs, our deceptions, and sins because they were instituted by the *Lamb of God who takes away the sins of the world.*[107] He said once: *Come to me, all who labor and are heavy laden, and I will give you rest.*[108]

Many intellectuals of our time have assured us that we don't have the right to call suicidal people "poor men." Many of them

---

[107] *Jn* 1:29.
[108] *Mt* 11:28.

151

want us to believe that man is a being for nothingness, a being destined for death and useless passion. If it is true, then Hemingway, Cobain, Marilyn Monroe, and many others, would be enviable and worthy of imitation. Their lives would be examples of the essence of human nature. We know that this is not the case. **On the contrary.** Let those intellectuals commit suicide, let them practice what they preach, rather than writing falsities that deceive others.

I want to finish with a passage from Chesterton, a champion for life:

"Not only is suicide a sin, it is the sin. It is the ultimate and absolute evil, the refusal to take an interest in existence; the refusal to take the oath of loyalty to life... A suicide is the opposite of a martyr. A martyr is a man who cares so much for something outside him, that he forgets his own personal life. A suicide is a man who cares so little for anything outside him, that he wants to see the last of everything. One wants something to begin: the other wants everything to end. In other words, the martyr is noble, exactly because (however he renounces the world or execrates all humanity) he confesses this ultimate link with life; he sets his heart outside himself: he dies that something may live. The suicide is ignoble because he has not this link with being: he is a mere destroyer; spiritually, he destroys the universe."[109]

For this reason Chesterton once wrote the following poem called, "Ecclesiastes."

There is one sin: to call a green leaf gray,

Whereat the sun in heaven shuddereth.

There is one blasphemy: for death to pray,

For God alone knoweth the praise of death.

There is one creed: 'neath no world-terror's wing

---

[109] G.K. CHESTERTON. *Orthodoxy* (Image Books: Garden City, NY:, 1959), 72-73.

Apples forget to grow on apple-trees.

There is one thing is needful everything

The rest is vanity of vanities."[110]

---

[110] Citation on website: http://www.poemhunter.com/poem/ecclesiastes.

CHAPTER 4

The Callings from God

"Jesus, looking at him, loved him" (Mk 10:21)

"...the Lord offers you new horizons; the Lord proposes higher goals to you and he calls you to give yourself to this love without reserve. To discover this call, this vocation, is to realize that Christ has his eyes fixed on you and he invites you, with his look, to total self giving in love. Before this gaze, before this love of his, the heart opens its doors wide and is capable of answering him yes."

Asunción, Paraguay, June 19, 1988.

1.

JESUS CHRIST, "ETERNALLY YOUNG"

"Life begins to dawn with contact with Jesus.
Far from him there is only solitude and death.
You are thirsty for life! Eternal life! Eternal life! Seek it and find
it in he who not only gives life,
but who is life itself."

Santiago, Chile,
April 12, 1987.

I

Fads pass quickly, and with them pass the typical personalities of the moment. What young person today remembers the "flappers," the "dandies"? They barely remember the "hippies." The figures of today are the "punk," the "snob," the "valley girl," the "homeboy" or the "gangsta." And in a few years, who will remember that valley girls and homeboys existed? They will be, like those mentioned above, museum pieces. When we see old pictures with strange glasses, hair styles and clothing, we laugh. In a few years, young people will no doubt laugh when they see pictures of their women relatives with haircuts that imitate Jennifer Aniston or Kate Moss. Obsolete things, out of style, museum pieces, they smell like moth balls! How out of fashion they will look to them!

It does not happen this way with Jesus Christ. He is "eternally young,"[111] by the strength of His resurrection, because He *will never die again*.[112] He will never "go out of style," or lose His relevance: *JESUS CHRIST is the same yesterday, today and forever.*[113]

Christ is not a remarkable relic of the past. No.

Christ is not a valuable museum without life. No.

Christ is not a wonder of the past, like the buildings of the Pharaohs, wearing away with wind, rain, sand and tourism. No.

Christ is not a great hero who is only remembered in epics of the past. No.

II

The third day after dying on the cross and being buried, Jesus Christ resurrected. He lives! In the present He lives! He will no longer die. He died only once in order to pay for our sins.

Today the greatest deed in the memory of the world continues to be enacted. Today it continues to conquer and captivate the hearts of men and women, children and the elderly, young people and adults. Today He is the most important person, the one whose "ratings" top all records. Just count all the people who come together every Sunday for the Holy Mass. No politician has so many people gathering for him every week. He is the most sought after and the most loved and followed. Jesus requires the most from us, because He requires *everything*.

Not only did He make all things, and *without him was not anything made that was made,*[114] but also *in him all things hold together.*[115] The fish, birds, flowers, angels, rivers,

---

[111] II Vatican Council closing speech to the youth.
[112] *Rom* 6:9.
[113] *Heb* 13:8.
[114] *Jn* 1:3.
[115] *Col* 1:17.

mountains, cities; men and women *exist* now, *today,* in this very moment because He *sustains* them in being.

All things have been created through him and for him,[116] but in His exaltation, in His glorification, He fills everything in the *pleroma,* in His fullness.[117]

He became **flesh,**[118] *to unite all things in him, things in heaven and things on earth.*[119] He regroups in Himself Adam, all of humanity, and the whole universe that sings His glory. As it is revealed in the book of Revelation: *worthy is the Lamb who was slain to receive power and wealth and wisdom and might and honor and glory and blessing.*[120]

Christ, the Word, is the beginning of the existence of all things by creation, and He is the beginning of the reconciliation and union of all creatures by the paschal mystery. He is the source of all the new creation.

Because of the transgression of only one man, Adam, *death reigned,*[121] by the justice of only one man, Jesus Christ, life reigns even more greatly.[122] Just as the bronze serpent that Moses raised up in the desert cured those who looked at it, Jesus Christ, raised up between heaven and earth, is the Savior of all men and He draws all men to Himself.[123]

Christ is the most current of current events and He will never go out of style; He is the event that will never pass.

---

[116] *Col* 1:16.
[117] Cf. *Eph* 4:10.
[118] *Jn* 1:14.
[119] *Eph* 1:10.
[120] *Rev* 5:12.
[121] *Rom* 5:17.
[122] Cf. *Rom* 5:17.
[123] Cf. *Jn* 12:32.

He is present, **alive**, *where two or three are gathered in my name, there I am in the midst of them.*[124]

He is present, **alive**, in the poor, the hungry, the persecuted and the sick.

He is present, **alive**, in children: *Whoever receives one such child in my name receives me.*[125]

He is present, **alive**, in Christians, living in their hearts by faith, as Saint Paul teaches in the letter to the Ephesians and Saint John teaches in his gospel: ***If a man loves me he will keep my word, and my Father will love him, and we will come to him and make our home with him.***[126]

He is present, **alive**, in the pastors who govern the People of God: ***he who rejects you rejects me.***[127]

He is present, **alive**, substantially, in the Eucharist, in the most solemn moment when the celebrant says: *This is my Body...this is the cup of my Blood...*

He speaks to us, today, through Sacred Scripture because all of Scripture refers to Him.

He speaks to us, today, in the Holy Mass with the strength of His sacrifice. It is a discourse that is very concise and at the same time ardent.

He speaks to us, today, through the voice of His Vicar, the Pope, the "sweet Christ on the earth," whom He commanded to ***Tend my sheep.***[128]

Only in Him "does the mystery of man take on light."[129]

---

[124] *Mt* 18:20.
[125] *Mt* 18:5.
[126] *Jn* 14:23; cf. *Eph* 3:17.
[127] *Lk* 10:16.
[128] *Jn* 21:16.
[129] *Gaudium et Spes*, 22.

Only He will give life to your mortal bodies.[130]

Only He has the words of eternal life. [131]

Only He took flesh from the most pure flesh of the Virgin.

Only He *is the Lord*![132]

Only He continues to stir up priestly and religious vocations: apostles, martyrs, preachers, missionaries. He also inspires us to pray for them, for their increase and for their holiness.

Only He stirs up holy spouses, who love each other after the example of the love of Christ for the Church and the Church's love for Christ.

Christ is not out of style.

Christ is not out of place.

Christ is not obsolete, Christ will never ever be out of style…

The heavens and the earth will pass, but His words will never pass,[133] because Jesus Christ is the same yesterday, today and forever.[134]

Today He is the same as yesterday.

May we always follow, with enthusiasm, this Christ who lives forever, who will no longer die, who has triumphed over evil, over sin and over death.

---

[130] Rom 8:11.
[131] Cf. Jn 6:68.
[132] *Jn* 21:7.
[133] Cf. *Mt* 24:35; *Mk* 13:31; *Lk* 21:33.
[134] Cf. *Heb* 13:8.

2.

THE GREAT ADVENTURE OF
KNOWING JESUS CHRIST

*"God's closeness to man through the Incarnation is the result
of a free act of love on his part. Without this loving closeness
humanity would be irretrievably lost."*

*Jarkarta, Indonesia,
October 10, 1989.*

There are some questions that have been asked in every time
to which every man must answer. They are questions that are so
fundamental that their answers are flavored by eternity.

Among these questions, one is particularly important. It is a
question that, if answered correctly, has an irresistible power
capable of raising the dead and moving mountains, of making us
walk on water. It is the question that Jesus Christ asks us.

And so, just as Jesus asked the apostles, I want to ask you
today, who is Jesus for you? I also want to help you to bring to
life the response.

✠   ✠   ✠

First we need to know that it is Jesus Himself, the Only son of
God and the Son of the Most Blessed Virgin who asks about the
love that you have for Him. Perhaps some of you are not able to
respond as Peter did: *Yes, Lord; you know that I love you.*[135] Perhaps

---

[135] *Jn* 21:15.

163

you haven't heard very much about Jesus or learned to love Him. The past doesn't matter. It is enough that, in this moment, you have the intention to love Jesus and it is enough that you begin to love Him and believe that He will continue to love you, ever more intensely.

Saint Paul could say: *I live by faith in the Son of God who loved me and gave himself for me.*[136]

Many people have received little teaching about the Bible in their lives. And many never even had catechism.

I once had the opportunity to go on a mission in the Islands of Paraná, in the Paraná Miní [a northern region of Argentina]. It had been thirty years since a priest had been there. There were cane fields and an abundance of goldfish that were kept in a kind of cage made out of reeds put underwater. The children surrounded me and I asked them a question about Bethlehem.

"All right, let's see...where was Jesus born?" No one knew the answer. How sad! This place had been thirty years without a priest. When you ask a child something, and he can't answer, he feels bad. So I looked for some way to help them feel better about not knowing where Jesus was born. I asked them: "And do you know what a manger is?" They didn't know that either. So I decided to change the questions: "So where did Jesus die?" "He died on the cross," they answered. They didn't know where He was born, but they did know that He had died on the cross.

"And why did He die on the cross?" They looked at me as if to say "you don't know?" "He died to save us from our sins" was the answer.

Jesus is made known to us by frequenting the sacraments. Many of you have had the opportunity to go to Confession. It is Jesus Himself, through the mouth of the priest, who says, "I forgive you," and the soul is cleansed of all sin. It is as if the soul were newly baptized. And why is the soul forgiven? Because it is

---

[136] *Gal* 2:20.

through the power of Jesus Christ Himself, that absolution is given in His Name. By going to Confession often and receiving the forgiveness of Jesus, one can begin to know Him who offers this forgiveness.

Though your sins are like scarlet, they shall be white as snow.[137] *There will be more joy in heaven over one sinner who repents than over ninety-nine righteous persons who need no repentance.*[138] These are the words of Jesus: *Those who are well have no need of a physician, but those who are sick.*[139] Why are there doctors? For the healthy? No, rather to cure the sick: *For I came not to call the righteous but sinners.*[140]

You also need to know and love the Eucharist, the Holy Mass. In a mysterious but real way, Jesus wanted to stay and subsist with His body and with His blood, with His soul and with His divinity in the Eucharist. This mystery can be understood by the ignorant of this world and by the most extraordinary minds, by the greatest geniuses, and the best theologians. They all stand trembling before the greatness of the mystery.

Jesus said: *He who eats my flesh and drinks my blood abides in me, and I in him.*[141] At the Last Supper He did what the priest does at Mass: He took the bread and He said: This is my body; He took the cup with wine and said: This is my blood,[142] and the bread became His body and the wine became His blood. By these very actions, the sacrifice of the cross is perpetuated in every Mass, just as if we were at the foot of Calvary where Jesus died.

And finally, I want to tell you that Jesus is also known in a very unique, personal and intimate way through His mother: the Most Holy Virgin. We will know and love Jesus in the measure that we know and love His Blessed Mother.

---

[137] *Is* 1:18.
[138] *Lk* 15:7.
[139] *Mt* 9:12.
[140] *Mt* 9:13.
[141] *Jn* 6:56.
[142] Cf. *Mt* 26:26-28; *Mk* 14:22-24; *Lk* 22:19-20.

When you know the Virgin Mary, she brings you to Jesus: *Do whatever he tells you.*[143] And when you know Jesus, He gives you His mother for your mother: *Woman, behold your son.*[144] Jesus said this pointing to St. John while hanging from the cross, and in the person of St. John we were all represented.

✠   ✠   ✠

Jesus has done so much for you! He gave Himself even unto death. He gave everything, to the point of forgetting Himself. He truly loves you.

And so I propose to you an adventure, the great adventure that every young person must undertake for himself. *This great adventure is the personal, intimate and irreplaceable knowledge of Jesus Christ.*

You are the age at which you must have this experience because what your parents or priests can tell you is no longer enough. You, by yourselves, must come to know Him who said: *I am the Way, and the Truth, and the Life.*[145]

In order to start this journey, you must learn the teaching of Jesus. The doctrine of Jesus has never been, nor ever will be, surpassed by anyone else because it is the highest and most sublime doctrine that has ever come out of the mouths of men. It is the doctrine that teaches forgiveness for enemies, loving one's neighbor and helping each other to live in solidarity, and defending and celebrating the lives of all, including the handicapped, the abandoned and those with mental and psychiatric illnesses. Why? *Because Jesus died for all.*

There is no person, even the most evil, to whom we do not owe respect, to whom we do not owe love. Why? *Because the son of God Himself poured out His blood for love of that person.*

And also for love of you.

---

143 *Jn* 2:5.
144 *Jn* 19:26.
145 *Jn* 14:6.

3.
ATTACKS AGAINST MARRIAGE AND THE FAMILY

"For the good of mankind the family
must be defended and respected."

Bamenda, Cameroon,
August 12, 1985.

The essence of marriage

One of the greatest thinkers of the West, and certainly the greatest theologian of all time, Saint Thomas Aquinas, says, in a beautiful comparison, that the family is like a spiritual womb.[146] Just as we need our mother's physical womb to begin our life and receive nutrients and care so as to develop and then be able to see the light of day, in a similar way every person also needs the second womb: the spiritual womb of the family. Because the family is the natural place where men, women and children feel protected, where they are helped, educated, and loved. This is the place where we are taught to do good, to avoid evil and to practice all the virtues. This family is what makes man authentically human. Attacks against the unborn in the modern world are increasing (as can be seen in the recent conference in Cairo), but our spiritual womb, the family, is also being attacked with increasing intensity. It is being attacked in the very essence of what the family is.

---

[146] St Thomas Aquinas. *Summa Theologica* II-II, 10, 2.

167

The family is the stable relationship of a man and a woman forever. This is the simplest and the most beautiful definition for the family and for marriage: *a man with a woman forever.* But in today's culture, the family is under siege, and pernicious attacks are raised against the natural law. Let's take a look at some of the ways these attacks are launched.

Attacks against the family

1.   **The belief that marriage** is between one man and many women. Unfortunately, this mentality is prevalent in Latin America today. We hear of Latin-American *machismo* which refers to a man who thinks he can be involved with other women and unfaithful to his legitimate wife. In legal terms, this is called "polygamy": The practice of polygamy still exists in some primitive villages in Asia and Africa where it is acceptable for a man to have several wives. It can also be successive, which is the case when a man has one woman after another and another and another; such as those who adhere to divorce as a way of life, or who see divorce as a real solution for their relationship problems. This is a "refined" or "legalized" polygamy, practiced under the pretext of maturity, respect for the private individual and the pluralism of culture.

2. **The belief that a family can be formed by one woman and many men.** This is a new form of destruction of the basic cell of society, the family. This takes place in the polyandry practiced openly in some regions of Asia and behind closed doors in the houses of prostitution in the West. Prostitution is defined as sexual relations between persons for money. In Buenos Aires, for example, in important hotels the bored wives of businessmen are presented with photo albums full of pictures of athletes who offer themselves for sex. They are pictured in different situations, with a car, dressed and undressed, advertising options where the sexual encounters can occur, and the wives end up going out with them and paying them.

3. **The belief that a marriage can be formed between homosexuals,** the marriage of a man with a man or a woman with a woman. Today, there is certainly an agenda that attempts to make homosexual relationships acceptable. Because of the

ethical night that has fallen over the world, and the moral darkness that has fallen over the conscience of so many, what was seen with such clarity in the past is not seen today. The elementary truth that an authentic marriage exists only between a man and a woman forever has been lost. As a result, there are some countries that have legalized this abhorrent practice of the joining of homosexual couples! Now, there is a push to obtain the right of homosexual couples to adopt children. Can you imagine what can happen in the heads of those children later in their lives? Which one is the father? Who is the mother? Clearly, the practice of artificial insemination, the unnatural use of what should be the source of life, is not the only problem here. If this becomes a common and legal practice as some advocate, the essence of family will be destroyed, along with the human race. This aberration of marriage will eventually give rise to further acceptance of other aberrations such as "trans-sexuality," the operation where an attempt is made to change the sex. When I was a seminarian and I taught catechism in the jail in Villa Devoto in Buenos Aires, which was a rather special environment, a trans-sexual person arrived who had the body of a woman, but he had a beard and identification papers for a man. The jail guard didn't know what to do, he said to him, "Do I send you to the women's block or the men's block?" Because according to the ID card he was a man but according to his appearance he was something else.

4. Group sex as a legitimate practice. This is called "group sex," in English or "round beds," in Creole. The idea of sexual relations among many men and women is a corruption found in two different ways: the so-called "communes" (some with hippie orientation, others with clearly Marxist orientation, as we will see later on), and the "partner switching," where couples get together for a party and afterward exchange husbands and wives with each other.

A report was done on the "Community of the South," a group or commune of Uruguayans who moved to Argentina. Following the Marxist doctrines with all their implications, they had everything in common, including their goods, their husbands and wives and their children. In the report they declared themselves convinced that in order to realize the goal of "no-property relations," "free" relations between human beings, it was necessary to fight against sexual exclusivity by which they mean relations with one partner forever. Some have claimed the necessity to integrate the sexual revolution into the socio-political revolution, while others question the limits on having new types of sexual relations. These cultural limits are considered to be the prejudices of Western Christian society. Such men are ungrateful people who don't have the right to celebrate Mother's Day. They know they were not born from many women, nor did many women carry them for nine months in their wombs.

Another opinion states that we all know that marriage, the traditional family, is the base of the social structure of domination. Therefore, it is necessary to reject the traditional conception of marriage of one man and one woman together forever, so that the man will abdicate his authority over his children and his "oppression" over his wife. This rejection further helps to liberate women, to fight against the prejudices of bourgeois morality and to love and be loved in a plurality of relationships. Along these same lines, the idea of stripping human relationships of all inhibitions and prejudices having to do with sexual pleasure is to make of them a source of subversive happiness. It is interesting to ask, who does the child kiss when he comes home from school? The community?

5. The belief that "trial marriage" is legitimate. This claim destroys the primordial and natural reality of family in which the "forever" part is upset. Trial marriage is the idea of living together as husband and wife without commitment. If the trial doesn't work out, the relationship dissolves. However, in the case that it dissolves, the one who usually gets the worse end of the deal is the woman. This is why, for two thousand years, the Church has defended, and will continue to defend, the dignity of women, and the stronghold that is marriage, even if it is unpopular. The Church has always been the voice of those who are without voice and who are unable to defend themselves and, in this particular case, for twenty centuries, for two thousand years, the Church has raised its voice to defend women and the unborn.

6. The denial of the sacramental nature of marriage. This belief posits that family exists merely on a natural level, forgetting that Jesus Christ raised marriage up to a sacramental level—so it is not only "a man and a woman forever," but "a man and a woman in God forever." Often marriage failures, incomplete families, or the difficulties in married life can be attributed to the fact that for this family God has become an unwanted guest. God is not given the place that he deserves, and so there is no guarantee of unity, fidelity, or fruitfulness. And in an environment like the one we live in, when God is forgotten, things become more and more materialized. The relationship between husband and wife, or parents and children, becomes materialized. And it is impossible to find the solution for the serious problems a family can face today in material things.

4.
THE CHRISTIAN VIEW OF
SEXUALITY IN THE FAMILY

*"The crisis of modern society will be overcome if marriage and
the family are given back
their true physiognomy and exact function.
This can be fully accomplished when the family is founded in
indissoluble and unique matrimony."*

Discourse, December 7, 1991.

Forgive me if I write boldly here, but it seems to be the only way to get the point across.

Who created man with different sexes? God. Therefore, the difference in sex is not bad, but very good. Why? Because God wanted it and made it that way. That there are men and women is desired by God.

Who was it who thought that men should have certain sexual organs and that women should have certain other sexual organs? The Creator Himself: God. Therefore, these sexual organs are created good.

Sex is truly a wonder because it is what guarantees the perpetuation of the species and those who have had the opportunity to study anatomy and physiology will attest to this. The transmission of genetic codes and the great advances science has made in this field have illustrated how marvelous human reproduction is.

But there is more. Who put the attraction between the man and the woman, a strong attraction that it is only surpassed by the instinct for self-preservation? It was God Himself. Therefore, sexual attraction in a man for a woman and in a woman for a man is also good. It was created by God Himself.

There is still more. The pleasure that is normally present when a man and a woman have sexual relations itself is good because it is what the Creator Himself wanted, who has given to the use of sex this quota of pleasure. This gift has been given for good reasons, not the least of which is to populate the world. Without sexual attraction or pleasure, the sacrifices needed to educate children would make the world still emptier than it is. And so, marriage is good, worthwhile, laudable and even meritorious. When spouses have sexual relations in an ordered way as God wants, they gain merit for eternal life: it is a good act that is according to the moral law; it is a worthy act that dignifies the spouses; it is a laudable act, deserving of praise; and it is a meritorious act that makes them holy. And this is so, because in God's plan, marriage and families have many purposes.

The first purpose is · the transmission of life, a miracle of birthing new beings who become children of God by Baptism and who are called by the same God to eternal life and holiness. To multiply this miracle of life is the great work of a woman, although it is not exclusively hers.

Further, God has created the concept of marriage and family in order that it be the place, or the environment, of the manifestation of mutual love. It is the environment in which a man and a woman reciprocally give themselves to one another in order *to achieve the communion of persons.* In this way, marriage and the family become a magnificent reflection of that community of three that is the Most Holy Trinity, the Father, the Son and the Holy Spirit. In the family, there is an *I* and a *you* so that they might become a *we.* This is why you must not let yourself be deceived by the distorted views of sex that are often seen on TV, radio, and in magazines.

God has made man and woman to unite to one another faithfully throughout their entire lives for the manifestation of mutual love and the transmission of life so that they might live the true communion of persons. There are only two views on this issue: God's view of husband and wife who are lords over sex, or the view that is popular today that men and women are slaves to sex. In other words, sex is made for men and women, not men and women made for sex. Men and women are much more than the act of sex and all the good things about it, because sex itself is not our ultimate end. And this is the key point in differentiating between these two diametrically opposed views.

When a man considers a woman as a sexual object he treats her like an object. When people consider others as sexual objects those "objects" lose their personhood, resulting in perversity. To clarify, I am going to use the example of a step-father who raped a two month old baby and then cut her with broken glass to make what he did look like an accident. This was a horrendous case!

The Christian view calls for using sex with responsibility according to God's law. When it is abused the woman becomes for the man, or the man becomes for the women, an object or a thing. As the great sexologist, Paul Chauchard said: "Sexuality has been reduced to genitals. Humanity has become a jungle where males and females lie in ambush to seize what allows them to satisfy their needs."

Just as people become enslaved to their drug and alcohol addictions, those who abuse sex become enslaved to their passions.

Therefore, we are dealing with two views that draw the line in black and white: the differences between the person, man or woman, who is lord of him or herself, and the person who is a slave to sex, to his or her inordinate passions. Pope John Paul II said that there is an anthropological difference, a difference in the conception of what man and woman are, in these two opposing views of sex. At the same time, there is a moral difference.

"In the light of the experience of many couples and of the data provided by the different human sciences, theological reflection is able to perceive and is called to study further the difference, both anthropological and moral, between contraception and recourse to the rhythm of the cycle: it is a difference which is much wider and deeper than is usually thought, one which involves in the final analysis two irreconcilable concepts of the human person and of human sexuality. The choice of the natural rhythms involves accepting the cycle of the person, that is the woman, and thereby accepting dialogue, reciprocal respect, shared responsibility and self-control. To accept the cycle and to enter into dialogue means to recognize both the spiritual and corporal character of conjugal communion and to live personal love with its requirement of fidelity. In this context the couple comes to experience how conjugal communion is enriched with those values of tenderness and affection which constitute the inner soul of human sexuality, in its physical dimension also. In this way sexuality is respected and promoted in its truly and fully human dimension, and is never 'used' as an 'object' that, by breaking the personal unity of soul and body, strikes at God's creation itself at the level of the deepest interaction of nature and person."[147]

I would like to end with perhaps one of the most brilliant texts about the beauty of human sexuality which points to the practice of chastity, be it the chastity of youth, the chastity of marriage, or the chastity of the widow. Chastity, in the context of marriage, means the ordered use of sex. These are the words of Saint Paul the Apostle: *"All things are lawful for me,"* but not all things are helpful. *"All things are lawful for me,"* but I will not be enslaved by anything. *"Food is meant for the stomach and the stomach for food,"* and God will destroy both one and the other. The body is meant not for immorality, but for the Lord, and the Lord for the body. And God raised the Lord and will also raise us up by his power. Do you not know that your bodies are members of Christ? Shall I therefore take the members of Christ and make them members of a prostitute? Never! Do you not know that he who joins himself to a prostitute becomes one body with her? For as it is written, "The two shall become one." But he who is united to the Lord becomes one spirit with him. Shun immorality. Every other sin which a man commits is outside the body; but the immoral man sins against his own body. Do you not know that your body is a temple of the Holy Spirit within

---

[147] Apostolic Exhortation, *Familiaris Consortio*, 32.

you, which you have from God? You are not your own; you were bought with a price. So glorify God in your body.[148]

---

[148] 1 *Cor* 6:12-20.

5.
CATHOLIC COURTSHIP I

"Young people: Do not let your future
be destroyed; do not let the richness of love
be snatched away from you!
Secure your future fidelity,
the fidelity of the future families
that you will form in the love of Christ."[149]

Lima, Perú,
June 19, 1988.

Before beginning on the topic of courtship and dating, it is important to keep two things in mind:

-the structure of man; and

-the vocation, or triple call of man.

a- Intelligence, will, and the passions exist in man. The dignity of man exists, when the superior potency dominates the others.

What is the superior potency of man? It is the intelligence that distinguishes man from animals.

So, man is more human when the intelligence dominates the other potencies, and not the other way around, which is when man resembles animals the most.

b- Every man has a triple call (or vocation) from God:

---

[149] Editorial translation.

-The first call is to existence. It is God who called us into being. We cannot choose to exist or ask to exist. It was God who called us into being.

-The second call is to the life of grace. We are called to the life of grace through the reception of Baptism and the Sacraments. Those people who have not yet received the sacraments are also called.

-The third call is to a certain state of life: the priesthood, religious life, or marriage. God calls us to be holy in the state that He chooses from all eternity, and that will bring us to happiness.

Courtship is the first step towards future marriage. Therefore, the marriage will reflect the courtship.

Because the majority of marriage failures begin while the couple is dating, we will study the characteristics of a good courtship.

Time of mutual acquaintance

The principle objective of a courtship is to determine whether or not the couple is compatible on many different levels: to see if they are "made for each other," if they could live the married life, and above all if they will be able to educate their children. There are several ways to discover if the marriage will work:

a-Discernment about whether he or she can successfully fulfill his or her role as a father or mother; and acquire knowledge about the work, character, virtues and vices of each other. Sometimes imagining someone as a father or mother can highlight flaws in the relationship over the long term. Many girls realize that they have to cut off the relationship when they think about their children and they see that the young man will not be able to be a good father.

b- Consideration of parents' opinions. Why is that?

-They (usually) have a more disinterested love;

-They have more life experience;

-They have known more people in their lives, including relatives and friends.

Advisably, one should never marry without the consent of the parents, except when one must make exceptions to the rule.

It is common for young people today to describe their parents as:

-old-fashioned;

-lacking understanding;

-out of step with the times;

-not realizing that things were different in their days.

Usually, people who get married without the approval of their parents fail in their conjugal lives.

The purpose of courtship then, is "mutual knowledge (or acquaintance) directed toward marriage," and to determine if they are "made for one another."

Limited acquaintance

What kind of knowledge is needed to become well-acquainted? Courtship is a time of limited and relative knowledge, not absolute knowledge. It can only be total and absolute in marriage. Many use the excuse of getting to know each other better to support pre-marital sexual relations, which has lamentable consequences.

a- Let's talk a little more about **pre-marital sex:**

According to a poll, "almost 80% of those polled are in favor of pre-marital sex and more than 50% are against abortion. 14% do not use any form of ingested birth control. 61% use condoms."[150] In situations where this early profanation of the

---

[150] Poll taken by UNICEF Argentina among youth in the first months of 1995. In *Viva* magazine, Sunday 8/13/1995, p. 56-62.

Sacrament of Marriage takes place, the woman gets the worst end of the deal:

-She loses her virginity.

-She feels enslaved to her partner who always looks for sex more and more often.

-She can't say no because she is afraid he will leave her, reproaching her for not loving him anymore.

-She lives in anguish that her parents will find out about the relationship.

-She suffers the annoyances of the marital act without the security and tranquility of marriage.

The man, on the other hand, is not in a hurry to get married because he gets the benefits of being married without actually making a commitment to marriage, and he is not the one who becomes pregnant. But the woman does, and this is a danger that is all too real for her to not fear it.

There was a young woman who traveled to Bariloche in the Andes Mountains with her classmates on a graduation trip. She met a young man there and had sex with him. When they were saying goodbye he gave her a package and told her to open it when she got home to Mendoza. When she opened it she found a flower and a note that said: "Welcome to the world of AIDS."

b- If there is an out-of-wedlock pregnancy, usually the woman is pressured to have an **abortion**. Abortion is an "unspeakable crime,"[151] with three aggravating circumstances:

-it is the *murder of an innocent*,

-defenseless and *un-baptized*,

-and *the regret* that a woman will carry for having killed her child will haunt her for the rest of her life.

---

[151] *Gaudium et Spes*, 51.

A young man who got his girlfriend pregnant once said: "Many friends came to me and told me to get an abortion for my girlfriend, that it was very simple, that everyone did it, and that I wouldn't end up tied down. I had the money to do it, but would I ever be able to watch a child play in the street again? I would have to turn away."

There is no doubt that the regret stays for life. In the film "The Silent Scream," by Dr. Bernard Nathanson (filmed during an abortion), the moment the suction instrument touches the bottom part of the placenta you can see the creature inside open its mouth (the Silent Scream) and desperately try to escape to the upper part of the placenta, seeking refuge. This moment might make us think (so ironically!) of a small frightened child who runs to his mother's skirts looking for protection. The gynecologist himself, Dr. B. Nathanson, who had performed thousands of abortions, swore never to do another abortion after seeing the film. He was convinced that he was looking at a person.[152]

Sometimes a woman gets an abortion badly done and can no longer have children. As gynecologist and obstetrician Dr. Juan Garrido, from the Gynecology department in the Hospital José Joaquín Aguirre in Santiago, Chile, said, "Specialists agree that sterility in the woman is among the gravest complications that come from abortion because it causes chronic inflammations and damage to the ovaries."[153]

Many women also die from abortions. In Argentina they say that there are about 350,000 abortions a year and about 350 women a year die from infections caused by abortions.[154] And we can add to that the number of women who die during an abortion, or the psychological damage they suffer. It is easy to

---

[152] "El aborto y el sentido común," and "¿Es el aborto un derecho?" *Nueva Cristiandad,* (Institución Social Católica).

[153] "El aborto causaría un tipo de cáncer," *Diaro LA NACION,* 4 Oct. 1981.

[154] Cf. "El aborto causaría un tipo de cáncer," *Diaro LA NACION,* 4 Oct. 1981.

extract a child from the womb; it is almost impossible to extract a child from the mind.

To people who argue that they don't have the money to raise children we should say:

-Abortion itself is expensive.

-If they don't have money they should kill the oldest child who has lived the longest. Would a mother be capable of doing this?

c- Since man is more cowardly, he will use **contraceptives**.

To those who advertise in favor of condoms and birth control we say:

-Condoms do not offer security; there are cases in which they fail.

-Since campaigns in favor of contraceptives have taken place, abortion and AIDS rates have risen.

-Since the use of contraceptives became widespread in 1977, cases of venereal diseases have greatly increased.

-Contraceptives cause problems such as pelvic inflammation or extra-uterine pregnancies.

These examples point out that nature responds when it is attacked. It will always be true that: "*God always forgives, men sometimes forgive, nature never forgives.*"

d- If sex takes place before marriage, the **wedding** will be without happiness, without dreams, without the hope of being able to receive or to give anything new. A very beautiful stage, the courtship, has been missed. On the other hand, sacrifices made to preserve purity until the wedding will bear fruit in the marriage.

We can see an example of this in a letter that a young woman wrote to a priest. It says:

"As a teenager I never heard the word purity, nobody ever told me about this great treasure that I had and that I needed to protect it with so much care. Even less did I know that my body was the temple of the Holy Spirit and that it should be respected for that reason.

"When I turned 14 or 15, I began to date, if it can even be called that. The only advice my mother gave me was that I should give my body to the boy until the day I get married, because if I didn't he would get tired and leave me.

"She never told me about purity, she never explained to me that true love does not depend only on this. She never explained to me what a good courtship is; neither did she tell me that I was too forward and that I wasn't old enough to be dating.

"You know, Father, sometimes I think about how my life has been, I think about the treasure that I lost, and I cry. I cry a lot, because it hurts me to think about what I'm going to do in the future, if I begin to date a good man, in order to form a very Christian home; because now I know that his virtues, his soul, his love for God, matter more than anything else. But really, I don't feel worthy of a man like that."

e- Finally, often during arguments in marriage, a woman will listen with pain to her husband's reproaches reminding her of her past shame.

For these reasons the Church, in insistently defending the sanctity of marriage, has done nothing other than defend women, children (who suffer the most) and the family so that women do not become mere objects of pleasure and the children aren't left to raise themselves.

And so we must say that courtship is a time of RELATIVE acquaintance, whatever friends, neighbors or parents might say. In courtship the "already, but not yet" is given: you should love each other already, but not as you will in marriage.

In courtship, you should seek spiritual union with each other. Bodies can be united in marriage only after spiritual union is established. If the union of bodies is sought outside of marriage, egoism, not true love, is present. If we seek only bodily union, disregarding the will of God, what distinguishes us from animals?

The fact that two people are not united by the sacrament means that the union is dissoluble. That's why the courtship is a time to say NO, if it is not heading to a good end. We have a very good example of this in the story of a heroic young woman: "Her parents strongly advised against the marriage, the groom was lazy and irritable. The day of their nuptials, the groom took her by the arm to lead her to the altar and she tripped over her long dress. He meanly reproached his fiancée in the following way: 'You're always so clumsy!' When the moment of consent arrived the groom gave his. When the priest asked the bride: 'Jane, do you accept John as your husband?' her voice was heard clearly and serenely: 'I do not.' She repeated the same answer when the priest asked her again, to the surprise of everyone. Today she is married to another man and she has several children who, when they find out what their mother did, will not stop thanking her until the end of time."

6.
CATHOLIC COURTSHIP II

"Two people becoming one in the mutual self-giving of
body and soul will only avoid enslaving domination and reciprocal
exploitation if it is united to an enduring mutual respect."[155]

Salzburg, Austria,
August 14, 1988.

We must see each other as people, not as objects to be used and then discarded. If you do not learn to respect each other while dating, you will not respect each other in marriage. And we can affirm that "A regular courtship leads to a bad marriage; a good courtship leads to a regular marriage; only a holy courtship leads to a holy marriage."

True love is not always rose-colored. In fact, true love is crucified because it demands forgetfulness of self for the good of the other. True love culminates in self-giving, sacrifice, fruitfulness, and in the search for the fullness of the one who is loved. The false love the modern world presents consists only in attraction, sympathy and emotion, it consists in liking, possessing and enjoying, since without self-giving and sacrifice for the other it becomes only different forms of egoism. If we stay just on the level of "liking" we have egoism, not love.[156]

---

[155] Editorial translation.
[156] Cf. *Nueva Cristiandad.* (Institución Social Católica). "¡Hola! Aquí te habla el Amor," and "Me gustas, te quiero, te amo."

Since we are talking about Catholic courtship, which must be holy, we will talk a little about the things that can prevent a courtship from being holy. Some things are:

Signs of affection

The emphasis on sex in advertisements, TV shows, and movies falsify real love. The flirtations, embraces, kisses and intimate dancing do not constitute a complete sexual relationship and make it appear that imaginary pleasures are more fascinating, lasting, stronger and more intimate than the real thing. In the end, these pseudo-affections are more desired than a genuine relationship.

But these "effusions" have serious consequences, for the woman and the couple:

a-THE WOMAN

-They often cause **frigidity;**

-Some doctors also assure that they can cause **sterility** in the marriage.

b-THE COUPLE

-These practices lead to **masturbation** (for both of them) and to seeking out prostitution houses (for the man). It is using sex egotistically, using the partner as an object of pleasure and nothing more. She, or he, is only there to satisfy personal enjoyment.

-When people habitually fall into the sin of masturbation, it becomes so chronic that they are incapable of engaging in the marital act of sex for love.

-These affections or masturbation is one of the principle causes of unhappy families. When one of the couple discovers that the other egotistically uses him or her as an object, the death of love is inevitable.

-This is the cause of bitter sadness, great disappointments, and frustrations. The fruit of egoism cannot be happiness or peace.

-Separation and marriage failures have other serious consequences for the children, who suffer the most. We have the example of a letter from "Johnny," the son of separated parents, who wrote: "Sweet Child Jesus: I beg you to take me to heaven. I would like to be an angel. I promise that I will be a very good angel and I will do everything you tell me to. But here I am very miserable. Did you know that daddy threw mommy out because he got married with another mommy? Mommy took me with her, but I've had a terrible time with her. I haven't had any candy since then. It's very cold here. Mommy always cries. Now there's another daddy who has come to see mommy, but she always cries a lot. The new daddy is drunk. Mommy has cried to the neighbors, saying that we are dying of hunger. I told mommy that I'm going to kill the new daddy. But mommy says that the Child Jesus will get mad. I learned in school that the angels have a very happy life, and they don't have to do anything else but obey you. That's why I would like to be an angel, because I am very miserable. Child Jesus, come soon to get me. I kiss your hands. Johnny."

All the sacrifices that are made for mutual respect in the courtship are nothing compared to the great and blessed fruits that the marriage will have because of those sacrifices.

Frequency of seeing each other

One of the customs or practices that have developed in dating is the great frequency a couple is together. They don't realize that being together morning, noon and night is a serious mistake that often causes them to lose the freshness of love, and submits them to a routine. This is because we have lost the importance of the *rite* and of the *party*. And what is that?

Saint Exupery writes admirably on rites in *The Little Prince*:

"'It would have been better to come back at the same hour,' said the fox. 'If, for example, you come at four o'clock in the afternoon, then at three o'clock I shall begin to be happy. I shall feel happier and happier as the hour advances. At four o'clock, I shall already be worrying and jumping about. I shall show you how happy I am! But if you come at just any time, I shall never know at what hour my heart is to be ready to greet you... One must observe the proper rites...'

"'What is a rite?' asked the little prince.

"'Those also are actions too often neglected,' said the fox. 'They are what make one day different from other days, one hour from other hours. There is a rite, for example, among my hunters. Every Thursday they dance with the village girls. So Thursday is a wonderful day for me! I can take a walk as far as the vineyards. But if the hunters danced at just any time, every day would be like every other day, and I should never have any vacation at all.'"[157]

With respect to this sense of party or excitement, it has been said:

"Regarding the encounter between a couple: habit and familiarity have a chilling effect on love. What we see, hear and experience every day loses its sense of unpredictability and uniqueness. In the end, the relationship loses its flavor, becoming as insipid as water. The worst mistake a couple can make is to be together too frequently: 'absence makes the heart grow fonder.'

"It is better for the couple to always think of each other, to continually long for the presence of the other, but to actually be together as little as possible. A date should always feel like a celebration, and you can't celebrate every minute of your life."[158]

How these everyday couples bore the rest of their families! The constant presence of the couple can create a lack of privacy in the home, the parents cannot watch TV in peace, the girlfriend stops fixing herself up as she should to look nice for her boyfriend, school work suffers and they each lose contact with their own friends.

---

[157] ANTOINE DE SAINT EXUPÉRY. *The Little Prince.* Trans. Katherine Woods. http://www.angelfire.com/hi/littleprince/frames.html, chap. 21.

[158] Editorial translation.

About meeting frequently in dangerous places, we can say with Saint Isidore: "It is impossible to be close to the serpent for a long time without getting bitten." *He who loves danger will perish by it.*[159] Saint Bernard said: "Isn't it a greater miracle to remain pure while exposing oneself to the occasion of sin than to raise someone from the dead? You can't do what is lesser (raise someone from the dead) and you expect me to believe you can do the greater?"

Age

How old should we be to begin to date? Love doesn't have an age: there are happy marriages where the couple met very young and also when they met at an older age.

In general it is inadvisable to start dating too young for several reasons:

-lack of maturity;

-lack of a sense of full responsibility;

-overlong courtship;

-the loss of the best years of youth, including time with other friends;

-loss of interest in university studies or a career;

-limited acquaintances; acquaintances and friendships will expand, giving enough time, allowing for a better choice.

Courtships are like fruits: they are good neither too early, because they need to ripen, nor too late because they fall and begin to go bad.

For example, an Argentine model got married at age 16 and separated by the time she was 17: Deborah de Corral. At 13 years old she lived without her mom, at 15 she became a model, at 16 she began to date, and very soon after she began to live with her

---

[159] *Sir* 3:26.

boyfriend, at 17 she separated from him. "I need to be alone for a time. I want to be at peace and get back into my work...I was only 16 years old and I was miserable."[160]

Religious dimension

What is the sign that a couple truly loves each other? The sign is growth in the love of God. Not loving God is a sure harbinger of failure in the marriage. If the couple loves God above all things, they will have a solid marriage, founded on rock,[161] and it will remain firm in spite of the rain of difficulties that will fall, the torrents of sacrifices that will come, and the winds of calumnies that will blow.

God wants marriage, which is why He made it a sacrament. A beautiful courtship is the preparation for a great union.

But how do we prepare for marriage? We prepare:

-by reading good books about marriage (encyclicals...);

-by the couple participating in apostolic works;

-by helping each other to fulfill the duties of his or her state of life;

-by keeping the first love alive;

-by receiving the sacraments frequently, especially Sunday Mass;

-by a fervent devotion to the Virgin Mary.

It is chaste young people who will form the most fruitful, solid, strongest, and happiest homes.

We have a beautiful example of Catholic courtship in Bartolomé Blanco Marques, a young man who died a martyr in

---

[160] Cf. Revista *Gente* 07/27/1993, pp. 36-39.

[161] Cf. *Mt* 7:25.

the Spanish Civil War on October 2, 1936, at 21 years of age. Before being shot for being Catholic he wrote four letters: three to his family and one to his girlfriend, in which he revealed the great sufferings of his noble soul:

"Provincial Prison of Jaén, October 1, 1936

"Maria of my soul,

"Memory of you will accompany me to the grave; as long as there are beats left in my heart, my heart beats with love for you. God has wanted to make these earthly affections sublime, ennobling them when we love each other in Him. And so, even in my last days, God is my light and my desire, but this doesn't impede the memory of the person I love most from being with me until the hour of my death... Now when there are only a few hours left before final rest, I only want to ask you for one thing: that in memory of the love we had, which is now increasing, you keep before you as your principle goal the salvation of your soul; because then we will be able to meet again in heaven, for all eternity, where no one will separate us. And so, until then, Maria of my soul! Do not forget that I will look down on you from heaven; make sure you become a model for Christian women, for at the end of the game earthly joys and goods are worth nothing if we do not succeed in saving our souls...

"Until eternity, where we will continue to love each other for all time.

-Bartolomé."

7.

I WILL FOLLOW YOU WHEREVER YOU GO

"...the Lord offers you new horizons; the Lord proposes higher goals to you and he calls you to give yourself to this love without reserve. To discover this call, this vocation, is to realize that Christ has his eyes fixed on you and he invites you, with his look, to total self giving in love. Before this gaze, before this love of his, the heart opens its doors wide and is capable of answering him yes."[162]

Asunción, Paraguay,
June 19, 1988.

Jesus Christ is truly worth the complete surrender of our lives to him.

He is the great captivator of hearts and the greatest lover of all time. He is the most ardent lover of eternity. He deserves the offering of an entire existence and much more.

What is it that really moves so many young people to offer themselves unconditionally to follow Him wherever He wants them to go?

Some people say it is because of the resurrection. That is not correct. No. With the resurrection it would be difficult to awaken vocations because people will think that we are advertising like those companies who play catchy jingles on TV: "If listening to

---

[162] Editorial translation.

this music makes your heart beat faster, apply to the University of _____, you will have a great future..."

According to others, the motivation to follow Christ is fear of hell, or frustration in love, or brain-washing, or coercion. However, if a young man or woman tries to consecrate themselves based on these reasons, the commitment won't last.

For my part, I believe that vocations to the priesthood and to consecrated life are produced by the CROSS OF CHRIST. The fact that He *who loved me and gave himself for me,*[163] and that His *love bears all things,*[164] moves people to give themselves. Christ loved unto death, so that a young person could never reproach Him for not loving enough. It calls. It burns. It attracts. It inflames.

The call then, is nothing less than a call to radically share the sufferings of Christ. It is not a call to have fun, but to *suffer*, as the Holy Spirit teaches: *My son, if you come forward to serve the Lord...prepare yourself for temptation.*[165] It is a call to *die every day.*[166] It is a call to crucify oneself with Christ.[167] It is a call to be like those condemned to death.[168] It is a call to go up to Calvary.

In a way, Jesus said it in general, and I think that it can be understood vocationally in particular: *And I, when I am lifted up from the earth, will,* which is to say, on the cross *draw all men to myself.*[169]

If a young man or woman is truly disposed to be *lifted up* with Jesus Christ, it is possible that he or she has a vocation. If he or she is frightened by this, there is probably no vocation. Those who have vocations are willing to do great, heroic and even epic things for Christ and His Church.

---

163 *Gal* 2:20.
164 1 *Cor* 13:7.
165 *Sir* 2:1.
166 1 *Cor* 15:31.
167 cf. *Gal* 2:19.
168 cf. 2 *Cor* 4:11.
169 *Jn* 12:32.

✠   ✠   ✠

Unfortunately, many people have discouraged religious vocations because they do not understand the nature of them. Some vocations are discouraged for bad or selfish intentions. Therefore, I would like to pause here briefly to consider some of the most common objections, in order to show, with the authority of the saints, that these objections don't have any foundation on the truth.

1. The sublimity of consecrated life

Entrance into religious life is, in itself, clearly, a great good. Saint Thomas says that anyone who doubts this "contradicts Christ,"[170] who made religious life the object of an evangelical counsel. He also states that not to realize that the vocation to the consecrated life is a greater good is to "*disparage Christ.*"[171] That is why Saint Augustine says, "The East," that is Christ, "calleth thee, and thou turnest to the West,"[172] or to man who is mortal and capable of error.[173]

In answer to the following objection: "It's ill-advised to enter religious life without seeking the counsel of many people and considering the matter a long time," Saint Thomas replies: "but for him who seeks to enter religion, there can be no doubt but that the purpose of entering religion to which his heart has given birth is from the spirit of God, for it is His spirit that *leads man into the land of uprightness* [*Ps* 142:10]."[174]

---

[170] ST. THOMAS AQUINAS. *Summa Theologica* II-II, 189 10 (Christian Classics: Allen, Texas, 1948): "derogat Christo".

[171] Cf. Ibid., ST. THOMAS AQUINAS, *Contra la pestilencial doctrina de los que apartan a los hombres del ingreso a la religion: "...iniuriam facit Christo..."*

[172] ST. AUGUSTINE. *De verb. Dom.,* Serm 100, c.2; ML 38, 604.

[173] ST. THOMAS AQUINAS. *Summa Theologica* II-II, 189, 10 (Christian Classics: Allen, Texas, 1948).

[174] ST. THOMAS AQUINAS. *Summa Theologica* II-II, 189, 10, ad 1 (Christian Classics: Allen, Texas, 1948).

Saint John Bosco teaches that "the religious state is a sublime and truly angelic state. Those who, for the love of God and their eternal benefit feel in their hearts the desire to embrace this state of perfection and holiness, **can have faith, without any doubt, that this desire comes from heaven**, because it is too generous and too far transcends natural sentiments."[175]

2. *Fear of a lack of strength*

Regarding the fear of not having the strength needed to persevere in a vocation, Saint Thomas says: "And here again there is no room for doubt about the entrance to religion, since those who enter religion trust not to be able to stay by their own power, but by the assistance of the divine power, according to Isaiah 40:31, 'They that hope in the Lord shall renew their strength; they shall walk and not faint.'"[176]

"The misgiving of those who hesitate as to whether they may be able to attain to perfection by entering religion is shown by many examples to be unreasonable. Hence Augustine says (*Conf.* viii, 11): ...*There were so many young men and maidens here, a multitude of youth and every age, grave widows and aged virgins...And she smiled at me with a persuasive mockery as though to say: 'Canst not thou what these youths and these maidens can? Or can they either in themselves, and not rather in the Lord their God?... Cast thyself upon Him; fear not.'* "[177]

Continuing, Saint John Bosco affirms: "And fear not, candidates, that you lack the necessary strength to fulfill the obligations that the religious state imposes; instead take great confidence, because God, who started the work, will bring to perfect fulfillment these words of St. Paul: *the one who began a good*

---

[175] ST. JOHN BOSCO. *Obras Fundamentales*, Ed. B.A.C., Madrid, 1979, 2ª. edición, p. 644. (Editorial translation).

[176] ST. THOMAS AQUINAS. *Summa Theologica* II-II, 189 10 (Christian Classics: Allen, Texas, 1948).

[177] ST. THOMAS AQUINAS. *Summa Theologica* II-II, 189, 10, ad 3 (Christian Classics: Allen, Texas, 1948).

work in you will continue to complete it until the day of Christ Jesus [Phil. 1:6]."[178]

3. Promptness in following a vocation

Saint Thomas considers whether it is advisable to enter religious life after having asking the advice of many people and then thinking about it for a long time. His response is that it is not advisable.

Advice and deliberation are needed for things in which the goodness is questionable, but not in the case of a vocation, which is advised by Jesus Himself and is, therefore, good. The apostles gave us example of this: Saint Peter and Saint Andrew, upon hearing Jesus' call *immediately, they left their nets and followed him*[179]; and Saint Paul, telling of his vocation, says that he responded *that instant, I did not confer with flesh and blood.*[180] Saint John Chrysostom comments: "Such obedience as this does Christ require of us, that we delay not even for a moment."[181]

a- Worldly men:

Commenting on this doctrine, Saint John Bosco says: "An extraordinary thing! Worldly men, when someone wants to enter a religious institute in order to obtain a life that is more perfect and safer from the dangers of the world, say that such a resolution requires much time, so as to ensure that this vocation truly comes from God and not from the devil."

b- Even in the case that it was a temptation from the Devil:

"But they don't speak so certainly when the same person tries to accept a position of honor in the world, in which there are many dangers of losing the soul. Far from this thinking, Saint

---

[178] ST. JOHN BOSCO, *Obras fundamentales*, Ed. B.A.C.: Madrid, 1979), 2ª. edición, p. 644. (Editorial translation).

[179] *Mt* 4:20.

[180] *Gal* 1:16.

[181] ST. JOHN CHRYSOSTOM, *Homilia XIV in Matth.*, quoted in *Summa Theologica* II-II, 189, 10.

Thomas says that the religious vocation should be embraced even if it were suggested by the devil, because one should always follow good counsel even when it comes from an enemy. And Saint John Chysostom affirms that God, when He deigns to make a similar call, wishes that we not vacillate for even a moment in putting it into practice."

c- Reasons for not drawing out the decision:

"Elsewhere, the same Saint says that when the devil can't dissuade someone from the resolution to consecrate himself to God, he uses any means possible to delay the implementation of that resolution, gaining much if he achieves a delay of one day or even one hour. Because after that day and that hour, new opportunities for corrupt influence arise, and it won't be very difficult to obtain a longer delay, until the young person who is called, finding himself weaker and less helped by grace, totally gives in and abandons his vocation."

d- Dangers of drawing it out:

"For this reason, Saint Jerome gave this counsel to those called to leave the world: 'I beg you to hurry up, and just cut, rather than untie, the cord that keeps the boat on the shore.' By this, the Saint means that, when you find yourself tied to a boat and in danger of drowning, you shouldn't delay by meticulously untying the cord, but just cut it; therefore, one who finds himself in the middle of the world should immediately free himself from it, in order to prevent, in the easiest way, the danger to one's soul."

e- Accept the first movements of grace:

"See what St. Francis de Sales writes in his work on the religious vocation: 'To judge a true vocation, you don't need to experience tangible proof, it's enough that the highest part of your spirit perseveres; for this reason, you must not believe yourself lacking a true vocation if, before you notice it, certain feelings you had at first seem not to last; on the contrary, you may feel repugnance and dismay that causes you to vacillate, fearing that all is lost.

"No, it's enough that your will remains firm in desiring not to abandon the divine call, that you stay inclined toward the call. To know if God wants you to be a religious, it's not necessary to hear God Himself speak or for an angel to be sent from heaven to show you His will. Neither is it necessary for ten experts to resolve if the vocation is or is not sure; what matters is to answer the call and embrace the first movement of grace without worrying about the repulsion or the tepidity which can appear thereafter and linger, because as you embrace that first movement of His grace, God will orchestrate all for His greater glory."[182]

4. Principal enemies

The principal enemies of following Christ in total surrender are usually parents. This is why Saint John Chrysostom teaches in general terms: When parents try to thwart spiritual things, they must not even be considered parents anymore.

With respect to this question, Saint Thomas responds: "Even as *the flesh lusteth against the spirit,*[183] so too carnal friends often thwart our spiritual progress, according to *Micah* 7:6, *A man's enemies are they of his own household.* Wherefore Cyril expounding *Luke* 9:61, *Let me first take my leave of them that are at my house,* says: 'By asking first to take his leave of them that were at his house, he shows he was somewhat of two minds. For to communicate with his neighbors, and consult those who are unwilling to relish righteousness, is an indication of weakness and turning back. Hence he hears our Lord say: *No man putting his hand to the plough, and looking back, is fit for the kingdom of God,* because he looks back who seeks delay in order to go home and confer with his kinsfolk."[184]

---

[182] ST. JOHN BOSCO, *Obras fundamentales* (Ed. B.A.C.: Madrid, 1979), 2ª. edición, p. 644-645. (Editorial translation).

[183] *Gal* 5:17.

[184] ST. THOMAS AQUINAS. *Summa Theologica* II-II, 189, 10, ad 2 (Christian Classics: Allen, Texas, 1948).

A vocation is such a delicate flower that it must be carefully protected. Saint Alphonsus, asking himself what in the world is required for losing a vocation, answers: "Nothing. One day of recreation, one word from a friend, one slightly unmortified passion, one affection, one anxious thought, or unrebuked fear is sufficient."[185] Nothing! ...in the world, or also in a seminary or convent where the spirit of Christ does not reign, rather the spirit of the world reigns, not the spiritual Israel, but the fleshly Israel. Because *the Spirit of truth, ... the world cannot receive, because it neither sees him nor knows him.*[186]

5. Doubts about a vocation

Saint John Bosco continues, teaching: "He who consecrates himself to God with holy vows makes one of the most precious and pleasing offerings to the Divine Majesty. But the enemy of our souls, understanding that, by these means, one escapes his dominion, is wont to disturb the mind with a thousand deceptions to cause the soul to retreat and to thrust it back into the torturous ways of the world.

"Of these deceptions, the primary one is the stirring up of doubts about our vocation, bringing discouragement, tepidity and occasionally, a return to the world, which we had recognized many times as treacherous, and which, for love of Jesus Christ, we had abandoned.

"If, by chance, dearest children, you are assaulted by this dangerous temptation, tell yourself immediately that, when you entered the religious institute, God granted you the incomparable grace of your vocation, and that, if this seems doubtful to you now, it is because you are a victim of a temptation that you caused, which you should disregard and fight against as a true insinuation from the devil. It is common for an agitated and doubting mind to say to itself: 'You could do much better in

---

[185] ST. JOHN BOSCO, *Obras fundamentales* (Ed. B.A.C.: Madrid, 1979), 2ª. edición, p. 647-648. (Editorial translation).
[186] *Jn* 14:17.

·other places.' Immediately respond with the words of Saint Paul: *Let each of you remain in the condition in which you were called.*[187] The Apostle also stresses the prudence of continuing firm in the vocation to which each one was called: *I therefore...beg you to walk in a manner worthy of the calling to which you have been called, with all lowliness and meekness, with patience.*[188] If you remain in your institute and faithfully observe the rule, be assured of your salvation.

"Sadly, experience shows that many that leave the religious life were fooled. Others fall into great dangers, causing scandal and greatly risking their salvation and the salvation of others.

"So while your soul and your heart are agitated by some doubts or passions, I strongly urge you not to give weight to them, because such thoughts cannot be in conformity with the Lord's will, who according to the Holy Spirit *was not in the wind.*[189] In those critical moments, I advise you to present yourself to your superiors, sincerely opening your heart to them and faithfully following their advice. Whatever their advice may be, put it into practice, and you shall not err. The advice of superiors is like that of Jesus who assures us that their answers are like his own: *He who hears you hears me*[*Lk* 10:16]."[190]

6. Conclusion

Each vocation is a masterpiece of God. The Divine Artisan has chosen certain men and women for His service from all eternity. Long before we decided to follow Him, He began to prepare us through our fathers and mothers and relatives, through education, gifts, talents, character, temperament, circumstances and events. The vocational decision itself is a marvelous work of grace. Those who ignore or deny that a

---

[187] 1 *Cor* 7:20.
[188] *Eph* 4:1-2.
[189] *1 Kg* 19:11.
[190] ST. JOHN BOSCO, *Obras fundamentales* (Ed. B.A.C.: Madrid, 1979), 2ª. edición, pp 663-664. (Editorial translation).

vocation to the consecrated life principally consists in an interior call: "the inner callings of the Holy Spirit…the impulses of grace…by inspiration of the Holy Spirit" [191]; will discourage, delay, fetter, or even impede candidates from actualizing their vocation. For the person who seeks to impede a vocation, or doesn't embrace it, Saint Thomas says: "whoever resists the prompting of the Holy Spirit with long consultations ignores or consciously rejects the power of the Holy Spirit." [192]

In the end, two heresies are still alive: that of Jovinian, (who lived in Rome and died in 406) who equated marriage to virginity; and that of Vigilantius in Gaul (370-490) who equated riches to poverty. Both heresies have a common denominator: they take men away from spiritual things, enslaving them to worldly things. This is what Satan does through carnal men, preventing people from being "transformed in view of eternity." [193]

The evil intention to separate men and women from the religious life has a precedent in the attitude of Pharaoh who reproached Moses and Aaron for wanting to take the chosen people out of Egypt: *Why do you take the people away from their work?* [194]

This Gnostic era of progressive Christianity that seeks to reduce Christianity from an event to an idea [195] has caused seminaries and novitiates to empty. This is because youth don't feel motivated to offer their lives for an idea, but they will for a Person. Formal Nominalism, the abandonment of being, doesn't get anybody excited and is endlessly boring. This is analogous to a pastor who made a procession for Corpus Christi without taking the Corpus, because "Christ is in the people." So we have Christ without Christ and the people adoring themselves;

---

[191] ST. THOMAS AQUINAS, *Contra Retraentes,* Chapter 9. (Editorial translation).

[192] ST. THOMAS AQUINAS, *Contra Retraentes,* Chapter 9. (Editorial translation).

[193] ST. THOMAS AQUINAS, *Contra Retraentes,* Chapter 9. (Editorial translation).

[194] *Ex* 5:4.

[195] Cf. *Vox Verbi,* 1 de abril de 1996, Año 3, n°60, pp. 30-32.

seminaries and novitiates emptied because they forgot the Event, they forgot about Christ and they adored their ideas about Christ. And they continue headstrong in these ideas, in spite of the evidence of their noxious fruits.

Many of those who are responsible for impeding vocations to consecrated life don't know why there is a lack of vocations and desertions from consecrated life. Sometimes, they even become an occasion of desertion when they argue that there was a lack of vocation. But when the Church calls through the bishop or through a religious superior, isn't this very act a confirmation that there is a true divine vocation? Saint Paul teaches, and it is a matter of faith, that: *For the gifts and the call of God are irrevocable.*[196] And so, those who are responsible, through crass or negligent ignorance, are incapable of giving a solution.

If these problems are not solved, New Evangelization will be very difficult. To think that there could be a New Evangelization without evangelizers is as absurd as the Gnostic omission of Christ in the Corpus Christi procession. This is why John Paul II said in Santo Domingo: "An indispensable condition for the New Evangelization is to be able to count on numerous qualified evangelizers. Therefore, the promotion of priestly and religious vocations…must be a priority for the Bishops and a commitment for all the people of God."[197]

---

[196] *Rom* 11:29.

[197] Inaugural discourse at Santo Domingo, 10/12/92. n. 26; cited in *The Santo Domingo Document*, Conclusions, 82. (Editorial translation).

CHAPTER 5

Deepening the Faith

"There is no other name under heaven by which we must be saved" *(Acts 4:1)*

"My dear young people: only Jesus knows what is in your hearts and your deepest desires. Only He, who has loved you to the end (cf. Jn 13:1), can fulfill your aspirations. His are words of eternal life, words that give meaning to life. No one apart from Christ can give you true happiness."

Message for the 18ᵗʰ World Youth Day, July 25, 2002.

1.

"AND THE WORD BECAME FLESH AND DWELT AMONG US" (JN 1:14)

"In the mystery of the Incarnation, the Son of God becomes visible in person: 'When the fullness of time had come, God sent forth his Son, born of woman' (Gal 4:4). God became man in Jesus Christ, who thus becomes 'the central point of reference for an understanding of the enigma of human existence, the created world and God himself.'"

Letter to Artists, 5,
April 4, 1999.

In the Great Jubilee celebrating two thousand years of the Incarnation of the Word, the Church is remembering one of the central mysteries of our faith: the mystery of Jesus Christ.

There is nothing in the world greater than Jesus Christ. This is why I believe that the great experience all the young people of every time must have, and in particular the youth of the third millennium, is the experience of Jesus Christ. This experience is very personal, but because I am speaking to many people instead of one-on-one this will be somewhat impersonal.

The encounter with Jesus Christ is personal between Him and each person in the intimacy of the conscience and in the hidden places of the heart and the soul. No two encounters with Christ are alike. The encounter of each soul with Jesus has singular characteristics because we are people; we are not numbers or robots.

My encounter with Jesus Christ is unique. No one can take my place; I am the one who has to make the effort so that the encounter may be real, fruitful and unforgettable; an encounter that truly marks me for my whole life.

There are particular points that must be kept in mind in order for this encounter to be authentic.

1. To unite yourself to His Person

When we "know" someone, we know his exterior, his face, his countenance and his body. We don't see his soul or "his person." However, the most important thing is "his person." We get to know what this soul, or what this person is like from what he does, what he says, and what his virtues are. Only then can we say that we really know him. It happens in a similar way with Jesus Christ.

Lamentably, the knowledge people often have of Jesus Christ is superficial, from the outside, merely a shell or a skin. We think that we know Jesus Christ because when we were little we learned to recognize Him when we see a crucifix, but if we have not yet arrived at His soul, at His heart, "His person," we don't really know Him.

To know Christ means that we know that He is the Son of God made man and that He is the Second Person of the Most Holy Trinity. Therefore, to unite myself to His Person means to unite myself to the Second Person of the Most Holy Trinity. To accomplish this I must be convinced of what Jesus did, His life and mission in this world, the chosen ones of His heart and, what He taught us.

In human acquaintance, when I know a person deeply, in mutuality, this person also knows me, because I have made the effort to know him. Similarly, when I know Jesus Christ, I become aware that He knows me deeply, in the deepest part of my consciousness. There is no one else who knows me as well as He does because He is more interior to me that I am to myself. And when this knowledge comes, it is necessarily followed by love: love Him, and love Him as only God can be loved, love

Him; with an unrestrained heart, with all the strength of the soul and heart, and with all the strength of the mind. Love Him with an affective love, which means with acts of love from my will by which I love Him, I seek His love and I let myself fall in love with Him, and with an effective love, which means doing what He wants. And there I discover that not only does He know me intimately, He loves me intensely.

At the opening in Rome of the Jubilee of the Youth in the year 2000, the Pope said to the youth: "Don't ever think then that you are unknown to him, as if you were just a number in an anonymous crowd. Each one of you is precious to Christ, He knows you personally, He loves you tenderly, even when you are not aware of it."[198]

Saint Catherine of Ricci said, "He exhausts Himself in giving us His grace."[199] In the case of our Lord we are in an order that is not merely the natural order, (His body…) but also supernatural (His divine nature, His divine person…); the knowledge we should have of Him is a supernatural knowledge by faith, hope and love. We must always ask for the grace to grow in faith and nourish our faith, and we must always ask, as one man asked in the Gospel: *I believe, Lord; help my unbelief!*[200]

The Pope, speaking to thousands of young people in Tor Vergata, outside of Rome, placed this question: "In the year 2000, is it difficult to believe?" And he answered: "Yes, it is difficult, we must not hide it." There are so many impious attacks against the faith coming from the media that the Catholic faith is becoming ever more difficult to live. And so we must cultivate a faith that is alive, valiant and effective. Developing a fearless faith, a faith that can bring us, as it has brought many of our brothers over this

---

[198] JOHN PAUL II, 15th World Youth Day, Welcoming Ceremony Address, August 15, 2000.

[199] "Egli si struggle a darvi delle grazie." DOMENICO DI AGRESTI, *Caterina de Ricci-L'esperienza spirituale della santa di Prato* (Edizioni Librería Cattolica: Prato, 2001), pg 87.

[200] *Mk* 9:24.

past century, to give our very lives for our Lord, being martyrs and suffering a bloody martyrdom. The faith that our Lord teaches is a faith that is defined by various characteristics:

a. Trust: When one authentically believes, he can say with the apostle Saint Paul: *I can do all things in him who strengthens me,*[201] or *I know whom I have believed.*[202] Faith that is merely intellectual is not enough. We need faith that gives us life, in spite of the difficulties we must endure. We must always trust in Him, because we know in Whom we put our trust no matter how difficult the times in which we live are, or how difficult fidelity to Jesus Christ is. If we truly believe in Him, we must not be afraid: He has said in several places in the Gospel: *Take heart, it is I; do not be afraid.*[203]

b. Hope: Which is the certainty that, if we do what we have to do, we will reach our reward. Hope is what must move us to act virtuously, so as to reach the knowledge of Jesus Christ our Lord.

c. Conviction: As Luigi Orione said, that only charity will save the world. And so *the love of Christ urges us on.*[204]

We must live charity as it was lived by Saint Alberto Hurtado, who sought out the poor, the needy, and the elderly. He opened the *Hogar de Cristo* (the Home of Christ), which is still in operation today, and is a monument to Christian charity.

2. Having His Spirit

Exterior union or fulfillment of certain rites or works is not enough; we must also have the spirit of Christ. There are few words in the Sacred Scripture as serious as those of Saint Paul in his letter to the Romans: *Anyone who does not have the Spirit of Christ does not belong to him.*[205] I can come from a good Catholic family, I

---

[201] *Phil* 4:13.
[202] *2 Tm* 1:12.
[203] *Mt* 14:27.
[204] *2 Cor* 5:14.
[205] *Rom* 8:9.

can be in a very Christian environment, from a truly Christian society, I can have received all of the sacraments just for the sake of receiving them, I can know the Gospel by heart, or even the whole Bible, but if I do not have the spirit of Christ, I am not of Christ. It is necessary to have His spirit, and so the apostle insists *be filled with the Holy Spirit.*[206]

And how do I know if I have the spirit of Christ? I know if I have the spirit of Christ in as far as the fruits of the Spirit can be seen in me.

And what are the fruits of the spirit?

Saint Paul tells us in the letter to the Galatians: *the fruit of the Spirit is love, joy, peace, patience, kindness, generosity, faithfulness, gentleness, and self-control.*[207] This spirit is the very kingdom of God, as the Apostle also says in the letter to the Romans: *For the kingdom of God is...righteousness and peace and joy in the Holy Spirit.*[208] Those who are moved by the Holy Spirit are sons of God.

3. *Assimilate His doctrine*

The Word was made flesh. As the Word was made flesh in Jesus Christ, the Word was also seen in the letters of the Gospels, because He wanted to leave us written documents. These written documents are transmitted to us by the Apostles and the Church and, through them the truth about Jesus Christ is made known to us.

This truth obligates us to know Him and to defend His doctrines. John Paul I said: "Today, only the faith that is defended survives."[209] One night in Tor Vergata, John Paul II remembered this statement. He wanted to give the youth a present, so that they would be able to be Christians of the Third

---

[206] *Eph* 5:18.
[207] *Gal* 5:22-23.
[208] *Rom* 14:17.
[209] JOHN PAUL I, *Illustrissimi : the letters of Pope John Paul I* trans. Isabel Quigly (Gracewing Publishing: Herefordshire, United Kingdom, 2001) p. 97.

213

Millennium: the Gospel. He said to them: "The word which it contains is the word of Jesus. If you listen to it in silence, in prayer, seeking help in understanding what it means for your life from the wise counsel of your priests and teachers, then you will meet Christ and you will follow him, spending your lives day by day for him!"[210]

To assimilate the doctrine of Jesus Christ is to be able to understand what the heart of the Gospel is, that is, what the Beatitudes are. To understand the heart of the Gospel is to understand that which is diametrically opposed to what the world wants. For example:

-The world desires riches; Jesus says: *Blessed are the poor in spirit.*[211]

-The world seeks vengeance; Jesus says: *Blessed are the meek, for they will inherit the earth.*[212]

-The world is hungry and thirsty for material things; Jesus Christ says: *Blessed are those who hunger and thirst for righteousness.*[213]

-The world does not forgive; Jesus says: *Blessed are the merciful.*[214]

-The world lives in excess, in idolatry of the flesh and of sex; Jesus says: *Blessed are the pure in heart.*[215]

-The world believes that it will resolve conflicts with wars, battles and struggles; Jesus says: *Blessed are the peacemakers.*[216]

---

[210] JOHN PAUL II, Address during the Vigil of Prayer at *Tor Vergata,* Saturday, 19 August 2000.

[211] *Mt* 5:3.

[212] *Mt* 5:5.

[213] *Mt* 5:6.

[214] *Mt* 5:7.

[215] *Mt* 5:8.

[216] *Mt* 5:9.

-The world is interested only in comfort and good times— what do others matter to me? Jesus says: *Blessed are you when men revile you and persecute you and utter all kinds of evil against you falsely on my account. Rejoice and be glad, for your reward is great in heaven.*[217]

Christ is the only one who has *the words of eternal life.*[218]

I am getting up there in years and I have heard many lies! I hear them on the radio, television, in the newspapers and books, in conversations and election promises. I don't know how many elections I've lived through in my country, but they are lying to you! Jesus Christ does not lie. He is the only one who does not lie and He is the only one who has the words of eternal life: *Heaven and earth will pass away, but my words will not pass away.*[219]

Styles, customs and fashions change. We might get all our nutrition from pills, everything could be made out of plastic...we might know the things that are to come...but Jesus Christ will never change. His Word will not change. *I the Lord do not change.*[220]

Jesus Christ is the same yesterday and today and forever.[221] That is why He said: *I am the Truth.*[222]

We must discover the sublimity and beauty of the doctrine of Jesus Christ. The doctrine of Jesus Christ is so extraordinary that still today, more than two thousand years after He taught it, it is extremely current. It is the only truly new doctrine because it is the most perfect. The sublimity of the doctrine comes from several factors that reveal its extraordinary excellence.

a. Its integrity: The doctrine of Christ gives complete teaching about God, humanity and the world. It solves the problems that have most tortured humanity throughout the ages

---

[217] *Mt* 5:11-12.
[218] *Jn* 6:68.
[219] *Mk* 13:31.
[220] *Mal* 3:6.
[221] *Heb* 13:8.
[222] *Jn* 14:6.

and in our current times: What is the origin of the world, of man, of evil? How do we fight against evil? How is there life after death in this world? What is man's end?

b. Its holiness: The doctrine provides norms that perfectly regulate the life of men. With respect to God, it gives norms of Christian worship, which is most perfect, the worship that the Incarnate Son of God Himself gives to the Father *in spirit and in truth.*[223] Through its teachings, we are taught to respect one another and love our enemies; to love sinners and the poor, i.e., the great signs of Christian love. We learn to respect ourselves as sons of God, and, as said by Saint Peter, to be by Baptism *participants of the divine nature.*[224] His doctrine gives us an effective means for fulfilling these norms through the example of our Lord Jesus Christ in His life and by grace that comes to us through the sacraments worthily received.

c. By the perfect reward that it gives us in this life: Peace of conscience and joy of the soul, even in the midst of crosses, constitute the greatest happiness to be had in this valley of tears.

d. The harmonious unity of all the dogmas among themselves: The unity of the Most Holy Trinity with the Incarnation of the Word; the mystery of Jesus Christ with the mystery of the Blessed Virgin; the mystery of the Church in the mystery of Christ; and harmony between faith and reason, and between the mysteries and the precepts of natural law.

e. It is most fitting, because it accommodates to all people, of every kind and condition, because it is profound and simple. The wise man, if he is truly wise, is as struck with admiration for this doctrine as an illiterate peasant, including men from every nation and region, across all time and in every place.

---

[223] *Jn* 4:24.
[224] 2 *Pt* 1:4.

Many who should reach sanctity do not because their nations are apostates of Jesus Christ. They seek false gods: the state, money, sex, and they fall into idolatry.

Assimilation of Christ's doctrine is to know the entire Catholic faith which is the *Catechism of the Catholic Church*. We should know it much better than we do. To assimilate His doctrine is also to be well-informed and to able to refute modern attacks launched by New Age and other sects.

4. Follow His commandments

They who have my commandments and keep them, he it is who loves me[225]; *Not everyone who says to me, 'Lord, Lord,' will enter the kingdom of heaven, but only the one who does the will of my Father in heaven.*[226]

Today the commandments of the law of God are not followed. Years ago, at the Cathedral of San Rafael on the occasion of the patronal feast, Bishop León Kruk, who presided at the Mass said at one point in his sermon: "Argentina's problems would be solved with two things." And I scratched my head and said to myself: "If the problems are so complicated, how are they going to be solved with just two things?" And he said: "With following two commandments: do not lie and do not steal." And he was right. Imagine what would happen if the politicians were to stop lying and "scraping a little off the top." That moment made me think of Alexander Solzhenitsyn who suffered in a Siberian concentration camp during the peak era of the soviet regime's power. He denounced the regime, saying in one of his books: "What can we do when faced with an empire of evil, a political empire dominated by lies? We must commit ourselves to one thing: to not consent to lies." Someone might respond: "What about the missiles and the atomic submarines they have?" But he was right. Once the people began to fight little by little against the lies, the regime fell like a castle made of sand.

---

[225] *Jn* 14:21.
[226] *Mt* 7:21.

When people no longer follow the commandments, they want to change them. Mr. Ted Turner, who owns CNN, has a lot of money and thinks he owns the world. He stated that we have to get rid of one of the commandments: "Do not commit adultery." With that statement he defined himself, since what he wants is to commit adultery. Another example occurred at the world summit meeting in Río de Janeiro from March 13-21, 1997, in which the participants wrote the so-called "Letter from the World," a horribly worldly letter in which they said the following: "We must fashion a new ethic for a new world, a new universal code of behavior: replace the ten commandments with the eighteen principles in this letter." Look! Do they believe they are Moses? And even Moses didn't invent the Ten Commandments, he received them from God. And what do they propose as the new commandments for the new world? One of the proposals is to insure the reproductive health of women and girls; another is to recognize the right of homosexuals and lesbians to legally marry and adopt children; another is the right to male and female sterilization, birth control and abortion, and post-coital birth contraception.[227]

How proud human beings are! This is the new ethic, the new rubbish that they want to impose: globalization, the new world order! They want to impose anti-commandments of the law of God! This also happens in our country, for example in the laws about reproductive health, the laws that forget that charity is the way to perfection or forget that, as Saint John says, *And this is love, that we follow his commandments; this is the commandment, as you have heard from the beginning, that you follow love.*[228]

5. *Frequent the sacraments*

Baptism. I want to emphasize the importance of the sacrament of Baptism and to urge that Baptism be sought for yourself and your children as soon as possible. In a case where

---

[227] Cf. AICA magazine, 4/30/97.
[228] 2 Jn 6.

there is a possibility of death, everyone has the responsibility and obligation to baptize. All we have to do is to pour a little water over the head of the person being baptized and say the words: "So and so, I baptize you in the name of the Father, and the Son and the Holy Spirit." This baptized person will go to heaven.

Confession. There might be among those who read these pages some people who have not been to Confession for many years, either because they never made their First Communion, or they did without going to Confession. Perhaps they confessed badly and since then have some scruple and don't want to try again. Maybe they had a negative experience and wish to avoid Confession. But it is Christ who said to us: *If you forgive the sins of any, they are forgiven.*[229] These are His words, and we have to receive the grace of forgiveness through the sacrament of Confession, Penance, or Reconciliation. Who the minister of the sacrament is doesn't matter; what matters is when the priest says: "I absolve you." It is Jesus Christ who forgives sins and gives us a clean slate.

We should frequent the sacraments. Saint John Bosco said: "Youth are formed by good Confessions and good Communions."

Communion. How can we not receive Jesus, who has desired to remain present under the appearances of bread and wine in order to be food for our souls? "Take and eat," "Take and drink." Take! Eat! Drink! He wanted to be our spiritual food and drink to give strength to our souls. If we fall into sin or if it is often very difficult for us to go against the grain, we have to draw near to the fount of grace that is Christ and worthily receive Communion. That is where we will receive the strength to do what we need to do, "even if they come slashin' at my throat,"[230] like Saint Maria Goretti or Blessed Pier Giorgio Frasatti. We must

---

[229] *Jn* 20:23.
[230] JOSÉ HERNÁNDEZ, *The Gaucho Martín Fierro*; trans. Frank G. Carrino, Alberto J. Carlos, Norman Mangouni (SUNY Press: Albany, 1974) p. 13 stanza 70.

receive Communion and get into the habit of going to Mass every Sunday. There is a very beautiful Apostolic Letter from Pope John Paul II about the day of the Lord (*Dies Domini*), in which he reminds us of the Sunday obligation. When a person receives Jesus he becomes like Jesus and receives His light, His strength, and the consolation that he gives us. He gives us all this together with the increase of sanctifying grace, the proper graces of the Eucharist. *My flesh is food indeed and my blood is drink indeed. He who eats my flesh and drinks my blood abides in me, and I in him.*[231]

6. Imitate His example

Let the same mind be in you that was in Christ Jesus.[232]

We must learn to love and serve as He does because that is what being a Christian means. Christians are asked to exemplify patience, meekness, humility and self-sacrifice as they willingly carry the cross of daily life. This means that following Christ involves enduring our defects and those of others, fulfilling the duties of state and striving to be just in our dealings. As Saint Paul the Apostle says: *For this slight momentary affliction is preparing us for an eternal weight of glory beyond all measure, because we look not at what can be seen but at what cannot be seen; for what can be seen is temporary, but what cannot be seen is eternal.*[233]

In Tor Vergata, the Holy Father challenged the youth to embrace a martyrdom of living in a countercultural way. He beautifully added: "It is Jesus in fact that you seek when you dream of happiness; he is waiting for you when nothing else you find satisfies you; he is the beauty to which you are so attracted; it is he who provokes you with that thirst for fullness that will not let you settle for compromise; it is he who urges you to shed the masks of a false life; it is he who reads in your hearts your most genuine choices, the choices that others try to stifle. It is Jesus who stirs in you the desire to do something great with your lives,

---

[231] *Jn* 6:55-56.
[232] *Phil* 2:5.
[233] *2 Cor* 4:17-18.

the will to follow an ideal, the refusal to allow yourselves to be grounded down by mediocrity, the courage to commit yourselves humbly and patiently to improving yourselves and society, making the world more human and more fraternal."[234]

7. Be in communion with His Church

Jesus said: *You are Peter, and on this rock I will build my church, and the gates of hell will not prevail against it.*[235] If we are with Peter, with the Pope, we need not fear, even before all the combined powers of hell, because *the gates of hell will not prevail against it.*[236] Jesus said to the Apostles and to his priests: *Whoever listens to you listens to me.*[237]

The experience of the Church brings us to the knowledge of how this communion is possible: it is possible through Jesus Christ, because He gives us His Spirit and teaches us to be united with one other. He teaches us that we must be concerned about the things of the soul, the important things that do not fade and do not die.

To experience the Church is also to experience the evil that exists among the people of the Church. Jesus Himself said this: *there will be wheat and chaff.*[238] If we were all wheat, the whole world would be Catholic. But because we have free will, there is wheat and chaff, saints and sinners. If one were to see that all Christians were saints, he would be forced to follow Jesus Christ. For example, we see that Judas was included in the Apostolic College. Wheat and chaff! It will be this way until the end of the world, and whoever thinks otherwise is utopian. There is no Church where only the good exists. The Church is holy because its source, means, and end are holy. But the Church has sinners in her womb; we are these sinners. That is why we always pray the

---

[234] JOHN PAUL II, Vigil of Prayer, Tor Vergata, Saturday, August 19, 2000.
[235] *Mt* 16:18.
[236] *Mt* 16:18.
[237] *Lk* 10:16.
[238] Cf. *Mt* 13:25.

act of contrition at the beginning of every Mass. That is why we have to go to Confession often. We are not angels; we were born in original sin and we commit many sins every day, *the righteous fall seven times a day.*[239] But, seeing evil in the Church, which can be one of the greatest temptations a Christian can have, must bring us to greater faith in Jesus, because He already prophesized this evil, two thousand years ago when He said:*"There will be wheat and chaff."*

And what is it that we must do? We must work so that we can be wheat. A reporter once said to me in a television interview: "I would be a Catholic, or, people say they would be Catholic, but in the end, those who go to Mass are bad, they are unjust, they don't pay what they owe, don't do what they should, etc." I told him: "Look, among the twelve apostles there was one who betrayed Jesus Christ, which represents 8.33%. Statistically speaking, we are more than a billion Catholics in the world today and that means there will be at least 83 million false Catholics. You work so that you are not one of them." Then he said: "Okay, let's go to a commercial break…"

8. Recognize Him in our brothers

In order to look for Christ in our brothers we think first of the poor. We look at the homes and the care given to handicapped children. They are cared for because they are Jesus Himself. *I was hungry and you gave me food, I was thirsty and you gave me something to drink.*[240] This is a great work! But we also must seek Christ in our husbands and wives, our children, students and all who surround us in our daily lives. *I was hungry and you gave me to eat.* Look at the religious who labor in works of mercy or who care for the poor…do you see the love they show? They understand that they are attending to and cooking for Jesus. *I was hungry and you gave me to eat.* How can we care for so many, or give food to so many? When there are young people who have the

[239] *Prov* 24:16.
[240] *Mt* 25:35.

interior spiritual disposition to do the best they can for the good of their brothers, we can nurture a great many people. This is the commandment that we have: *Those who love God must love their brothers and sisters also.*[241]

9. See Him in His saints

One of the splendid things about the Church is the saints. There is no one who is like Jesus, but a saint reveals one aspect of the face of Jesus. For example, we see poverty in Saint Francis of Assisi, confidence in the providence of God in Saint Luigi Orione, love of children and youth in Saint John Bosco, love of sacred doctrine in Saint Thomas Aquinas, and apostolic zeal in Saint Paul, who was willing to make himself an anathema in order to save his brothers.[242] There are the saints of this century, the martyrs, who were willing to give their lives before giving in. Thousands and thousands of them have poured out their blood giving testimony of Jesus Christ. How many have died crying out "Viva Cristo Rey!"[243]

Saints reveal to us the strength of Jesus Christ who was the first martyr and the prototype of all martyrs. The Apocalypse says, the saints are *true words of God.*[244] In revealing God to us, the saints are a concrete example of what we should be. For example, I had the privilege to meet Mother Teresa of Calcutta and to speak with her…she was an extraordinary little woman who, walked with energy in spite of her eighty years. She was worried because there were great floods and dead bodies were floating around in Bangladesh, and she, who was in Rome, had to do something. The next day she was meeting with Saddam Hussein because she was taking her Missionaries of Charity to Baghdad to care for the poor in an Islamic country, while she herself was really poor. Or consider John Paul II who lived an extraordinary life, working sixteen hours a day. When he arrived in Tor Vergata

---

[241] *1 Jn* 4:21.
[242] Cf.*Rom* 9:3.
[243] Long live Christ the King!
[244] *Rev* 19:9.

outside of Rome for the youth jubilee in 2000, there were millions of young people wanting to see him. He drove around for a long time in a jeep so that the youth could see him close up, even though there were huge screens. Then he walked with his cane, to the place where he would speak, and there he greeted everyone. Zenit says that he cried to see so many young people cheering. In the end he responded with these words: "Rome will never forget this sound." It is the biggest pilgrimage that has ever happened in all the history of the Eternal City.

So, like the saints, today everyone must learn to say: "Lord, what do you want me to do?" Like the Blessed Virgin: *Behold I am the handmaid of the Lord; let it be to me according to your word.*[245] "Lord, I want to listen to your word, I want to be faithful to your word, and to do what you want, even if it is something difficult, something very difficult."

10. Love His Mother

Whoever loves the Most Holy Virgin can be sure that she will contrive to bring him to Jesus Christ. I also had the joy of meeting ninety-three year old, Sister Lucia, one of the visionaries of Fatima, on the occasion of the beatification of her cousins, Jacinta and Francisco. She was lucid, she radiated great happiness! To think that she had played with those cousins that the Pope beatified on that day! She is a holy woman, extremely devoted to the Blessed Virgin. The Blessed Virgin, our mother, appeared to her and gave her an urgent message for the people of this century: "Pray the rosary every day," "offer sacrifices for sinners." And in the third part of the secret, recently revealed, the angel says firmly: "Penance, penance, penance."

Do we want to know Jesus? Let us love His mother. Let us listen to her, obey her requests and take her advice. Let us pray the rosary every day, do penance, and offer sacrifices for the salvation of sinners.

---

[245] *Lk* 1:38.

When he was at Fatima on that enormous field in front of a million people, the Pope remembered what the Virgin said: "Today, many souls are condemned because there is no one to pray for them."

✠   ✠   ✠

May no one, due to fear or for any other reason, fail to receive Jesus in Holy Communion and go to Confession frequently. May no one fail to aim at holy things or begin to better know the only Lord who merits being served, Jesus Christ!

"It is Jesus in fact that you seek when you dream of happiness; he is waiting for you when nothing else you find satisfies you; he is the beauty to which you are so attracted; it is he who provokes you with that thirst for fullness that will not let you settle for compromise; it is he who urges you to shed the masks of a false life; it is he who reads in your hearts your most genuine choices, the choices that others try to stifle. It is Jesus who stirs in you the desire to do something great with your lives, the will to follow an ideal, the refusal to allow yourselves to be grounded down by mediocrity, the courage to commit yourselves humbly and patiently to improving yourselves and society, making the world more human and more fraternal."[246]

---

[246] JOHN PAUL II, Prayer Vigil in Tor Vergata.

2.

WHO ARE YOU LORD?
(ACTS 9:5)

"The Redeemer of the world!
The good has its source in Wisdom and Love.
In Jesus Christ the visible world
which God created for man
recovers again its original link
with the divine source of Wisdom and Love.
Indeed, "God so loved the world
that he gave his only Son."

Redemptor Hominis,
March 4, 1979.

"Who are You, Lord?"

I am the Way and the Truth and the Life.[247]

1. Who are you Lord?

-I am the Way…

Why Lord, are You the Way?

-Because… *I am the good shepherd. The good shepherd lays down his life for the sheep.*[248]

-*I am the good shepherd. I know my own and my own know me.*[249]

---

[247] *Jn* 14:6.
[248] *Jn* 10:11.

-*I am the gate for the sheep*[250] ... *whoever enters through me will be saved.*[251]

-*The Word became flesh,*[252] *I am the Son of God,*[253] *do you say of him...,* '*You are blaspheming,*' *because I said,* '*I am the Son of God'?*[254] '*Are you the Christ, the Son of the Blessed?*' *And Jesus said,* '*I am,*[255] *the Messiah, the Christ who was to come. I who speak to you am he,*[256] It *is you who say that I am king.*[257]

-With Jesus there is no room for fear because He gives strength and confidence: *Take heart, it is I; have no fear*[258]; *It is I; do not be afraid.*[259]

Youth of the third millennium, are you willing to walk along this Path with energy and courage, this Path that is Jesus Christ Himself, who is the same yesterday, today and forever?

2. Who are You, Lord?

-I am the Truth

Why Lord, are You the Truth?

-*You call me Teacher and Lord; and you are right for so I am.*[260]

-*Teacher, we know that you are true and teach the way of God truthfully,*[261] the disciples of the Pharisees say to him.

---

[249] *Jn* 10:14.
[250] *Jn* 10:7, New American Bible Version (hereafter simply NAB).
[251] *Jn* 10:9, NAB.
[252] *Jn* 1:14.
[253] *Mt* 27:40.
[254] *Jn* 10:36.
[255] *Mk* 14:62; cf. *Lk* 22:70.
[256] *Jn* 4:26.
[257] *Jn* 18:37, New Jerusalem Bible Version (hereafter simply NJB).
[258] *Mt* 14:27, *Mk* 6:50.
[259] *Jn* 6:20.
[260] *Jn* 13:13.
[261] *Mt* 22:16.

-Learn from me; for I am gentle and lowly in heart.[262]

-Again Jesus spoke to them, saying 'I am the light of the world; he who follows me will not walk in darkness, but will have the light of life.'[263] *As long as I am in the world, I am the light of the world.*[264]

-The words that I have spoken to you are Spirit and life.[265]

-Saint Peter says to him: *You have the words of eternal life.*[266]

-What I say, therefore, I say as the Father has bidden me.[267]

-For this was I born, and for this I have come into the world, to bear witness to the truth. Everyone who is of the truth hears my voice.[268]

Youth of the third millennium, are you willing to undertake all of the sacrifices required to let the truth of Jesus Christ, who is full of grace and truth, reign in your hearts and your souls?

3. Who are You, Lord?

-"I am…the Life"

Why Lord, are you Life?

-Because *I am the living bread which came down from heaven.*[269] He is the Eucharist. The Mass.

-I came that they may have life, and have it abundantly.[270]

-I am the resurrection and the life.[271] *See my hands and my feet, that it is I myself,*[272] revealing Himself alive with the wounds from the nails.

---

[262] *Mt* 11:29.
[263] *Jn* 8:12.
[264] *Jn* 9:5.
[265] *Jn* 6:63.
[266] *Jn* 6:68.
[267] *Jn* 12:50.
[268] *Jn* 18:37.
[269] *Jn* 6:51; cf 35, 41, 48.
[270] *Jn* 10:10.

-I am the true vine, and My Father is the vinedresser[273]*; I am the vine, you are the branches.*[274]

-He is the Savior. *Whom do you seek?' They answered Him, 'Jesus of Nazareth.' Jesus said to them, 'I am He.'* [275] The angel had commanded Saint Joseph, *you shall call His name Jesus, for He will save His people from their sins.*[276]

-And so, when Saint Paul asks Him: *Who are you Lord?* The Lord responds, *I am Jesus...I am Jesus of Nazareth.*[277]

-I am the first and the last, and the living one.[278]

-I am he who searches mind and heart,[279] He who knows every man and woman to the depths of their conscience and their soul.

-I am the root and the offspring of David.[280]

-And the Apostles confess: *We have believed and come to know, that you are the Holy One of God.*[281]

Youth of the third millennium, John Paul II cried: "Dear young people, may it be your holy ambition to be holy, as He is holy...do not be afraid to be the saints of the new millennium!"[282] To do this, always be faithful to the *Way*, the *Truth* and the *Life*.

---

[271] *Jn* 11:25.
[272] *Lk* 24:39.
[273] *Jn* 15:1.
[274] *Jn* 15:5.
[275] *Jn* 18:4-5.
[276] *Mt* 1:21.
[277] *Acts* 9:5, 22:8.
[278] *Rev* 1:17.
[279] *Rev* 2:23.
[280] *Rev* 22:16.
[281] *Jn* 6:69.
[282] JOHN PAUL II, Message to the Youth, 15th World Youth Day, 3.

Our Lady Patroness of Youth will always protect you. In her womb *the Word became flesh and dwelt among us,*[283] and together with Him, the Head, she spiritually gave birth to us, His Body, the members of that Head, forming only one mystical Body, the Head and the members.

---

[283] *Jn* 1:14.

3.

YOU HAVE WORDS OF ETERNAL LIFE (JN 6:68)

In Capernaum, Our Lord teaches for the first time the reality of the Eucharist that He was going to institute on Holy Thursday by telling His disciples clearly that His flesh was going to be food and His blood was going to be drink, and that this flesh and this blood, would be *for the life of the world.*[284] Upon hearing this, many of them said: *This is a hard saying; who can listen to it?*[285]

---

[284] *Jn* 6:51.
[285] *Jn* 6:60.

And then our Lord, who knew their thoughts, gave them the key to interpreting the sermon of the bread of life. The key is not in a materialistic interpretation of the words, but in a supernatural interpretation that flows from faith. He told them: *It is the Spirit that gives life, the flesh is of no avail.*[286] Those present who were scandalized understood in a carnal way what should be understood in a supernatural way: *The words that I have spoken to you are Spirit and life. But there are some of you that do not believe.*[287] There will always be people in every community who are missing the essentials: living with fearless faith in our Lord. St. John makes a rather important annotation: *For Jesus knew from the first who those were that did not believe, and who it was that would betray him.*[288] These two acts are related. He who does not believe is going to hand over Jesus because he has already handed Him over in his heart. By not believing, not having faith, he has already betrayed Him and for that reason he will hand Him over.

This crucial moment of our Lord's preaching caused many of His disciples to fall away. It is this essential mystery, the Eucharist, that makes the Church what it is.

Jesus, like us, has experienced apostolic and pastoral failures. We often come up against hardness of heart, people who refuse to believe in spite of our best efforts. Or the hardness of consciences that don't want to take a step toward conversion and keep affirming themselves in their own judgment, even going against the words of Jesus Christ. And that is when Jesus asks the Apostles a question, a question that Peter will answer.

Jesus said to the Twelve, 'Will you also go away?'[289] Jesus does not take freedom away from anyone. He didn't take it away from the Apostles, nor does He take it from us. He doesn't take away our freedom when we decide on a vocation, entering the novitiate or the seminary, or becoming a priest. Jesus never takes away our

---

[286] *Jn* 6:63.
[287] *Jn* 6:63-64.
[288] *Jn* 6:64.
[289] *Jn* 6:67.

freedom. He desires and hopes for our answer to be given in freedom, because He wants it to be a conscious, responsible answer that is made in love. If there is no freedom, there is no love.

And so Simon Peter responded: *Lord, to whom shall we go? You have the words of eternal life; and we have believed, and have come to know, that you are the Holy One of God.*[290] These are very beautiful words that express in a concise way the reality of Jesus, which must be the center of our faith.

Saint Peter addresses Christ personally, using *"You,"* a personal pronoun, as Christ addressed him in a personal way. Peter addresses Christ as a person, not as a theory, scientific explanation, or belief. And that *"You"* in that moment on the lips of Peter, has a particular resonance because a moment before that he had said to Him, *Lord, to whom shall we go?...*That *"You"* is the Lord! In Greek it is *"Kyrios,"* a word the Septuagint had used when the Bible was translated from Hebrew to Greek, which was the *lingua franca* a century before the coming of our Lord. Every time the sacred tetragram, *Yahweh* appeared in the Hebrew, the word *"Kyrios"* was used. *Kyrios* is the Lord. *Kyrios* is Yahweh. *Kyrios* is God. A few moments later, Saint Peter reinforces this when he says: *We have believed, and have come to know, that you are the Holy One of God.* The Holy One, *"Kadosh"* is God Himself. What is it that Jesus Christ has as something characteristic and substantial? He has *words of eternal life.* These words are not accidental, foreign or occasional, but constitutive, essential and characteristic. That is to say, these words give life and are life. And they don't give just any life, they give eternal life! These words do not pass away, fade or change, but endure and will continue to endure: *Heaven and earth will pass away, but my words will not pass away.*[291] Today we are overwhelmed by an avalanche of a culture of death, for example with New Age ideas which are even manifested in some of the

---

[290] *Jn* 6:68-69.
[291] *Mt* 24:35.

members of the Catholic Church. And this gives the impression that we are passé or out of style. But it is they who are out of style! Because this will pass as many things have passed. However, the words of Christ will not pass away, because they are *words of eternal life*. These are not weak words, like the words of men, who say one thing today and another thing tomorrow, who play with words and juggle ideas. It is as if Peter had said: *"You have words that will not pass away."*

"You have words of eternal life" is like saying: "You **alone** ("alone" in the sense that no word of Jesus ever stops being a word of eternal life, even when He teaches about the existence of hell and eternal condemnation. Also when He speaks of the primacy of charity, and when He speaks of the final judgment) are the one who has the words of eternal life." ...**All of the words of Jesus are words of eternal life.** We must incarnate all of them in ourselves, because no word of Jesus is passing, changeable, trivial or superfluous.

And it is also to say: "You are the **only one** who has words of eternal life." No other man has them, because no other is God, and no other has taught doctrine as admirable as the doctrine the Lord taught, or done miracles or prophecies to show the truth of what He taught, as He did. He is the only one. All the great men in the history of the world and of our country, not even all of them put together, have words of eternal life. Jesus is the only one!

In addition, we can and must understand that, *"You always have words of eternal life."* These words continue to be heard throughout the centuries with the same force they had the first time they were spoken, and they will continue to be heard with the same force, because they do not die, they don't lose strength; they do not need anyone to empower them...because they are words of eternal life!

And this must be our deepest conviction. Otherwise, we deserve the reproach that the great theologian Melchor Cano gave when he complained about certain bishops, priests, religious and laymen, who were responsible in their times, as others are now, for relaxing the identity of Christian life, seeking in other places what can only be found in Jesus. He said that these men do not believe, and therefore, ultimately, they are traitors: "One of the things that makes me unhappy with these fathers is that instead of turning gentlemen into lions, they make chickens out of them..." Those who, by the position they occupy, cause people to lower their guard, depositing them into the swamp of progressivism, they say that everything is alright, nothing's wrong; they make compromises, and destroy the only truth that saves, which is the truth of Jesus Christ.

This is the world in which we find ourselves today. A woman once told me that she heard someone asking a favor from Judas Iscariot on the radio. For those who ask for graces from the tooth fairy or from singers, "saint ABBA" or "saint Madonna" are confused and ignorant. Those who do not have faith, and hand Jesus over and betray Him, take advantage of the credulity of many people for commercial reasons.

Let us make it our goal to put into practice what we say in our Constitutions: "We want to be founded in Jesus Christ who *has come in the flesh,*[292] and only in Christ, and always in Christ. We want Christ to be in everything and in all, and all of Christ."[293]

The Most Holy Virgin understood more than anyone that the words of her Only Son were words of eternal life and will always be so for all generations of men. Only Christ had them and taught them to His disciples who participated in them. She understood that His words would not be subjected to the inconstancy of the times and fashions, that they would never grow old and would never be surpassed. Many would give their lives for them, that they would never deceive anyone. May she who kept these words in her heart remind us of this.

---

[292] *1 Jn* 4:2.
[293] Constitutions of the Institute of the Incarnate Word, 7.

4.

THE ACTUALITY OF THE INCARNATION OF THE WORD[294]

"In Christ, religion is no longer a 'blind search for God' (cf. Acts 17:27) but the response of faith to God who reveals himself. It is a response in which man speaks to God as his Creator and Father, a response made possible by that one Man who is also the consubstantial Word in whom God speaks to each individual person and by whom each individual person is enabled to respond to God. What is more, in this Man all creation responds to God."

Tertio Millenio Adveniente, 6,
November 10, 1994.

In this time of "militant atheists," archaic laity, moral eclipses, or hidden or public apostasies and anti-Christian media, it is interesting that the most current and present reality is the fact that the Word become flesh.

This is the case for several reasons:

1. There is no one more actual than God, who is the creator of everything that exists, preserves creation in existence and even governs it with His providence. He is the "***Ipsum esse subsistens***," the subsistent Act, the infinite being who ***became man***.

---

[294] We have decided to include this chapter, even though at some points it could be difficult to understand, because it briefly presents a reality that the youth of our times encounter when they begin higher studies.

2. The Word of God made flesh means that the divine nature and the human nature are united in the one divine Person of Jesus Christ. This is the great mystery of the hypostatic union—union in the Person—that will never end. Therefore, it is always actual. This unending union of both natures in the divine Person was defined as a dogma of faith, because Marcellus of Ancyra (d. circa 374) who was condemned as a heretic in the Second Ecumenical Council of Constantinople (381),[295] was against it. In response to his false doctrine, the phrase: "of his kingdom there will be no end"[296] was added to the symbol of the faith. Yes, the union between the two natures in Jesus Christ will remain for eternity; the Incarnation of the Word is absolutely actual.

3. The actuality of the mystery of the Incarnation can also be seen by the spread, among others, of Hegelian ideas in philosophy and Marxist ideas in sociology, since they flow from a caricature of the Incarnation.

First of all, we should take note of the spread of Hegel's doctrines. Massimo Borghesi's[297] testimony is enough, which summarizes Hegel's book in an article: "Hegel, the master of all—even of Catholics."[298] Take note of this concise affirmation: master of all—even of Catholics. It is not necessary here to dwell on the diffusion of Communism.

According to the Catholic doctrine that is more than twenty centuries old, God is infinitely transcendent—He is even closer to us than we are to ourselves. He creates man and the world freely. There are two immanent divine processions ("immanent" means that they "remain in Him"): the generation of the Word and the spiration of the Holy Spirit. In the fullness of time, the Word, without ceasing to be God, assumes the human nature in unity of Person, in the womb of the Virgin Mary. It is the

---

[295] Cf. DZ 85.

[296] *Lk* 1:33; Dz 86, cf DZ 283.

[297] *L'eta dello Spirito in Hegel.* Dal Vangelo 'storico' al Vangelo 'eterno,' Studium (Roma, 1995).

[298] Article published in the *Revista 30 Días,* Año III, n.1, 1996, pp. 36-39.

greatest communication and communion between God and creatures. What an august, impenetrable and marvelous mystery!

In his letter to the Philippians, Saint Paul describes the Incarnation as the "negation of God"; [he] *emptied himself*,[299] which is to say "He made Himself nothing." The Vulgate *"exinanivit"* and the Greek "ἑαυτὸν ἐκένωσεν," are translated as "He emptied Himself." A bad understanding of these concepts, which express transcendent realities, causes false readings.[300]

There is a false interpretation of this passage in the Lutheran Reformation, which influenced Hegel and his dialectic, and it rests on the so-called "second moment," "antithesis," "negation," "contradiction," or above all, "alienation."

The emptying of the Word *is not ontological,* as if He were to stop being God and begin to be something else. When the Word empties Himself He gives Himself to us as an example of humility, by hiding the glory and power of the divinity.

By losing sight of the *sapiential* vision of the Christian mysteries, Lutheranism only focuses on what they mean *for us,* for *praxis,* and is not concerned with the metaphysical and contemplative aspect of the Incarnate Word, only its dramatic aspect. According to this doctrine, it doesn't matter that Christ has two natures in one Person, it only matters that He has come to take away our sins and to give us His justice.

From there it is just a small step to confuse the language used, the association and mutual interchange of divine and human properties, attributes, and operations that refer to *only one concrete subject,* Jesus Christ. Thus we say, and it is true, that "God was born in Bethlehem," that "God died on the cross," which doesn't mean that He was born or died in His divinity, but rather that He was born and died according to His humanity. However, that

---

[299] *Phil* 2:7.

[300] For more on this and what follows, see: JULIO MEINVIELLE, *El poder destructivo de la dialéctica marxista* (Buenos Aires, 1973) p. 40ff.

humanity has been assumed by the divine Person of the Word, it is true that God was born and died, as a man.

Luther, on the other hand, interpreted the *"kenosis,"* the emptying, of God, as if at the Incarnation God were to give up the attributes of His divine nature, His immutability, and His infinite power, and to take up creaturely conditions. Centuries later, Lutheran theologians would interpret the Incarnation as if the Word were not to have being outside of His humanity, nor were His humanity to have being outside of the Word. Behind this great error is the error of *Nominalism,* which teaches that being is univocal, not analogical. Nominalists refute the idea that there are two ways to have being (God, who is being by essence and creatures who are being by participation). Instead, they maintain that there is only one way to have being. From this false belief comes the absurd notion that what God has, creatures do not have, and what creatures have, God does not have.

The Hegelian and Marxist systems are based on alienation. Hegel calls it *Entäusserung,* the substantive form of the phrase *hat sich selbs geeussert,* which is how Luther translated "he emptied himself" from the Vulgate. Therefore, in Hegel the "Word" empties Himself until He becomes part of the Absolute Spirit that encompasses the identity of identity and of non-identity. He rejects the transcendent God in the famous analogy of the master and the slave. The master is the transcendent God and the slave is the consciousness. However, the slave will become master of his master when he manages to absorb the divinity into the immanence of the consciousness. And so, the exaltation of the faith of the Church follows from the *kenosis,* while the conversion of divinity into consciousness follows from the negation of the divinity as transcendence.

So, "the master of all, even of progressive Catholics," takes the idea of *process or procession* from the Trinity, and the idea of *self-movement or alienation* from the Incarnation and transfers this from theology to a *concept.*

The most dangerous part of all of this is that the dialectic is caused by opposition, contradiction and negation; it is not moved by being, but by nothingness. The great destructive power that these systems have comes from the nothingness that they contain.

The free Protestant inquiry gave birth to savage liberal Capitalism. The misreading of the *kenosis* hymn that Protestantism made gave birth to the Hegelian dialectic, whose right side produced Nazi totalitarianism and whose left side produced Marxist totalitarianism, enslaving entire peoples with terror for as much as seventy years. This goes to show that we reap what we sow. The false interpretation of the *kenosis* also speaks to us of the perennial value of the Incarnation, as the negative of a photograph would.

My dear young people, let us not fall into the false and nefarious dialectics that the globalized world sets before us today, obliging us to side with one position necessarily against another.

Remember that when we were children we knew how to break false dialectics between two good things. When we were asked, "Who do you love more, your mom or your dad?" We would answer, "Both!" And if the things they want to make us choose between are both evil, then without ambiguity we must say that we don't want either.

Tertullian would compare the scandal of the Incarnation to the scandal of the cross, because the scandal of the cross could not have happened without the scandal of the Incarnation: Which is more unworthy of God, which is more likely to raise a blush of shame, that *God* should be born, or that He should die? That He should bear the flesh, or the cross? Be circumcised, or be crucified? Be cradled, or be coffined? Be laid in a manger, or in a tomb?... Spare the whole world's one only hope, you who are destroying the indispensable dishonor of our faith. Whatsoever is unworthy of God, is of gain to me. I am safe, if I am not ashamed of my Lord... The Son of God was crucified; I am not ashamed because men must needs be ashamed *of it.* And the Son of God died; it is by all means to be believed, because it is absurd... But how will all this be true in Him, if He were not Himself true—if He really had not in Himself that which might be crucified, might die, might be buried, and might rise again?... Thus the nature of the two substances displayed Him as man and

God,—in one respect born, in the other unborn; in one respect fleshly, in the other spiritual; in one sense weak, in the other exceedingly strong; in one sense dying, in the other living... Wherefore halve Christ with a lie? He was wholly the truth.[301]

Let us be faithful to the true doctrine about the Incarnation of the Word, which has been infallibly taught by the Catholic Church for 2,000 years. And may we know how to be filled with a holy astonishment at the reality of the event that divides the history of the world into a before and an after.

Even the greatest anti-Catholic thinkers can't think except in dependence on the great mysteries of the Catholic faith, even though they seek to deform them.

May the Virgin Mary, who was a ciborium for nine months, a monstrance for 33 years and a luna for 2,000 years for the Word of God Incarnate, make us know Him, love Him and serve Him ever more intensely.

---

[301] Cf. *De Carne Christi* [*On the Flesh of Christ*] ch. 5, v. 4.

5.

THE NEGATION OF THE INCARNATION

> *"The mystery of the Incarnation reveals God's astonishing love, whose highest personification is the Holy Spirit, since he is the Love of God in person, the Person-Love...the glory of God is revealed in the Incarnation more than in any other work."*
>
> *Wednesday Catechesis, May 27, 1998.*

The feast of Epiphany celebrates the manifestation of the Lord. In the Eastern Churches it is celebrated on the same day as the Baptism of our Lord in the River Jordan, the Adoration of the Magi and the first miracle of our Lord at the wedding at Cana.

In the liturgical readings of the feast of the Epiphany we remember in a special way what Saint Paul says when he speaks of the revelation of the mystery of the Incarnation of the Word; and the mystery is that the pagans also fully participate in Him. This is the feast on which we remember the entrance of the gentile peoples, the non-Jewish peoples, into the Church and the kingdom of God.

I

The negation of the Incarnation of Christ by those who don't believe is a reality Sacred Scripture warns us about. It was already happening in apostolic times:

For many deceivers have gone out into the world, men who will not acknowledge the coming of Jesus Christ in the flesh; such a one is the deceiver and the antichrist.[302]

Children, it is the last hour; and as you have heard that antichrist is coming, so now many antichrists have come; therefore we know that it is the last hour. They went out from us, but they were not of us; for if they had been of us, they would have continued with us; but they went out, that it might be plain that they all are not of us.[303]

Who is the liar but he who denies that Jesus is the Christ? This is the antichrist, he who denies the Father and the Son. Anyone who denies the Son does not have the Father. He who confesses the Son has the Father also.[304]

Beloved, do not believe every spirit, but test the spirits to see whether they are of God; for many false prophets have gone out into the world. By this you know the Spirit of God: every spirit which confesses that Jesus Christ has come in the flesh is of God, and every spirit which does not confess Jesus is not of God. This is the spirit of the antichrist, of which you heard that it was coming, and now it is in the world already.[305]

Let no one deceive you in any way; for that day will not come, unless the rebellion comes first, and the man of lawlessness is revealed, the son of perdition, who opposes and exalts himself against every so-called god or object of worship, so that he takes his seat in the temple of God proclaiming himself to be God...For the mystery of lawlessness is already at work.[306]

II

The same considerations were made in the era of the Church Fathers. Commenting on the second to last text above, Saint Augustine said: "'Every spirit that confesses that Jesus Christ came in the flesh, is of God.' Then is the spirit that is among the heretics, of God, seeing they 'confess that Jesus Christ came in

---

[302] 2 *Jn* 7.
[303] 1 *Jn* 2:18-19.
[304] 1 *Jn* 2:22-23.
[305] 1 *Jn* 4:1.
[306] 2 *Thes* 2:3-4,7.

the flesh'? Aye, here perchance they lift themselves up against us, and say: You have not the Spirit from God; but we confess 'that Jesus Christ came in the flesh:' but the apostle here has said that those have not the Spirit of God, who confess not 'that Jesus Christ came in the flesh.' Ask the Arians: they confess 'that Jesus Christ came in the flesh': ask the Eunomians; they confess 'that Jesus Christ came in the flesh': ask the Macedonians; they confess 'that Jesus Christ came in the flesh': put the question to the Cataphryges; they confess 'that Jesus Christ came in the flesh': put it to the Novatians; they confess 'that Jesus Christ came in the flesh.' Then have all these heresies the Spirit of God? Are they then no false prophets? Is there then no deception there, no seduction there? Assuredly they are antichrists; for 'they went out from us, but were not of us.'

"What are we to do then? By what do we discern them? You have already heard what was said above, 'Whosoever denies that Jesus Christ is come in the flesh, the same is an antichrist.' There also we asked, Who denies? because neither do we deny, nor do those deny. And we found that some do in their deeds deny; and we brought testimony from the apostle, who says, *For they confess that they know God, but in their deeds deny him.*[307] Thus then let us now also make the enquiry in the deeds not in the tongue. What is the spirit that is not from God? That 'which denies that Jesus Christ is come in the flesh.' And what is the spirit that is from God? That 'which confesses that Jesus Christ is come in the flesh.' Who is he that confesses that Jesus Christ is come in the flesh? Now, brethren, to the mark! Let us look to the works, not stop at the noise of the tongue. Let us ask *why* Christ came in the flesh, so we get at the persons who deny that He is come in the flesh. If you stop at tongues, why, you shall hear many a heresy confessing that Christ is come in the flesh: but the truth convicts those men. Wherefore came Christ in the flesh? Was He not God? Is it not written of Him, *In the beginning was the Word, and the Word was with God, and the Word was God?*[308] Was it not He that

---

[307] *Titus* 1:16.
[308] *Jn* 1:1.

did feed angels, is it not He that does feed angels?...Wherefore then came He in the flesh? Because it behooved us to have the hope of resurrection shown unto us. God He was, and in flesh He came; for God could not die, flesh could die; He came then in the flesh, that He might die for us. In what way did He die for us? *Greater charity than this has no man, that a man lay down his life for his friends.*[309] Charity therefore brought Him to the flesh. Whoever therefore has not charity denies that Christ is come in the flesh. Here then do you now question all heretics. Did Christ come in the flesh? 'He did come; this I believe, this I confess.' Nay, this you deny. 'How do I deny? You hear that I say it!' Nay, I convict you of denying it. You say with the voice, deniest with the heart; sayest in words, deniest in deeds. 'How,' do you say, 'do I deny in deeds?' Because the end for which Christ came in the flesh, was that He might die for us. He died for us, because therein He taught much charity. 'Greater charity than this has no man, that a man lay down his life for his friends.' You have not charity, seeing you for your own honor dividest unity. Therefore by this understand ye the spirit that is from God. Give the earthen vessels a tap, put them to the proof, whether haply they be cracked and give a dull sound: see whether they ring full and clear, see whether charity be there. You take yourself away from the unity of the whole earth, you divide the Church by schisms, you rend the Body of Christ. He came in the flesh, to gather in one, you make an outcry to scatter abroad. This then is the Spirit of God, which says that Jesus is come in the flesh, which says, not in tongue but in deeds, which says, not by making a noise but by loving. And that spirit is not of God, which denies that Jesus Christ is come in the flesh; denies, here also, not in tongue but in life; not in words but in deeds. It is manifest therefore by what we may know the brethren. Many within are in a sort within; but none without except he be indeed without."[310]

Do not think that these teachings are things of the past.

---

[309] *Jn* 15:13.
[310] ST. AUGUSTINE, Homily 6 on the First Epistle of John.

III

In spite of the great Jubilee celebrated in 2000, in which we solemnly remembered the mystery of the Incarnation of the Word, and in spite of the new awareness it brought, and the multitude of people who participated in the celebration, the negation of the incarnation is still a painful and clear reality.

The Holy Father recently taught in a letter to the Dominicans[311]: "From the outset, one of the first tasks assigned to your Order was the proclamation of the truth of Christ in response to the Albigensian heresy, a new form of the recurrent Manichaean heresy with which Christianity has had to contend from the beginning. At its core there lay the denial of the Incarnation, a refusal to accept that *the Word was made flesh and dwelt amongst us, full of grace and truth.*[312] To respond to this new form of the old heresy, the Holy Spirit raised up the Order of Preachers, men who would be pre-eminent for their poverty and mobility in the service of the Gospel, who would unceasingly contemplate the truth of the Incarnate Word in prayer and study, and through their preaching and teaching would pass on to others the fruits of that contemplation. *Contemplata aliis tradere*[313]: the motto of the Order became its great call to action, and it remains such to this day…

"It is clear that the ancient afflictions of the human soul and the great untruths never die but lie hidden for a time, to reappear later in other forms. That is why there is always need for a new evangelization of the kind to which the Holy Spirit is now summoning the whole Church." (A new evangelization is always necessary, first of all, in ourselves. When the priest or the layman ceases to evangelize himself, he begins to become careless which could lead to scandal). "We live in a time marked in its own way

---

[311] JOHN PAUL II, Letter to the Master General of the Order of Preachers, 28 June 2001. All citations in this section are from this source. The paragraph divisions are ours.

[312] *Jn* 1:14.

[313] Transmit what is contemplated.

by a denial of the Incarnation. For the first time since Christ's birth two thousand years ago, it is as if he no longer had a place in an ever more secularized world. Not that he is always denied explicitly: indeed many claim to admire Jesus and to value elements of his teaching. Yet he remains distant: he is not truly known, loved and obeyed, but consigned to a distant past or a distant heaven.

"Ours is an age which denies the Incarnation in a multitude of practical ways, and the consequences of this denial are clear and disturbing." (The negation of the Incarnation is seen, above all, in the abasement of the human being, which couldn't be otherwise).

1. "In the first place, the individual's relationship with God is seen as purely personal and private, so that God is removed from the processes that govern social, political and economic activity." What this means is that the negation of the Incarnation which ultimately seeks to separate people from God can be seen in many forms, including social, political and economic activity, liberalism, Marxism, technocracy, and laicism. The world that man constructs without God turns against man. When he doesn't want God to reign, man enslaves himself.

2. "This leads in turn to a greatly diminished sense of human possibility, since it is Christ alone who fully reveals the magnificent possibilities of human life, who truly 'reveals man to himself.'"[314] When a sense of human possibilities decreases, men and women fall into marginalization, social exclusion, the plague of unemployment, the exploitation of workers, and the accumulation of riches in the hands of a few while the poor grow poorer, increase in number, and have less and less participation in common wealth. Healthy creativity is lost.

3. "When Christ is excluded or denied, our vision of human purpose dwindles; and as we anticipate and aim for less, hope gives way to despair, joy to depression." Saint Paul teaches that

---

[314]*Gaudium et Spes*, 22.

we must not *be submitted to the elements of the world,*[315] which, in the end, is clearly manifested in all known forms of addictions: alcohol, drugs, speeding, money, sex without responsibility, power, internet and television, and irrational violence. Man falls into existential meaninglessness and the loss of the self control of a Christian. Reductionism in human existence enslaves man to things that are inferior to him. This is why humanity in the modern world more or less, thinks the same way and believes what the mass media under the dictatorship of the "givers of meaning" repeats daily.

4. "There also appears a profound distrust of reason and of the human capacity to grasp the truth; indeed the very concept of truth is cast into doubt. To their mutual impoverishment, faith and reason part company, degenerating into fideism on the one hand and rationalism on the other."[316] Man makes himself a slave to his subjective caprice and to the dictates of relativism. The image of relativism can be seen in "talk show" television programs that feature lifestyles of prostitutes, gays and lesbians as if they were legitimate habits of being: "You who are a prostitute, what can you tell us about sex? You who are gay, what can you tell us? You who are a lesbian, what do you think of love? You who are a transvestite, what do you think about abortion?" Everything is the same: "Nothing is true or false, but depends on the angle from which it is seen." That is their creed.

So man is not interested in the truth. He is not interested in extra-mental reality, or what is outside, over and superior to him…"I make the truth; I am the measure of all things." That is the summary of their lives.

5. "Life is not valued and loved; and hence the advance of a certain culture of death, with its dark blooms of abortion and euthanasia." Contraception, anti-life ideologies, cloning, divorce, widespread suicide, the killing of the innocents, the death of the

---

[315] Cf. *Gal* 4:3.
[316] Cf. *Fides et Ratio,* 48

soul from not having recourse to the grace given by the sacraments. Therefore, men and women live like animals, without sacraments: they don't go to Confession, don't receive Communion, don't go to Mass on Sundays, they don't receive the Anointing of the Sick, or get married in the Church. They do anything in order to destroy the divine image of marriage and the family, and the dignity of human work.

6. "The body and human sexuality are not properly valued and loved; hence the degradation of sex which shows itself in a tide of moral confusion, infidelity and the violence of pornography." Men and women are pushed to all kinds of pathological sexual extremes: pedophilia, cross-dressing, sadism, masochism, and pornography in magazines, newspapers, movies, radio, television and the internet. Virginity and purity are held in contempt. Humanity suffers a true eclipse of ethics and morality.

7. "Creation itself is not valued and loved; hence the spectre of destructive selfishness in the misuse and exploitation of the environment." Creation is the great page written by God, and every effort is made to destroy the image of God written on it so that man would forget that *all things were made through him, and without him was not anything made that was made.*[317] Look at what is left of the Sea of Azov.

According to the Holy Father, the practical negation of the Incarnation of the Word is perceived in the social and public orders of peoples, in the possibilities of man and his very existence, in not loving life, the body, or creation. These are just a few examples that could be expanded upon.

"In such a situation, the Church and the Successor of the Apostle Peter look to the Order of Preachers with no less hope and confidence than at the time of your foundation. The needs of the new evangelization are great; and it is certain that your Order, with its many vocations and outstanding heritage, must play a vital part in the Church's mission to overturn the old untruths

---

[317] *Jn* 1:3.

and proclaim the message of Christ effectively at the dawn of the new millennium."

IV

Recently, the then Cardinal Joseph Ratzinger recalled: "The world has athirst to know, not our ecclesial problems, but the fire that Jesus came to bring to the earth.[318] [...] The central problem of our times is that the historical figure of Jesus Christ has been emptied of all meaning. An impoverished Jesus cannot be our one Savior and mediator, the God with us: Jesus is replaced with the idea of the 'man of the kingdom' and he is converted into empty hope. We must return with clarity to the Jesus of the Gospels, for it is He alone that is the true Jesus of history [Cf. *Jn* 6:68]."[319]

V

Let us reaffirm our faith in Jesus Christ.

May we know how to say to him with deeds and in truth: *You are the Christ, the Son of the living God.*[320]

---

[318] Cf. *Lk* 12:50.

[319] CARDINAL JOSEPH RATZINGER, *Intervención en la X Asamblea general ordinaria del Sínodo de los Obispos, 6 de octubre de 2001.* (Editorial translation).

[320] *Mt* 16:16.

6.
ALL IS YOURS

"Remember that the human person and respect for the human person is the path to a new world. The world and humanity are deprived of their life-breath if they are not open to Jesus Christ. Open your hearts to him and thus start out on a new life, a life in harmony with God and which responds to your legitimate aspirations to truth, goodness and beauty."

Camagüey, Cuba,
January 23, 1998.

I

Our Lord Jesus Christ says that a tree is known by its fruits. You will know them by their fruits. *So, every sound tree bears good fruit, but the bad tree bears evil fruit. A sound tree cannot bear evil fruit, nor can a bad tree bear good fruit.*[321] By using this same principle, we can know educational establishments, specifically, Catholic schools. And what are the fruits that a Catholic school should produce?

The primary fruit that Catholic schools must produce is the formation of the youth to be authentic disciples of Christ. Catholic schools must form Christian youth to be disciples of Christ, and who want to live according to the Gospel of Our Lord:

---

[321] *Mt* 7:16-18.

-Authentic disciples of Christ must be formed so that what Saint Paul says might come true in them: *It is no longer I who live, but Christ who lives in me.*[322]

-In addition, those disciples can truly carry Christ within themselves when they become fathers and mothers of families, religious, or professionals. In a special way they would become witnesses of the love of Christ before the world.

II

Why Christians are often not formed can be explained by various reasons:

1. We don't present Jesus Christ as we should. What is the principle of Christian life? Jesus Christ is central! We don't follow a man, or a priest, or a religious, but Jesus Christ our Lord. On the contrary, Catholics are formed with prejudices, who don't know how to live and work as Christians, who rebel against their parents and are disrespectful and promiscuous. Is this what it is to be Catholic?

2. Moreover, this lack of formation happens because no one has taught them what Saint Paul preached with such force and such clarity: *So let no one boast of men. For all things are yours, whether Paul or Apollos or Cephas or the world or life or death or the present or the future, all are yours; and you are Christ's and Christ is God's.*[323]

III

"*All things are yours.*" What does that mean?

1. Man does not glory in the inferior things that are subject to him. Neither should he glory in the things of this world, for as high as they seem they have all been put under the feet of Jesus Christ. Among the things that are under man—and at his service—are primarily the ministers of Christ including the Pope,

---

322 *Gal* 2:20.
323 *1 Cor* 3:21-23.

who are set in place to minister to the faithful, **"whether Paul or Apollos or Cephas"** (Cephas is Peter, the Pope). In the religious orders, priests and religious are also at the service of the faithful. **"All is yours"** because it is at the service of the chosen ones of God.

2. Neither should human beings glory in the exterior things of this world. **"The world"** is under each faithful person and serves him in that it satisfies his needs or it helps him to the knowledge of God.

3. We must not glory in the things of this world because they serve man by satisfying his needs, nor should we glory in **"life or death,"** in all the goods of family, or particular goods, not even in all the evils of this world. Life is at our feet as far as it serves to merit us eternal life; death is also at our feet in that it opens the way for eternal rewards.

4. **"The present or the future"**: All things are for our service and they fade as we do. The present must help us to merit for the other life, and the future we can reserve for the reward.

IV

All things are yours, all things are for us to use, all things are at our service for everything, *God works for good with those who love him, who are called according to his purpose.*[324]

The entire world is ruled by a triple law:

1. Everything is orientated to the Saints: the first ordinance is that all things are at the service of authentic men and women who are the chosen ones, those who are predestined to rejoice eternally in the glory of God.

2. The second ordinance is that of those who are faithful toward Christ.

3. The third is that of Christ as man who orders all to God.

---

[324] *Rom* 8:28.

So let no one boast of men. *For all things are yours, whether Paul or Apollos or Cephas or the world or life or death or the present or the future, all are yours; and you are Christ's and Christ is God's.*[325]

I ask for the grace that Catholic educational institutions might form "kings and lords" who know how to exercise "dominion and kingship" over all the things that are under them. I ask that they might know how to overcome the trends that lead to unhappiness, to escape, to nonsense, to nothingness, which, in the end, is death. This is not what Jesus Christ wants for us, since He teaches us to love to the point of giving our lives for others.

---

[325] *1 Cor* 3:21-23.

7.
PORTRAITS OF THE PASSION

"My dear young people,
at the conclusion of the Holy Year,
I entrust to you the sign of this Jubilee Year:
the Cross of Christ!
Carry it throughout the world
as a symbol of Christ's love for humanity,
and announce to everyone that only
in the death and resurrection of Christ
we can find salvation and redemption."

Rome, April 22, 1984.

I propose to you that with our minds and imagination we follow along with different scenes of the Passion of the Lord, just as if there were images from a slide projector on a screen.

First Scene: On the other side of the torrent of Kidron

In the Valley of Kidron, there are "branches of wrinkled olive trees, almost human like, which sway as if they wanted to cover I don't know what kind of invisible eyes in order to forget what they had seen."[326] What did the olive trees see? They saw the horror, and all of them, by the solidarity of nature, are silent witnesses of Gethsemane. There they listened to the God-Man

---

[326] JOSÉ MARÍA PEMÁN, *De cómo las cosas se asociaron a la Pasión de Cristo,* quinto de los *Ocho ensayos religiosos, Obras Completas,* III (1948) 1258-1275, cit. en *La Pasión según Pemán* (II EDIBESA: Madrid, 1997) p. 68, edición preparada por José Antonio Martínez Puche. (Editorial translation).

say: *My soul is very sorrowful, even to death.*[327] There they heard the God-Man say: *Abba, Father, all things are possible to you; remove this chalice from me.*[328] We can hear, offstage, the voice of the prophet Isaiah: *The Lord has laid on him the iniquity of us all.*[329]

And He sweated blood.

Second Scene: In a corner of the Gospel

"In a corner of the Gospel, in the patio of the Sanhedrin, there is a golden and dancing creature, subtle and inconstant. It is called Fire. It was caught onto a pile of wood in the center of the patio. The servants had lit it to warm themselves. Now it is dawning. Everyone has left. Among the pieces of wood the death of the fire is soft and gentle like twilight. How can such a restless and fickle creature die thus, with such peace, undone into dust and ash?" Pemán asks himself. And he continues, "Because the fire was all flicker and movement, it never stayed for two minutes together in the same form. He also, each minute, rejected the posture of the minute before, not only three times, but hundreds and thousands. How then, has he managed that death of peace and tranquillity, soft as a sunset? He has managed it because he knew how to erase his own inconstancy and how to be consumed in pure ardor; because there has been sin, but also penitence; because there has been denial, but also weeping; because while he danced his dance of vacillation, he was being consumed by Love. Peter, Peter, when the Lord passed through the gallery adjoining the patio, He looked at you with the tenderness of forgiveness because you have a soul aflame and a heart of fire."[330]

---

[327] *Mt* 26:38; *Mk* 14:34.

[328] *Mk* 14:36.

[329] *Is* 53:6.

[330] JOSÉ MARÍA PEMÁN, *De cómo las cosas se asociaron a la Pasión de Cristo*, quinto de los *Ocho ensayos religiosos, Obras Completas*, III (1948) 1258-1275, cit. en *La Pasión según Pemán* (II EDIBESA: Madrid, 1997) p. 69, edición preparada por José Antonio Martínez Puche. (Editorial translation).

The Lord was severely beaten.

Third Scene: The taunts in the Sanhedrin

They *mocked him*[331]; they *beat him*[332] with closed fists; they *slapped him*[333]; with open hands or possibly with clubs; they *spat in his face.*[334] Spitting is a very serious injury according to Holy Scriptures, as related in the case of Miriam, the sister of Moses in the book of Numbers. *Moses cried to the Lord, 'Heal her, O God, I beg you.' But the Lord said to Moses, 'If her father had but spit in her face, should she not be shamed seven days?'*[335] In the book of Deuteronomy, in the law of the Levites, a brother was obligated to take the place of a dead spouse and espouse his sister-in-law. If the brother did not take in the woman, God said: *If he persists, saying, 'I do not wish to take her,' then his brother's wife shall go up to him in the presence of the elders, and pull his sandal off his foot, and spit in his face; and she shall answer and say, 'So shall it be done to the man who does not build up his brother's house.'*[336] Christ's tormentors *also blindfolded him,*[337] as they sarcastically asked the *Messiah*[338] to *Prophesy!*[339] who was hitting Him; they plucked out the hairs of His beard.[340]

And Jesus bled.

Fourth Scene: In Pilate's Court

There also the Lord suffered scourging and nakedness as well as many other injuries. They stripped Him of His clothes[341];

---

331 *Lk* 22:63-64.
332 *Mk* 14:65; ραπίσμασιν.
333 *Mt* 26:67; *Mk* 14:56; ερἁπισαν.
334 *Mt* 26:67; *Mk* 14:65.
335 *Num* 12:13-14.
336 *Dt* 25:9.
337 *Lk* 22:64; *Mk* 14:65.
338 *Mt* 26:68.
339 *Lk* 22:64; *Mt* 26:68; *Mk* 14:65.
340 Cf. *Is* 50:6.
341 Cf. *Mt* 27:28.

they gave Him a robe or a mantle[342] that represented royal robes, and they *plaited a crown of thorns and put it on his head*[343] as a sign of royal dignity. They put a reed in His hands as a scepter.[344] They saluted Him in mockery[345]; they *took the reed and struck him on the head*,[346] making the thorns penetrate deeper into His scalp. They *spat upon him*[347]; there the spit of the Jews mixed with our spit (the pagans); they *struck him.*[348]

"When God created the worlds, he created them with extravagance and waste... One kind of grass would have been enough for herds to graze and the overflowing of varieties, colors and shapes that cover the meadows was not necessary. One kind of flower would have been enough to make honey; the lavishness of a garden was not necessary. But the Lord," Pemán continues, "worked like a doting father who can't spoil his newborn son enough. It was all a multiplying of species, a total waste of colors and shapes and varieties. And amid this overflow of gifts and indulgences, the Jujube, a small fruit-bearing tree with a thousand and one uses, also fell from between the fingers of God into Palestine. Its fruits, which are red and sweet, are good and refreshing for livestock as well as sweet for their pastors. Its branches, which have large, sharp thorns, are useful for the boundaries of human egoism, marking out private property and making fences for farms."[349] And also from the hands of God fell "the reed, a light and resistant reed, similar to the rush brought carefully by that splendid father to this country of livestock and wagons, apt for supporting a person on the road,

---

[342] Cf. *Mt* 27:28; *Mk* 15:17;*Jn* 19:2.
[343] *Mt* 27:29; *Mk* 15:17; *Jn* 19:2.
[344] *Mt* 27:29.
[345] Cf. *Mt* 27:29; cf *Mk* 15:18; cf. *Jn* 19:3.
[346] *Mt* 27:30; *Mk* 15:19.
[347] *Mt* 27:30; *Mk* 15:19
[348] *Jn* 19:3.
[349] JOSÉ MARÍA PEMÁN, *De cómo las cosas se asociaron a la Pasión de Cristo*, quinto de los *Ocho ensayos religiosos, Obras Completas*, III (1948) 1258-1275, cit. en *La Pasión según Pemán*, (II EDIBESA: Madrid, 1997) p. 69-70, edición preparada por José Antonio Martínez Puche. (Editorial translation).

hurrying along an animal, or for making a simple flute. And there they were for centuries and centuries, the Jujube and the reed, generously offering men fruit, fences, flutes and canes."[350]

In another scene, some soldiers from the Roman legion appear: "Some soldiers of the Roman legion...went to the Jujube, and laughing cruelly, they cut a thorny branch and fashioned it into a crown. They went to the riverbank and cut a reed into the form of a rough scepter. Where are they going, those soldiers of Rome, with their scepter of reed and their helmet of thorns? They are seeking the supreme prodigal, extravagant and generous, who, for the love of men, made thousands of flowers when one would have been enough. They are seeking him who made the Jujube sweet for pastors, the reed resistant for the weary and hollow for flautists."[351]

And Jesus bled.

Fifth Scene: Golgotha

Golgotha with three crosses appears in our image; the holy women are at the foot of the cross, the people are crying out— the masses never know what they do—shaking their heads, throwing dirt into the air, according to their custom. Let's zoom in with our projector. We see the majestic and dignified face of Jesus. What stateliness! We draw closer and we see His eyes, those sweet, penetrating eyes, that loved with their gaze as they loved the rich young man, that penetrating gaze that pierces the soul. The gaze of Jesus Christ was an intelligent gaze: He knew perfectly well what He was doing. Of all those who were there as spectators, almost nobody knew what was happening, except the Virgin. But Christ knew what He was doing, and He was doing it freely, with full consciousness and will. He knew that He was saving the men and women of all times!

---

[350] Ibid, p. 70. (Editorial translation).
[351] Ibid, p. 70. (Editorial translation).

If in that moment we had been able to observe the eyes of Jesus as we can do today with the eyes of Our Lady of Guadalupe using a high resolution microscope, we would see many things reflected in them. Among those things we would see ourselves reflected there, in this precise moment. We would see ourselves because we **are** in the pupils of the Lord. This is theologically certain because, by divine science, He knows absolutely everything. We would see in those eyes of Jesus all of us who are here: the priests, the seminarians, the sisters, the families who are with us…the huge multitudes of generations upon generations.

Jesus sees and knows everything: the one whom He called as a child, whom He called as a youth, whom He called as an adult; the form and the way in which He called them. And in that moment our Lord was clearly conscious that what He was doing was going to benefit every individual. In that moment, He wanted to die on the cross and offer His life, because it was necessary for our eternal salvation.

Describing that face, in which there was no longer any beauty, we can listen to the voice of Isaiah from offstage: *He had no form or comeliness…as one from whom men hide their faces.*[352] There is not a healthy part in Him. The agony of the redeemer arrives at its end: *… He bowed his head and gave up his spirit.*[353] And so to fulfill the prophecy, a soldier would pierce His heart, and from that heart, which so loved mankind, would flow blood and water.[354]

And Jesus bled and bled.

The Last Scene: In Heaven

A woman, who gave blood from her blood so that her only Son could shed His blood for us, and who remembers always,

---

[352] *Is* 53:2-3.
[353] *Jn* 19:30.
[354] Cf. *Jn* 19:34.

with the memory that mothers have heard, the last words of her son on the cross: *Behold, your son.*[355]

Saint Andrés Avelino called the Virgin: "la faccendiera d'il Paradiso", which is to say, "the hard worker of Heaven", she who has much work to do in Heaven. The saint likes to portray her as "familiarly and humanly involved in her constant supplication, in her dispatching of graces and favors."[356]

Most Holy Virgin, forgive us if we give you so much work! But you are the only one who can make it possible that we not render the blood of your Son fruitless for us.

---

[355] *Jn* 19:26.

[356] JOSÉ MARÍA PEMÁN, *De cómo las cosas se asociaron a la Pasión de Cristo,* quinto de los *Ocho ensayos religiosos, Obras Completas,* III (1948) 1258-1275, cit. en *La Pasión según Pemán,* (II EDIBESA: Madrid, 1997) p. 42, edición preparada por José Antonio Martínez Puche. (Editorial translation).

8.

GOD THE FATHER AND THE
PASSION OF THE SON

*"No one has ever seen God,' writes St. John, in order to
stress the truth that 'the only Son, who is in the bosom of the
Father, he has made him known.' This 'making known' reveals
God in the most profound mystery of His being, one and three,
surrounded by 'unapproachable light.' Nevertheless, through this
'making known' by Christ we know God above all in His
relationship of love for man: in His 'philanthropy.' It is precisely
here that 'His invisible nature' becomes in a special way 'visible,'
incomparably more visible than through all the other 'things that
have been made': it becomes visible in Christ and through Christ,
through His actions and His words, and finally through His death
on the cross and His resurrection."*

Dives in Misericordia, *November 30, 1980.*

The whole course of the life of Our Lord Jesus Christ is
marked with explicit and insistent references to His Heavenly
Father. As we read in the Letter to the Hebrews when Christ
becomes man in the womb of the Virgin, He cries, *Behold, I have
come to do your will.*[357] From the first moment of His earthly
existence and in the last moments of His earthly existence, He
makes reference to the Father: *Father, into your hands I commit my
spirit!*[358]

---

[357] *Heb* 10:9.
[358] *Lk* 23:46.

I

Jesus Christ establishes Himself as the great revealer of the Father. I want to specifically point out all the times that Jesus referred to the Father during his Passion. As you know well, the passion has a prior sacramental dimension which is the Last Supper, followed by the painful and bloody Passion itself that begins in Gethsemane.

And when the hour came, He sat at table, and the apostles with Him. And he said to them, *I have earnestly desired to eat this Passover with you before I suffer; for I tell you I shall not eat it until it is fulfilled in the kingdom of* **God**. And He took a chalice, and when He had given thanks He said, *Take this, and divide it among yourselves; for I tell you that from now on I shall not drink of the fruit of the vine until the kingdom of* **God** *comes.*[359]

* The Passion is sacramentally preceded and begins in the Cenacle. Christ reminds us that it is the Father who gives us the kingdom:

And I assign to you, as my Father assigned to me, a kingdom, that you may eat and drink at my table in my kingdom, and sit on thrones judging the twelve tribes of Israel.[360]

* He teaches us that these moments are moments of *passing,* which refers to the Passover:

Now before the feast of the Passover, when Jesus knew that His hour had come to depart out of this world to the Father—that passing is the Passover—having loved His own who were in the world, He loved them to the end—and in later verses—*Jesus,*

---

[359] *Lk* 22:14-18. Jesus had often spoken of heaven as a banquet. Now, when announcing the immanence of his death to his disciples, he promises them that He will celebrate a new, much more splendid banquet with them, in heaven, and He expresses it with the words *new wine.* The central idea of this promise is the reunion of the disciples and the master in a greater intimacy, a powerful thought of consolation in this moment of saying goodbye.

[360] *Lk* 22:29-30.

*knowing that the **Father** had given all things into his hands, and that he had come from **God** and was going to **God**.*[361]

* He also taught us in these moments, that in the house of our Father (a metaphor referring to heaven) there are many rooms:

*Let not your hearts be troubled; believe in **God**, believe also in me. In my **Father's** house are many rooms... I go to prepare a place for you. And when I go and prepare a place for you, I will come again and will take you to myself, that where I am you may be also. And you know the way where I am going.*[362]

* When He reveals the Father, He also reveals, in a very eloquent way, His own mystery. Christ is con-substantial with the Father, of the same substance, the same divine nature, numerically one, but He is also man, because He assumed a human nature in the womb of the Virgin. Thomas says to Him:

'Lord, we do not know where you are going; how can we know the way?' Jesus said to him, 'I am the way, and the truth, and the life[363]*; no one comes to the **Father**, but by me. If you had known me, you would have known my **Father** also.'*[364]

* So, whoever knows Jesus knows the Father, because they have the same divine nature, numerically one:

*'Henceforth you know him and have seen him.' Philip said to him, 'Lord, show us the **Father**, and we shall be satisfied.' Jesus said to him— mournfully— 'Have I been with you so long, and yet you do not know me,*

---

[361] *Jn* 13:1,3.

[362] *Jn* 14:1-4.

[363] Because of sin man had lost the way to life, without any hope of finding it again. Jesus presented Himself to the world as truth, as light that drives away error and indicates the way to heaven. Only He is the way, because He is the only mediator to reach the **Father**. But He is also life, He is the only one who has and gives life.

[364] *Jn* 14:5-7.

Philip? He who has seen me has seen the Father; how can you say, 'Show us the **Father**'?[365]

* And then He expresses the mysterious and real relationship between Himself and the Father, the Father and He, because they are only one thing.

Do you not believe that I am in the **Father** *and the* **Father** *in me? The words that I say to you I do not speak on my own authority; but the* **Father** *who dwells in me does his works. Believe me that I am in the* **Father** *and the* **Father** *in me; or else believe me for the sake of the works themselves.*[366]

* He expresses His death in a very beautiful and gentle way. He has already said that it is a "passing." Now He will insist on the idea that it is a journey.

Truly, truly, I say to you, he who believes in me will also do the works that I do; and greater works than these will he do, because I go to the **Father**. *Whatever you ask in my name, I will do it, that the* **Father** *may be glorified in the Son; if you ask anything in my name, I will do it.*[367]

* He tells the apostles not to be afraid, and that He will pray to the Father so that the Father will send them the Holy Spirit.

If you love me, you will keep my commandments. And I will pray the **Father**, *and he will give you another Counselor, to be with you forever [Jn 14:15-16].* [368]

---

[365] *Jn* 14:7-9; The **Father** and the Son are one thing; that is why where the Son is the **Father** is also. Jesus demonstrates His consubstantiality with the **Father** with an argument taken from His words and from His deeds: His transcendent doctrine cannot be human; His miracles exceed the forces of nature: they are words and deeds of God.

[366] *Jn* 14:10-11.

[367] *Jn* 14:12-14.

[368] The Greek word *Paraclite* means interceder, defender, and in a derived sense, consoler. It is the Holy Spirit, who we call another consoler, because Jesus is also a consoler.

* He insists on the mutual adhesion that there is between Himself and the Father, the Father and Himself.

*In that day you will know that I am in my **Father**, and you in me, and I in you. And he who loves me will be loved by my **Father**, and I will love him and manifest myself to him.*[369]

* Furthermore, the fact that He is in the Father, that the Father is in Him, and that He is in us, means that within our souls, the Most Holy Trinity, and therefore, the Father lives.

Judas (not Iscariot) said to him, 'Lord, how is it that you will manifest yourself to us, and not to the world?' Jesus answered him, 'If a man loves me, he will keep my word, and my Father will love him, and we will come to him and make our home with him.[370]

* He loves the Father:

*But I do as the **Father** has commanded me, so that the world may know that I love the **Father**.*[371]

* He presents the Father as if He were a country farmer:

*I am the true vine, and my **Father** is the vinedresser. By this my **Father** is glorified, that you bear much fruit, and so prove to be my disciples.*[372]

*The heavenly Father has great dreams for us; His glory is that we bear much fruit, which is why Saint Irenaeus, a great Father of the Church, said: "The glory of God is a living man."[373]

As the Father has loved me, so have I loved you; abide in my love. If you keep my commandments, you will abide in my love, just as I have kept my

---

[369] *Jn* 14:20, 21.
[370] *Jn* 14:22-23.
[371] *Jn* 14:31.
[372] *Jn* 15:1,8.
[373] *Adversus Haereses* IV, 20, 7. (Editorial translation).

Father's commandments and abide in his love. These things I have spoken to you, that my joy may be in you, and that your joy may be full.[374]

*He calls us friends. He reminds us of the obligation we have to love one another.

This is my commandment, that you love one another as I have loved you. Greater love has no man than this, that a man lay down his life for his friends. You are my friends if you do what I command you. No longer do I call you servants, for the servant does not know what his master is doing; but I have called you friends, for all that I have heard from my Father I have made known to you. You did not choose me, but I chose you and appointed you that you should go and bear fruit and that your fruit should abide; so that whatever you ask the Father in my name, he may give it to you. This I command you, to love one another.[375]

*The Father is in the Son and the Son is in the Father in such a way that whoever hates the Son hates the Father.

*If I had not come and spoken to them, they would not have sinned; but now they have no excuse for their sin. He who hates me hates my **Father** also. If I had not done among them the works which no one else did, they would not have sinned; but now they have seen and hated both me and my Father. It is to fulfill the word that is written in their law,*[376] *'They hated me without a cause.' But when the Counselor comes, whom I shall send to you from the **Father**, even the Spirit of truth, who proceeds from the **Father**, he will bear witness to me; and you also are witnesses, because you have been with me from the beginning.*[377]

*There will be difficulties.

I have said all this to you to keep you from falling away. They will put you out of the synagogues; indeed, the hour is coming when whoever kills you will think he is offering service to God. And they will do this because they

---

[374] *Jn* 15:9-11.
[375] *Jn* 15:12-17.
[376] *Ps* 35(34):19; 69(68):5.
[377] *Jn* 15:22-27.

have not known the Father, nor me. But I have said these things to you, that when their hour comes you may remember that I told you of them.[378]

*The Father is so infinitely generous that Jesus repeatedly promises that the Father will give us all things.

'A little while, and you will see me no more; again a little while, and you will see me.' Some of his disciples said to one another, 'What is this that he says to us, 'A little while, and you will not see me, and again a little while, and you will see me'; and, 'because I go to the Father'?'... Truly, truly, I say to you, if you ask anything of the Father, he will give it to you in my name.[379]

*It is on this occasion that Jesus tells us: *The Father loves you.*

'In that day you will ask in my name; and I do not say to you that I shall pray the **Father** *for you; for* **THE FATHER HIMSELF LOVES YOU**, *because you have loved me and have believed that I came from the* **Father***. I came from the* **Father** *and have come into the world; again, I am leaving the world and going to the* **Father***.' His disciples said, 'Ah, now you are speaking plainly, not in any figure! Now we know that you know all things, and need none to question you; by this we believe that you came from God.*[380]

*The Father's love is such that Jesus is never alone, just as we are never alone; we are in the grace of God.

Jesus answered them, 'Do you now believe? The hour is coming, indeed it has come, when you will be scattered, every man to his home, and will leave me alone; yet I am not alone, for the **Father** *is with me. I have said this to you, that in me you may have peace. In the world you have tribulation; but be of good cheer, I have overcome the world.*[381]

*And they also mutually glorify each other:

---

[378] *Jn* 16:1-4.
[379] *Jn* 16:16-17, 23.
[380] *Jn* 16:26-30.
[381] *Jn* 16:31-33.

When Jesus had spoken these words, he lifted up his eyes to heaven and said, 'Father, the hour has come; glorify thy Son that the Son may glorify thee'...

*This is so important that it means eternal life.

*...since thou hast given him power over all flesh, to give eternal life to all whom thou hast given him. And this is eternal life, that they know thee the only true God, and Jesus Christ whom thou hast sent. I glorified thee on earth, having accomplished the work which thou gavest me to do; and now, **Father**, glorify thou me in thy own presence with the glory which I had with thee before the world was made.*[382]

*He asks the Father to watch over us.

*Holy **Father**, keep them in thy name, which thou hast given me, that they may be one, even as we are one.*[383]

*He prays for those who were there, and for everyone gathered together here today and for those who will come throughout the centuries.

*I do not pray for these only, but also for those who believe in me through their word, that they may all be one; even as thou, **Father**, art in me, and I in thee.*[384]

*Christ prays so that we might be together with the Father and with Him:

---

[382] *Jn* 17:2-5; On this occasion Jesus speaks as a priest and as a victim before going up to the altar of the cross. He asks for His own glorification as a reward for having fulfilled the work that His **Father** had given Him. He asks Him to sanctify His disciples and to keep them united in charity, and last He prays for those who will believe by the words of His disciples, that they will also be united in faith and love.

[383] *Jn* 17:11; "Keep them in thy name" which is to say, in the right understanding of you that you have given me. We prefer this rendering to the version in the Vulgate, which says: keep in your name those who you have given me.

[384] *Jn* 17:20-21.

That they also may be in us, so that the world may believe that thou hast sent me...Father, I desire that they also, whom thou hast given me, may be with me where I am, to behold my glory which thou hast given me in thy love for me before the foundation of the world. O righteous Father, the world has not known thee, but I have known thee; and these know that thou hast sent me. I made known to them thy name, and I will make it known, that the love with which thou hast loved me may be in them, and I in them.[385]

II

When the bloody passion begins in Gethsemane, Jesus prostrates Himself on the rock of the agony three times and He cries out three times:

And he withdrew from them about a stone's throw, and knelt down and prayed, 'Father, if thou art willing, remove this cup from me; nevertheless not my will, but thine, be done.'[386]

Again, for the second time, he went away and prayed, 'My Father, if this (the chalice) cannot pass unless I drink it, thy will be done.' And again he came and found them sleeping, for their eyes were heavy.[387]

*Three times. A prayer of supreme tenderness: *Father;* of extreme anguish: *let this cup of suffering pass from me*, and of supreme abandonment to the will of God: *not my will but thine.* And He sweated blood. And later, hanging on the cross, in His first words he refers to the Father:

Father —again with supreme tenderness—*forgive them; for they know not what they do.*[388]

*Forgive them. This is the heroic mercy of our divine Savior. He is asking the Father to forgive those who had crucified Him. They do not know what they are doing. And also, when hanging on the cross, He speaks in His native language, Aramaic:

---

[385] *Jn* 17:21, 24-26.
[386] *Lk* 22:41-42.
[387] *Mt* 26:42-43.
[388] *Lk* 23:34.

'Eloi, Eloi, lama sabachthani?' which means, 'My **God***, my* **God***, why hast thou forsaken me?'* [389] *And some of the bystanders hearing it said, 'Behold, he is calling Elijah.'* [390]

*A prayer of supreme desolation, the greatest desolation that has ever existed in a human heart. After wetting His lips with the sponge dipped in vinegar and saying that it is finished, *consumatum est,* He said:

When Jesus had received the vinegar, he said, 'It is finished'... Then Jesus, crying with a loud voice, said, 'Father, into thy hands I commit my spirit!'[391] *...and he bowed his head and gave up his spirit.*[392]

*The most beautiful definition of death is: to give the soul to God. Dear brothers, Jesus refers to the heavenly Father during His Passion so many times! The Father is truly the unwavering reference point for Him—as He should be for us—because He is the principle of everything. It was the Father who created us and who sent His Son to die on the cross to save us. It is the Father who sends the Holy Spirit to sanctify us so that we can be saved and reach heaven to rejoice in happiness without end.

May the Blessed Virgin, our Mother, example of a faithful daughter of the heavenly Father, teach us to love our only Lord more each day.

---

[389] Words with which Psalm 22(21) begins.
[390] *Mk* 15:34-35.
[391] Cf. *Ps* 31(30):6.
[392] *Jn* 19:30; Lk 23:46.

9.
WE BELIEVE
IN THE RESURRECTION

"The tomb is empty. It is a silent witness to the central event of human history: the Resurrection of our Lord Jesus Christ. For almost two thousand years the empty tomb has borne witness to the victory of Life over death. With the Apostles and Evangelists, with the Church of every time and place, we too bear witness and proclaim: "Christ is risen! Raised from the dead he will never die again; death no longer has power over him."[393]

Homily Jerusalem, Basilica of the Holy Sepulcher, March 26, 2000.

Dear young people, I want to tell you in broad strokes about my first contact with Jesus Resurrected. I will do it in the way of *captatio benevolentia* only for rhetorical reasons. I say for rhetorical reasons because by quickly telling this story I want to stir up in you memories of what has been your own personal story with Jesus Resurrected.

I

I was about four years old and living in my grandparents' house where we had moved after my maternal grandfather died. I remember that they rang the bells at about ten in the morning on Holy Saturday. Pius XII hadn't reformed Holy Week yet. To my astonishment my Spanish grandmother dipped her fingers in tap-water and wet her eyes when the bells rang. I had to do the same. From then on, I always waited for the day when what

---

[393] Cf. *Rom* 6:9.

happened on no other day would happen: wetting the eyes with water. I didn't know exactly what it meant then and I still don't. Maybe it was meant to show a cleaning of the eyes in order to better see the truths of the Faith, or to show sympathy with Christ who had suffered His Passion. I don't know.

I experienced the second contact when I learned the catechism and had to memorize the Apostles Creed. There was a strange phrase: "He resurrected on the third day." It was explained to us, but it was still a mysterious thing: He resurrected!

As altar boys, it was exciting on Holy Saturday when we heard the singing of the *Exultet* after the lighting of the Paschal Candle and the three repetitions of *Lumen Christi*. It was a wonderful thing to realize that one was before something great, even without knowing exactly what it was. It was sung in Latin, and it was something that captured the heart. The singing of the *Exultet!*

Other contacts with Jesus resurrected: The Sacred Heart of Jesus. He appeared to Saint Margaret Mary Alacoque with His heart in His hand: *Voilá,* behold the heart that has loved man so much!

Years ago, I had an experience in my youth (18 or 19 years old) as a student in the Catholic University. A professor who had recently come from Europe with his new diploma under his arm, suggested difficulties about the resurrection that we had never heard of and had never even occurred to us. This intelligent, but foolish man produced an effect in my soul for which I will be truly grateful throughout life. This is how it was:"If this man, who is rationalist, believes in the resurrection, then the resurrection certainly happened." That was the reaction that he produced in me, and it was interesting because I saw the resurrection from an apologetic point of view.

My next experience of the resurrection was much more significant. In a Sacred Scripture class in a seminary, the professor denied the bodily resurrection of Jesus Christ. He claimed that Christ died and was resurrected in the same moment. And we, amid exclamations, were all shocked by his words. I said, "Great, so all the Jews were witnesses of the resurrection!" But he answered: "No, because the body resurrected but not the corporality." That is the same as speaking of a square circle.

Another experience was when I first wrote theologically about the resurrection of our Lord, published in the Journal *Mikael*.[394]

I can say that it was all of this that, in some way, led to the celebrations and festivities that take place in all our houses to remember the Resurrection of our Lord in the Easter Octave, those eight whole days of celebration because the Lord has resurrected!

After this long *captatio*, I want to address three points on the resurrection.

II

A. The resurrection is a miracle.

The resurrection is a miracle among miracles. As a miracle it belongs to the study of Fundamental Theology, but it is also a mystery, and these two facts are not mutually exclusive. They are two aspects of the same reality, like the two sides of one coin: miracle and mystery. The mystery is the study of Dogmatic Theology. For this reason a seminarian must spend whatever time is necessary to know the Resurrection of the Lord under these two aspects, the aspect of miracle and the aspect of mystery.

Under the aspect of miracle, the resurrection has an apologetic bivalence, or double aspect. In the first place, it is the fulfillment of a prophecy, an intellectual miracle, by which Our Lord, in an anticipated way, repeatedly said that He would resurrect and He did. In the second place, by its bivalence, it is the fulfillment and actualization of a physical miracle. This is an entirely original miracle never seen in either pagan mythology or

---

[394] Cf. CARLOS MIGUEL BUELA, "La Resurrección, ¿Mito o Realidad?" *Mikael,* n.6, 1974, pp. 17-38.

any other religion. Jesus, as He said in several parts of the Gospel, raised Himself from the dead.[395]

Sometimes Scripture says that God raised Him; for example, in the first discourse of Saint Peter. This was the most effective way to speak to the Jews to whom they could not yet speak directly of the divinity of Jesus. Technically, it is the most exact way to speak of the resurrection because neither the soul of Christ nor the body of Christ, but His divinity,[396] worked the miracle.

In the Gnostic times in which we live—times of the crudest rationalism in the Church—heresies about the resurrection have multiplied. We must learn to refute these heresies.

One Tuesday night at the desk of Father Julio Meinvielle, someone began to speak against the resurrection of our Lord. Father Julio, who was very intelligent, refuted him with fervor and authority. He knew the resurrection so well, especially from an apologetic point of view, that in the end the man admired his faith. The father, who was quite angry, answered: "Don't admire me for anything, I do this because of my habit!" (the cassock), as if to say to him, "It is my duty."

Rationalists such as Harnack, R. Bultmann, M. Dibelius and certain liberal Protestants such as Von Hase, Th. Keim,[397] and O. Pfleiderer have denied the existence of the prophecies about the resurrection.

Moreover, there are those who deny the fact of the resurrection itself. In this vein there are six principal tendencies:

---

395 Cf. *Jn* 10:17-18.

396 Cf. SAINT THOMAS AQUINAS, *STh*, III, 53,4, ad.1.

397 Both Von Hase (*Geshichte Jesu mach akademischen Vorlesungen*) and Th. Keim (*Die Geschichte Jesu von Nazara*) exclude all supernatural elements from the life of Jesus. Cf. FRANCISCO VIZMANOS-IGNACIO RIUDOR, *Teología Fundamental para seglares* (B.A.C.: Madrid, 1963), p 448.

-The school of *fraud*, which is the old theory of the Jews: the disciples of Christ feigned the resurrection and stole the body. Today Reimarus and Holtzman belong to this school, while Reville accuses the Pharisees themselves of having stolen the body of the Lord.

-The school of *natural explanation:* Gottlob Paulus, Schleiermacher, K. A. Von Hase. They say Jesus didn't die on the cross; He was only the victim of a faint from which He was able to recover because of the coldness of the tomb and the earthquake. He sat up and left the tomb dressed in the clothes of a gardener.

-The *mythical* school, with Strauss, A. Meyer and A. Loisy. For them the resurrection is a creation of the community under the influence of the Old Testament.

-The *symbolic* school, which pretends to distinguish the paschal announcement, composed of narrations about the reanimation of the body of Jesus, the empty tomb and apparitions, from the paschal faith, or the persuasion of the faithful concerning Jesus' victory over death and His new glorious life in the Father and the souls of the faithful. Ch. Guignebert and M. Goguel belong to this school.

-The *syncretistic school,* which seeks arguments from other religions, such as in the poem "Gilgamesh." P. Jensen, H. Gunkel, J. Frazer and W. Bousset belong to this school.

-The *visionary* schools, which reduce everything to mere illusions. They are divided into three main groups: *subjective visions* (A. Loisy), *objective visions* (Lotze, Th. Keim and A. Hoffmann) and *mystical visions* (R. Otto).

All of these schools, even though they have been refuted,[398] must continue to be refuted.

---

[398] Cf. Both Von Hase (*Geshichte Jesu mach akademischen Vorlesungen*) and Th. Keim (*Die Geschichte Jesu von Nazara*) exclude all supernatural elements from the

B. The resurrection is a miracle that must be known.

We must know clearly, especially from the point of view of the *preambula fidei,* three central points: first, that Christ prophesized His resurrection; second, that He truly died; and third, that He truly resurrected.

From a scientific and human point of view, we must be certain that the Gospels transmit to us the truth about Jesus and that they are historical documents.

Three of the four Gospels dedicate a chapter to the resurrection of the Lord; Saint John dedicates two chapters. Saint Paul speaks of the resurrections in eleven of his fourteen letters. Saint Peter talks about the resurrection three times in his first letter. In the Acts of the Apostles we find that the six discourses of Peter and the six discourses of Paul all speak about the resurrection. These witnesses have the quality of the Apostles. Then there are the five hundred people the Lord appears to,[399] of whom Paul says, *most of whom are still alive,*[400] and the thousands of Jews who saw the empty tomb...

We must know the objective foundation of the testimonies:

-The empty tomb[401]; the impossibility of the body being stolen by the Apostles, Joseph of Arimathea, the Jews or by the Romans.[402]

-The unexplainable transformation of the Apostles and disciples, who were *afraid,*[403] *who were behind closed doors,*[404] who

---

life of Jesus. Cf. FRANCISCO VIZMANOS-IGNACIO RIUDOR, *Teología Fundamental para seglares* (B.A.C.: Madrid, 1963), 450 ff.

[399] *1 Cor* 15:6.

[400] Cf. *1 Cor* 15:6.

[401] Cf. *Mt* 28:6; *Mk* 16:6; *Lk* 24:3; *Jn* 20:2; *Rom* 6:4; *1 Cor* 15:4; *Acts* 13:30.

[402] Cf. FRANCISCO VIZMANOS-IGNACIO RIUDOR, *Teología Fundamental para seglares* (B.A.C.: Madrid, 1963), p 458.

[403] Cf. *Jn* 20:19.

[404] Cf. *Jn* 20:19.

didn't believe,[405] or who *doubted,*[406] as in the case of Thomas the Apostle, which is related in the Gospel. [407]

-The fruit obtained in the conversion of the whole world; Saint Augustine says that if Christ did not resurrect and if that miracle is not believed, the greater miracle is that without the resurrection having happened, everyone still believed in Jesus Christ.[408]

-The foundation of the apparitions: there are twelve apparitions described in detail in the Gospels, and there are many more that are not described in detail but recorded in general, such as we see in the first chapter of the Acts of the Apostles.[409] They are objective and real apparitions, because of the circumstances that accompany them and the impossibility of reducing them to mere allusions or subjective illusions.

C. The resurrection is a mystery.

Finally, the mystery: the resurrection as a mystery, object of dogmatic theology, and therefore, of faith.

Since it belongs to faith, the resurrection is assented to through contemplation: there Christ presents Himself to us as the conqueror of death. All that His glorious body means—and ours will be similar to His body—is therefore a model for our future resurrection. He is *to unite all things in him, things in heaven and things on earth.*[410]

Dear Young People:

Let us allow ourselves to be permeated by the mystery of the resurrection of Our Lord.

---

[405] Cf. *Lk* 24:11; *Mk* 16:11,13.
[406] Cf. *Mt* 28:17.
[407] *Jn* 20:25.
[408] Cf. SAINT AUGUSTINE, *The City of God*, 22, 5.
[409] *Acts* 1:3.
[410] *Eph* 1:10.

Every day we eat a living body: the body of Christ Resurrected. Every day we rejoice in the closeness of a living, resurrected being: *I am with you always, to the close of the age.*[411]

We must allow ourselves to be formed by the King of life and never to be slaves of the culture of death.

We must be fearless and intrepid witnesses of the resurrection.

We ask this of the Blessed Virgin Mary.

---

[411] *Mt* 28:20.

10.

ᚠULL OF ᏀRACE

"My dear young people, you are more or less the same age as John and you have the same desire to be with Jesus. Today, it is you whom Jesus expressly asks to receive Mary 'into your home' and to welcome her 'as one of yours'; to learn from her the one who 'kept all these things, pondering them in her heart' (Lk 2:19)."

Message for the 18th World Youth Day, March 8, 2003.

Mary in the mystery of Christ

Dear young people, in accord with John Paul II, I would like to reflect with you on the mystery of the Blessed Virgin Mary. She "is definitively introduced into the mystery of Christ through the Annunciation by the angel. The divine messenger says to the Virgin: *Hail, full of grace, the Lord is with you.*[412] Mary *was greatly troubled at the saying, and considered in her mind what sort of greeting this might be*[413]: what could those extraordinary words mean, and in particular the expression 'full of grace' (kecharitoméne)." [414] These words, specifically the expression: *full of grace,* in Latin *gratia plena,* in Greek *kecharitoméne. Full of grace,* as we say to the Blessed Virgin every time we pray a Hail Mary.

---

[412] *Lk* 1:28.
[413] *Lk* 1:29.
[414] *Redemptoris Mater,* 8, about the Blessed Virgin Mary in the life of the pilgrim church. Cf Ignace De La Potterie, SJ, *kecharitoméne in Luca 1:28,* (Ed. Pt. Inst. Bíblica: Roma, 1991), 49; Javier Sanchew-Blanco, *Sentido de kecharitoméne en el saludo del Ángel a Santa María,* (Fe Católica: Madrid, 1966), 18.

Full of Grace and Blessed

In meditating on these words, we will first consider how the Blessed Virgin, *full of Grace*, is full of all blessings from God. Saint Paul the Apostle says in the letter to the Ephesians: *Blessed be the God and Father of our Lord Jesus Christ, who has blessed us in Christ with every spiritual blessing in the heavenly places, even as he chose us in him before the foundation of the world, that we should be holy and blameless before him. He destined us in love to be his sons through Jesus Christ, according to the purpose of his will, to the praise of his glorious grace which he freely bestowed on us in the Beloved. In him we have redemption through his blood.*[415] In this text from the letter to the Ephesians we are given the "significant echo"[416] of what the angel says to the Blessed Virgin Mary. Soon after the words from Saint Gabriel the Archangel, the Blessed Virgin received another greeting from her relative, Elizabeth, who called her: *Blessed are you among women.*[417]

The double greeting

Why *full of grace?* Why *blessed among women?* Because she received the blessing that Saint Paul speaks of in Ephesians: God the Father has filled us up *in the heavens in Christ.* This is "a spiritual blessing which is meant for all people,"[418] and to all women, from all times, cultures and tongues. It is a blessing "which bears in itself fullness and universality ('every blessing'). It flows from that love which, in the Holy Spirit, unites the consubstantial Son to the Father. At the same time, it is a blessing poured out through Jesus Christ upon human history until the end: upon all people. This blessing, however, refers to Mary in a special and exceptional degree."[419] The angel greets her with *full of grace* and Elizabeth greets her with *blessed are you among women.* The reason for this double greeting from the angel and Saint Elizabeth is that "in the soul of this 'daughter of Zion' there

---

[415] *Eph* 1:3-7.
[416] *Redemptoris Mater*, 8.
[417] *Lk* 1:42.
[418] *Redemptoris Mater*, 8.
[419] *Redemptoris Mater*, 8.

is manifested, in a sense, all the 'glory of grace,' which 'the Father...has given us in his beloved Son."[420] When the angel says *rejoice,* he does not say *Rejoice Mary,* but rather *Rejoice full of grace.* Full of grace! It is a name proper to the Most Holy Virgin. He doesn't call the Virgin "by her proper earthly name: Myriam (= Mary), but by this new name: 'full of grace.'"[421]

What is grace?

And why that name? In the Bible, grace means a special gift from God, from the God who is love.[422] The fruit of that love is election: it is the love of God that chooses this man, this woman, that man and that woman, as He chose the Virgin. This election is the eternal will of the Father to every man and woman; it is the grace that vivifies and sanctifies the elect. The blessing for man *with every spiritual blessing in the heavenly places,* that of *being adopted sons in Christ,* He who is eternally the *Beloved* of the Father,[423] is made reality in this way.

Full of Grace: a singular blessing

Full of grace means a completely unique blessing. Before the creation of the world, the Holy Virgin was chosen as mother of His Son in the incarnation. Mary is united to Christ in a completely exceptional way. She is uniformly loved in this eternal lover, in this Son co-substantial with the Father, in whom is concentrated all the glory of grace. The Vatican Council says that Mary "stands out among the poor and humble of the Lord, who confidently hope for and receive salvation from Him."[424]

Full of Grace: Divine Maternity

What is this singular, exceptional and unique thing that the Blessed Virgin was chosen for? She is chosen by God to be the

---

[420] *Redemptoris Mater,* 8.
[421] *Redemptoris Mater,* 8.
[422] Cf. *1 Jn* 4:8.
[423] Cf. *Redemptoris Mater,* 8.
[424] *Lumen Gentium,* 55.

mother of His Son. That is why she is *full of grace*. The greeting and the name *full of grace* refer above all, to the election of Mary as the mother of the Son of God, implying that this plentitude of grace indicates the supernatural gift of God from which Mary benefits because she has been destined and chosen to be the mother of Christ. This election is fundamental for our good because in this election, the divine design, which is salvific with respect to all men, is fulfilled. That is why the election of Mary is completely exceptional and unique.

From here flows the singularity and uniqueness of her place in the mystery of Christ.[425]

Full of Grace: Exceptional and unique

Mary is *full of grace, gratia plena*. This can be seen quite clearly in the Gospel of Luke. The divine messenger says: *Do not be afraid, Mary, for you have found favor with God. And behold, you will conceive in your womb and bear a son, and you shall call his name Jesus. He will be great, and will be called the Son of the Most High.*[426] And when the Virgin responds to the angel: *How shall this be, since I have no husband?* she receives confirmation from the angel and the explication of the proceeding words. The angel says to her: *The Holy Spirit will come upon you, and the power of the Most High will overshadow you; therefore the child to be born will be called holy, the Son of God* [Lk 1:35].[427]

Full of Grace: zenith of all graces

Full of grace: In that moment, humanity reaches the zenith, the highest summit of all the gifts of graces from the Father to humanity. The annunciation is the revelation of the mystery of the incarnation at the very beginning of its fulfillment on the earth. It is a zenith among all the gifts of grace in the history of man and of the universe. Mary is *full of grace*, because the

---

[425] Cf. *Redemptoris Mater*, 9.
[426] *Lk* 1:30-32.
[427] Cf. *Redemptoris Mater*, 9.

incarnation of the Word, the hypostatic union of the Son of God with human nature is fulfilled precisely in her. So the council says that Mary is "Mother of the Son of God, by which account she is also the beloved daughter of the Father and the temple of the Holy Spirit. Because of this gift of sublime grace she far surpasses all creatures, both in heaven and on earth."[428]

Full of Grace: Free of all sin

Gratia plena means another thing: that the Most Holy Virgin was free of all sin, even from original sin,[429] which is why we call her "Immaculate." (From this comes the old traditional greeting of Spanish speaking people "Ave María purísima" responded to with "sin pecado concebida"). From the very instant that she began to exist in the womb of her mother, Saint Anne, Mary was already free from sin, because she was freed in foreknowledge of the merits of her Son on the cross. This is why we read in the letter to the Ephesians: *The God and Father...freely bestowed on us in the Beloved...in him we have redemption through his blood.*[430] And so, it is said in so many ecclesial documents that the Blessed Virgin was redeemed "by a special grace and privilege of God."[431] In the Blessed Virgin, the glory of grace is made present. The liturgy does not hesitate to call her "mother of her Creator,"[432] and to greet her with the words that Dante Alighieri puts into the mouth of Saint Bernard: "Daughter of thy Son."[433] And Mary receives from this new life a plenitude that corresponds to the love of the

---

[428] *Lumen Gentium*, 53.

[429] Cf. SAN GERMÁN COST., In Annuntiationem SS. Deiparae Hom.: PG 98, 327s; san Andrés Cret., Canon in B. Mariae Natalem, 4: PG 97, 1321s.; In Nativitiatem B. Mariae, I: PG 97, 811s; Hom. In Dormitionem S. Mariae 1: PG 97, 1067s.

[430] *Eph* 1:3, 7.

[431] *Ineffabilis Deus*, Pope Pius IX, December 8, 1854.

[432] Liturgy of the Hours of 15 August, Assumption of the Blessed Virgin Mary, Hymn at First and Second Vespers; Saint Peter Damian, *Carmina et preces*, XLVII: PL 145, 934.

[433] DANTE ALIGHIERI, Published 1909 P.F. Collier online book p 424 trans.: Henry F. Cary.

Son for the mother, and consequently, to the dignity of divine maternity. This, in the annunciation, the angel calls *full of grace.*[434]

Full of Grace: Enmity with evil

Full of grace also means that, in her, there has arisen a radical opposition to evil, an enmity created by God Himself, as He had already announced at the beginning of humanity.[435] A Son is coming to the world, of the *line of the woman* who overthrew the evil of sin at its very root: *she will crush the head of the serpent.* Those are the words of the proto-evangelium. This enmity between the full of grace and the prince of evil announced at the beginning is confirmed in the Apocalypse, the book of the final realities of the Church and of the world, where the sign of the *woman* appears again, this time *a woman clothed with the sun.*[436] Mary, the Mother of the Incarnate Word, as John Paul II calls her in *Redemptoris Mater,*[437] is situated in the very center of that enmity, of the struggle and of the war that follows the history of humanity on earth and even the history of salvation. In this place, she who belongs to the "humble and poor ones of the Lord," carries in herself the "glory of grace" like no other human being does, with which the Father "bestowed on us in the Beloved." This plenitude of grace, this *gratia plena* of Mary, is what gives her and defines in her an extraordinary greatness and a unique beauty of her whole being. *He chose us in him before the foundation of the world... He destined us in love to be his sons through Jesus Christ.*[438] Thus, Mary remains before God and humanity. And if today we are gathered here it is because in some way the greatness of the *full of grace* has enthralled us and the unmarred beauty of her being has stolen our hearts. This election is stronger than all the experiences of evil and sin that we could fall into, stronger than all the enmity with

---

[434] Cf. *Redemptoris Mater*, 10.
[435] Cf. *Gen* 3:15.
[436] *Rev* 12:1.
[437] Cf. *Redemptoris Mater*, 10.
[438] *Eph* 1:4, 5.

which the history of man has been so marked. In this history Mary continues to be a sign of sure hope.[439]

Full of grace: Spes Nostra

The youth must recognize the enmity of the world whether they want to or not. If they are true children of Mary they must also participate in that irreducible enmity that doesn't know compromise and cannot be negotiated. If you are with Christ or against Christ, you are with Mary or against Mary. We must put greater trust in our mother in heaven, the *full of grace*, who, as the saints of all times have sung, is *spes nostra*, our sure hope.

To her we entrust all the young people of the whole world, the good and the bad, that her generous and abundant blessing might descend over them and that we might truly recognize her Son, our only Savior.

We conclude with a phrase attributed to Saint Gregory Nazianzus: "You have been called *kecharitoméne* because in you all treasures of grace are hidden."

---

[439] Cf. *Redemptoris Mater*, 10.

11.

MARY IS THE MOTHER OF GOD

"Mary is Mother of divine grace, because she is the Mother of the Author of grace. Entrust yourselves to her with complete confidence! You will be radiant with the beauty of Christ. Open up to the breath of the Spirit, and you will become courageous apostles, capable of spreading the fire of charity and the light of truth all around you. In Mary's school, you will discover the specific commitment that Christ expects of you, and you will learn to put Christ first in your lives, and to direct your thoughts and actions to him."

Message for the 18th World Youth Day,
April 13, 2003.

The sublime fact of the Incarnation of the Word compels us to know the Incarnate Word better. To know the Word is to know His mystery, his Person, what the faith tells us about Him, what the doctrine He taught is, and what it is that He wants from us. To know the Word is to know how to defend our faith in the Incarnate Word.

When I was out of the country some time ago, a European layman, who was a seminary professor, aggressively asked me how it was possible to call the Virgin Mary the Mother of God, "Can God have a mother?" His question revealed his denial of the divine maternity of the Blessed Virgin Mary, and his lack of understanding of the mystery of the Incarnation of the Word.

How can it be that cultured people who have received ample professional formation are ignorant of such elementary and fundamental truths of the Catholic faith? God in His divine nature does not have a mother. Insofar as He is God He did not have a cradle, use diapers, hold a bottle, or play with toys. God is pure spirit and has no body, no bones or muscles, blood pressure or illness. He has no beginning and no end. God is eternal.

But if God becomes man, which means that in addition to having a divine nature, He assumes a true human nature (which is precisely the Incarnation of the Word), then there must be a woman who gives Him human nature. And by being united to the person of the Word, the second person in the Trinity, that human nature is a human nature that does not have a human person, because the place of the human person is occupied in a much more wonderful way, by the person of the Word.

Therefore, our Mother begets a human nature that is substantially united to a divine person and she is the Mother of God! Because Christ her son, in addition to being man, is God! And this is elementary. [440] To deny this truth is to flaunt ignorance. A reading of the *Catechism of the Catholic Church* will verify that this is a dogma of faith defined by the council of Ephesus. [441]

In the region where the council fathers met, Greek was the language spoken. The precise, technical word they used to refer to the Virgin Mary was *Theotokos*, which means Mother of God! We pray it in the second part of the Hail Mary: "Holy Mary, Mother of God..." If this were not so, there would be no incarnation! If the Virgin is not the Mother of God, then she is the mother of a man. There would be no incarnation because there would be two subjects: one divine and the other human. For there to be an incarnation, God must assume a human nature and these two natures must be substantially united. The union has to take place in the divine person, the second person of the Most Holy Trinity, the person of the Word, "so that a Trinity and not a Quaternity might be believed in." [442]

---

[440] Cf. *Catechism of the Catholic Church*, n. 495.
[441] Cf. DH 251.
[442] ST. AUGUSTINE, *On the Predestination of the Saints*, Book I, ch. 31.

To be ignorant of this is to be ignorant of the most elemental things, and creates confusion, even in consecrated souls. After that encounter a seminarian came and asked me exactly the same question. When confusion enters a consecrated soul, that soul will not remain consecrated for long, because not knowing that Jesus Christ is true God and true man, and that He is One because both natures are united in Him, then what is the point of sacraments, religious life, virginity, poverty, and obedience? If the one we see on the cross does not have a human nature united hypostatically to a divine person, then our sins are not expiated, because He would be just a man. And so Baptism wouldn't wash away our sins, nor would Confession, and the Eucharist wouldn't be the Body and Blood of the Lord, together with His soul and His divinity.

If this core truth is no longer believed, the sacraments and the Church would fall and many priests will devote themselves to temporal concerns and stop believing in eternal truths. It is necessary to always go deeper into these truths of the faith because they are capable of moving our hearts to imitate the Lord. Further, we must be able to respond when we hear these truths being debunked and denied. John Paul I said: "Today, in faith, one only has what one defends."[443]

If there is something in the faith that we are not capable of defending it is because we do not have faith; we do not have faith as we should have it. And so, let us always ask the Blessed Virgin for the grace to defend with the greatest possible strength, the truth that the Word became flesh.

---

[443] ALBINO LUCIANI, *Ilustrísimos Señores* (Madrid, 1978), 93. (Editorial translation).

12.

THE SECOND COMING

"The memory of God's work reaches its climax in the
resurrection of Christ and is projected onto the eschatological event
of the parousia. We thus catch a glimpse, on this night of
Passover, of the dawning of that day that never ends, the day of the
Risen Christ, which inaugurates the new life, the 'new heavens
and a new earth.'"

Easter Vigil Homily, 2004.

I would like to address one of the great mysteries of the faith: the Second Coming of our Lord.

We must ask to grow in faith and we profess it in the Creed: "and from thence he will come to judge the living and the dead," we ask for it in the Our Father: *thy kingdom come*[444] and it also appears in other places: *Come, Lord Jesus!*[445]

In general, this mystery is not part of the consciousness of the believer, and it is very common that when we sing the canticle of the Apocalypse, *for the marriage of the Lamb has come, and his Bride has made herself ready,*[446] we do not realize that it refers to the second coming.

---

[444] *Mt* 6:10.
[445] *Rev* 22:20.
[446] *Rev* 19:7.

Who waits for the coming of the Lord?

From a very young age I have had the grace to read the Apocalypse and good commentaries on the second coming of the Lord. The writings of Father Leonardo Castellanni, with books such as *"Cristo, ¿vuelve o no vuelve?"*, *"Los papeles de Benjamín Benavides"* and *"El Apocalipsis según San Juan,"* and others are worth mentioning.

The second coming is a truth of the faith, and therefore not a matter of opinion. As noted, we confess it in the Creed. The Lord also taught it in his eschatological discourse when He said: *so will be the coming of the Son of man.*[447] Everything will pass away, only the word of Christ will not pass away. The world will end and will die, not of a natural death, but only when God ordains it.

When will this happen?

We do not know the day or the hour, because it is part of the saving message.[448]

Christians must be prepared because the hour of death is uncertain, as is the hour of the end of the world.

Some may claim that they know, but Saint Thomas Aquinas affirms the "falseness of these calculators."[449] We should not expect an encyclical from the Pope or a pastoral letter from a bishop telling us when the second coming will be. If Christ did not reveal it to the Apostles, even less will He reveal it to us. It is part of revelation that we do not know the time. Revelation tells man "all truth in respect to matters necessary for salvation."[450] He tells us nine times in the Apocalypse, *I am coming soon*, and so, at some point, He will come.

---

[447] *Mt* 24:27, 35; Cf *Mk* 13:31; *Lk* 21:33.
[448] Cf. *Mt* 25:13.
[449] ST. THOMAS AQUINAS, S. Th. Suppl. 77, 2.
[450] ST. THOMAS AQUINAS, S.Th. I-II, 106, 4, ad. 2.

This uncertainty helps us to bring order to those things that will not end with our death.

And what are these things?

The first is our life. Scripture says: *remember the end of your life, and then you will never sin.*[451]

The second is family, including society. These are all things that fall under our responsibility to order according to the will of God.[452]

This truth of the faith defends us against ideologies, so present in our times that affect a large part of the world. Truth defends us against cultural fads, what the media seeks to impose on us, and what seems to be the tendency of the future. One day the Antichrist will reign, but we must still remain faithful to Christ, even at the risk of our lives. Not too long ago in Germany and other countries they said "better to be red than dead"; and they joined the ranks of communism, which fell miserably a few years later, because they did not want to listen to the Word of God.

But there will be signs!

We do not know when the end of the world will be, but we do know that there will be signs:

Some minor signs are:

a. *Wars and rumors of wars... there will be famines and earthquakes.*[453]

b. The abomination of desolation will come.[454] How many religious houses can be characterized as the abomination of desolation!

---

451 *Sir* 7:36.
452 Cf. ST. THOMAS AQUINAS, *S. Th.,* Supp. 88, 3, ad 4.
453 Cf. *Mt* 24:6,7 and parallels.

To these are added other signs that are also in the Gospel.

The major signs are:

a. *And this gospel of the kingdom will be preached throughout the whole world.*[455]

b. Universal apostasy. Our Lord says: *when the Son of man comes, will he find faith on earth?*[456] Also in the eschatological sermon in Matthew: *And because wickedness is multiplied, most men's love will grow cold.*[457]

Have you not seen that we are living in an eclipse of morality and ethics because of the excess of evil on a planetary level?

Saint Paul teaches: *Let no one deceive you in any way; for that day will not come, unless the rebellion comes first.*[458]

c. The coming of the Antichrist who will have a totalitarian and universal reign: *and the man of lawlessness is revealed, the son of perdition, who opposes and exalts himself against every so-called god or object of worship, so that he takes his seat in the temple of God, proclaiming himself to be God... For the mystery of lawlessness is already at work.*[459]

The Popes have warned us about the gravity of the state of contemporary society

Blessed **Pius IX**: "even trample underfoot the rights both of the sacred and of the civil power.

"For this is the goal of the lawless activities against this Roman See in which Christ placed the impregnable foundation of His Church.

---

[454] Cf. *Mt* 24:15, among others.
[455] *Mt* 24:14.
[456] *Lk* 18:8.
[457] *Mt* 24:12.
[458] 2 *Thess* 2:3.
[459] 2 *Thess* 2:3-4, 7.

"This is the goal of those *secret sects* who have come forth from the darkness to destroy and desolate both the sacred and the civil commonwealth…

"This is the goal too of the *crafty Bible Societies* which renew the old skill of the heretics and ceaselessly force on people of all kinds, even the uneducated, gifts of the Bible…The commentaries which are included often contain perverse explanations; so, having rejected divine tradition, the doctrine of the Fathers and the authority of the Catholic Church, they all interpret the words of the Lord by their own private judgment, thereby perverting their meaning…

"Also perverse is the shocking theory that it makes *no difference to which religion* one belongs, a theory which is greatly at variance even with reason…They pretend that men can gain eternal salvation by the practice of any religion…

"The sacred celibacy of clerics has also been the victim of conspiracy…

"This is the aim too of the prevalent but wrong method of teaching, especially in the philosophical disciplines, a method which deceives and corrupts incautious youth in a wretched manner…

"To this goal also tends the unspeakable doctrine of Communism, as it is called, a doctrine most opposed to the very natural law…

"To this end also tend the darkest designs of men in the clothing of sheep, while inwardly ravening wolves. They humbly recommend themselves by means of a feigned and deceitful appearance of a purer piety, a stricter virtue and discipline; after taking their captives gently, they mildly bind them, and then kill them in secret. They make men fly in terror from all practice of religion, and they cut down and dismember the sheep of the Lord.

"To this end, finally—to omit other dangers which are too well known to you—tends the widespread disgusting infection from books and pamphlets which teach the lessons of sinning…"[460]

Leo XIII: "Now, the source of these evils lies chiefly, We are convinced, in this, that the holy and venerable authority of the Church, which in God's name rules mankind, upholding and defending all lawful authority, has been despised and set aside."[461]

Saint Pius X: "When all this is considered there is good reason to fear lest this great perversity may be as it were a foretaste, and perhaps the beginning of those evils which are reserved for the last days; and that there may be already in the world the 'Son of Perdition' of whom the Apostle speaks. Such, in truth, is the audacity and the wrath employed everywhere in persecuting religion, in combating the dogmas of the faith, in brazen effort to uproot and destroy all relations between man and the Divinity!

"While, on the other hand, and this according to the same apostle is the distinguishing mark of Antichrist, man has with infinite temerity put himself in the place of God, raising himself above all that is called God; in such wise that although he cannot utterly extinguish in himself all knowledge of God, he has condemned God's majesty and, as it were, made of the universe a temple wherein he himself is to be adored. 'He sitteth in the temple of God, showing himself as if he were God'."[462]

Benedict XV: "of all being most deeply distressed by the spectacle presented by Europe, nay, by the whole world, perhaps the saddest and most mournful spectacle of which there is any record.

"Certainly those days would seem to have come upon us of which Christ Our Lord foretold: 'You shall hear of wars and

---

[460] PIUS IX, Encyclical *Qui pluribus*, 13-17.
[461] LEO XIII, *Inscrutabili Dei Consilio*, 3.
[462] ST. PIUS X, *E Supremi Apostolatus*, 5.

rumours of wars - for nation shall rise against nation, and kingdom against kingdom [Mt 24:6, 7]."[463]

Pius XII: "The consequence is that the moral values by which in other times public and private conduct was gauged have fallen into disuse; and the much vaunted civilization of society, which has made ever more rapid progress, withdrawing man, the family and the State from the beneficent and regenerating effects of the idea of God and the teaching of the Church, has caused to reappear, in regions in which for many centuries shone the splendors of Christian civilization, in a manner ever clearer, ever more distinct, ever more distressing, the signs of a corrupt and corrupting paganism: 'There was darkness when they crucified Jesus'.

"...they spoke of progress, when they were going back; of being raised, when they groveled; of arriving at man's estate, when they stooped to servility. They did not perceive the inability of all human effort to replace the law of Christ by anything equal to it; 'they became vain in their thoughts.'[464]

"...It is true that even when Europe had a cohesion of brotherhood through identical ideals gathered from Christian preaching, she was not free from divisions, convulsions and wars which laid her waste; but perhaps they never felt the intense pessimism of today as to the possibility of settling them."[465]

Humanity does not have the strength to take away the stone which she herself has constructed, trying to impede Your return. Send Your angel, oh Lord! And make our night be illumined like day.

How many hearts, Lord, await You! How many souls are consumed to hasten the day in which You will only live and reign in hearts. Come, Lord Jesus!

---

[463] BENEDICT XV, *Ad Beatissimi Apostolorum*, 3.
[464] *Rom* 1:21.
[465] *Summi Pontificatus*, 30-31, 33.

There are so many signs that Your return is not far away![466]

John XXIII: "our age is marked by a clear contrast between the immense scientific and technical progress and the fearful human decline shown by its monstrous masterpiece... transforming man into a giant of the physical world at the expense of his spirit, which is reduced to that of a pygmy in the supernatural and eternal world."[467]

Paul VI: Speaking of the situation in the Church says of the spirit: "a danger bordering almost on vertiginous confusion and bewilderment can shake the Church's very foundations"[468] ; "a moment of self-destruction"[469]; "through some crack, the smoke of Satan has entered into the temple of God."[470]

John Paul II: "it is certain that the Church of the new Advent, the Church that is continually preparing for the new coming of the Lord, must be the Church of the Eucharist and of Penance."[471]

Indications?

These indications have been denounced by Popes for more than a century and these aspects of the reality occurring inside the Church are manifested by university teachings, lack of priestly and religious vocations, confusion in so many Christians and the rule of relativism. Not pointing out the Christian roots of Europe is a sign of the apostasy that afflicts us. Cardinal Luis Billot, SJ, thought that the verse in Luke 21:24 referred to Israel: *they will fall by the edge of the sword, and be led captive among all nations; and Jerusalem will be trodden down by the Gentiles, until the times of the Gentiles are fulfilled,* the last part of which would seem to have begun to be

---

[466] Easter Homily, April 21, 1957 (Editorial translation).
[467] *Mater et Magistra,* 243.
[468] *Ecclesiam suam,* 26.
[469] Speech in the Lombardo Seminary 12/7/68. (Editorial translation).
[470] PAUL VI, Homiliy, June 29, 1972.
[471] *Redemptor hominis,* 20.

fulfilled in 1948, against what had happened for almost twenty centuries.

The scripture talks about the destruction of Babylon at a certain time.[472] What seemed impossible before has happened in Hiroshima and Nagasaki in the Second World War.

Large armies are mentioned in the Apocalypse: *The number of the troops of cavalry was twice ten thousand times ten thousand.*[473] Today, only taking China into account, we can amass such an army.

In *Rev* 13:15 John speaks of the living image of the Beast seen across the whole world. For example, this can be done today, with satellite TV.

The lack of perseverance in religious life often points to lack of faith, where instead of being faithful to the Gospel, the world no longer waits for the second coming, but enslaves itself to the ideologies of the moment, be they political, social, economic or cultural. It is Christ who will judge the world, not the world who will judge Christ. And this can happen because they do not see, or they do not want to see reality, like an ostrich that hides its head to avoid seeing approaching danger.

Possible spiritual rebirth

The possibility of a great spiritual rebirth should also be taken into account, according to what some saints have thought:

Saint John Bosco says that throughout the whole world there will appear a sun so bright the likes of which have not been seen since the flames at the Cenacle, nor will be seen unto the end times.

Saint Luigi Orione warns us not to be like doom-sayers who believe that the world will end tomorrow...we are on the edge of a great era.

---

[472] Cf. *Rev* 18:9-10, 17, 19.
[473] *Rev* 9:16.

Saint Louis Marie de Montfort prophesied that the saints of the last times will exceed all known saints in the power of their words and deeds as the greatest trees surpass the simplest shrubs.

We must learn to live and grow in faith, as we pray in the Holy Mass: "Almighty and ever-living God, strengthen our faith, hope, and love. May we do with loving hearts what you ask of us and come to share the life you promise."[474] We ask this grace of the Blessed Virgin Mary.

---

[474] *Roman Missal*, 30th Sunday in Ordinary Time, Opening Prayer.

13.

SIGNS OF THE TIMES

"With the eyes of faith we can see history,
especially after the coming of Jesus Christ,
as totally enveloped and penetrated
by the presence of God's Spirit.
It is easy to understand why,
today more than ever, the Church
feels called to discern the signs
of this presence in human history,
with which she—in imitation
of her Lord—'cherishes
a feeling of deep solidarity.'"

Catechesis, September 23, 1998.

Some time ago I was able to visit Spain and make a pilgrimage to Daimiel, south of Madrid. There the Passionist Fathers had an empty seminary which is now a retreat house for spiritual exercises. During the Spanish civil war the militia arrived and told the seminarians to leave and choose another place to go. They consumed the hosts in the tabernacle. Father Nicéforo, the rector of the seminary, gave them a beautiful admonition and then they left the seminary in different groups. Although they knew that they were going to be killed, they left with hope of salvation. The military arrested them the next day and shot them. Some were not killed, but were badly wounded. However, after recovering from the wounds in the hospital, they were also killed. One of them was Blessed Honorino de la Dolorosa, nineteen years old. Initially, he was shot in the shoulder, which bled profusely and caused him much pain. He was brought to the hospital where no one wanted to care for him because to do so would endanger them. As he was bleeding onto the floor, one of the people who saw it asked him if he suffered much. He answered: "*Yes, but I am a Passionist.*" This is a great example for today.

I

I would like to give an idea of the signs of the times. Things are not at all well with, perhaps, a bloody persecution brewing. We have the testimonies of several European bishops:

-The first is from the Archbishop of Madrid, Cardinal Antonio María Rouco Varela, who stated during a meeting of Regnum Christi and the Legionaries of Christ that took place in the Francisco de Vitoria de Pozuelo de Alarcón University, that: "In Europe we are witnessing a gigantic crisis of faith, a silent apostasy from the faith is happening with greater or lesser intensity in all the countries of Europe."[475]

-The second testimony is from the Bishop of Mondoñedo-Ferrol, Mons. José Gea Escolano, who declared that "The church cannot remain silent before the moral degradation that the government plans for legislation in Spain on the topic of equating homosexual unions to marriage. We are aware that sometimes we bother people when we speak, and some politicians ask us to be silent, but a Church that doesn't speak out is good for nothing. The Church must guide its faithful in questions that have bearing on faith and morals."[476] The fervor with which the politicians claim to give stability to something that in itself is characterized by instability is striking. "In Canada, Argentina and various North American states, measures are being taken to legalize homosexual 'marriage.' A new Dutch study confirmed that *homosexual unions last, on average, only a year and a half.* The study, done by Dr. Maria Xiridou, is based on the health registers of young sodomites served by the Municipal Health Services of

---

[475] Madrid, 6/11/04, publicado en AICA (Agencia Informativa Católica Argentina, dependiente de la Conferencia Episcopal Argentina). (Editorial translation).

[476] Santiago de Compostela, 8/10/04, AICA. (Editorial translation).

Amsterdam and was published in the latest edition of the magazine AIDS."[477]

-The third testimony is from the Archbishop of Toledo, the Primate of Spain, Mons. Antonio Cañizares Llovera, who denounced the attacks on the Church from the powers and the mass media, who "are even ready to tear apart the Church." Mons Cañizares explained that "The Church, in her pilgrimage though the twentieth century and the beginnings of the twenty first century, has suffered much persecution and has had to wage a difficult battle against the powers of darkness. Never in history has she been harassed as she has been in these times,"[478] to wit: the martyrs of Daimiel, Barbastro, and so many others. According to the Primate of Spain, what is happening in the Church in Spain now is even more serious than what happened to the Church during the civil war, including the tribulations that the Church has had to suffer throughout history.

-The fourth testimony comes from the Archbishop of Valencia, Mons Agustín Garcia-Gasco, who expressed his concern for the "growth of organized anti-religious trends and an intolerant laicism against Christians, **national-laicism.**" He determined that "Intolerant laicism is like a caricature of those who don't profess any religion, an antireligious prejudice whose primary promoters want to expel religion from the social sphere and then eliminate it in humanity, so that religious principles end up disappearing from human consciousness."[479]

II

The laity has also given testimony:

-In an interview in the Italian newspaper *Il Messagiero,* the writer, Vittorio Messori, announced that in Europe anti-Catholicism has replaced anti-Semitism. Buttiglione pointed out

---

[477] Amsterdam, 7/8/04, AICA. (Editorial translation).
[478] Madrid, 8/10/04. AICA. (Editorial translation).
[479] Valencia, 22/10/04. AICA. (Editorial translation).

that it has been said that, "Catholics, smokers, and hunters are the three categories that are not protected by political correctness, and one can speak badly about them freely." "Thanks be to God that anti-Semitism is over, but it was substituted by anti-Catholicism." According to the writer, "blacks, women, sodomites or Jews were the object of sarcasm and criticism. Now, luckily, those categories can no longer be attacked, but I don't see why they then have to attack others."[480]

-When the appointment to the European Court of Buttiglione, an intellectual Catholic and personal friend of John Paul II, was vetoed, the Communion and Liberation movement denounced the "cultural totalitarianism what denies freedom of conscience, thought, and opinion," that, in their opinion "is being introduced in Europe." Their Information Office in Spain called it "dangerous" that Europe "rejects her Judeo-Christian roots, since she will then be without roots at all."[481]

III

The declarations of Cardinal Renato Martino that have appeared in the newspaper *Corriere della Sera* are even stronger. He has extensive diplomatic experiences that encompass the sixteen years he was the papal representative to the United Nations. Now he has been named president of the Council for Justice and Peace by the Pope. He compiled and presented a book about Pope John Paul II and his diplomatic activity during the years of his pontificate called *"Giovanni Paolo II e le sfide della diplomazia,"* which contains his discourses to diplomats. The Cardinal denounced the existence of new Holy Inquisitions, full of money and arrogance. "One can freely insult and attack Catholics and no one says anything... If other beliefs were attacked we would see what would happen." "Most harsh words" were said publicly by a Cardinal of the Church to the Sala Stampa.

---

[480] Roma 5/11/04. AICA. (Editorial translation).
[481] Madrid 4/11/04. AICA. (Editorial translation).

And then he says: "in Europe, a rich and powerful lobby is against the Pope," meaning that they do not want to listen to the words of the Pope. He says "lobbie potenti" that are in the continental countries (also in Europe), which are "rich and well off." According to the Cardinal, regarding the voices of the Pope and the Catholic Church, "they disappear amid the noise and commotion orchestrated by the powerful cultural, economic, and political interest groups, that are driven above all by the prejudice against all that is Christian."[482]

These interest groups have enormous power and an *a priori* prejudice against all Catholic Christians. These lobbies promote confusion, especially in the area of gender identity, and they seek to destroy marriage between a man and a woman. They believe that they can do whatever occurs to them, and so they discriminate and intimidate with public pressures, to mock people, especially Catholic people. In no way do they want anything Catholic.

There was an incident where a Bishop of Russia legitimately returned to a Russian airport, but had his visa confiscated, barring him from entering the country. Later, the Pope named him a Bishop in Poland and a Russian Bishop with a Russian passport, who was previously an auxiliary bishop in Belarus, was named in that Diocese. But meanwhile, who spoke up and said something? There is not a single power that will defend the Catholic Church. That is why Cardinal Martino says: "We face a mythical democracy, a mock democracy, if you don't think like me, you're out; your opinion is not accepted." And also, commenting on such strong words from Cardinal Martino, Riccardo Pedrizzi, responsible for the politics of the family in the newspaper *Alleanza Nazionale*, has said that "these interest groups are the

---

[482] Cf ZENIT ZI04101809 10-18-2004, Italian version: "le voci del Santo Padre e della Chiesa cattolica sono poco ascoltate" quanto addirittura deliberatamente fatte sparire, sommergendole nel frstruono e nel baccano orchestrate da potenti lobbies culturali, economiche e politiche mosse prevalentemente dal pregiudizio verso tutto quello che è christiano". (Editorial Translation).

ones who are intolerant and anti-democratic…today those who are truly attacked and oppressed are the Christians."

In summary, there is a conflict between two philosophies. On one side are those who believe in God and on the other side are those who argue for immanentism. Let us always ask Jesus, through the Blessed Virgin, to be faithful and to know that we are truly in a more difficult situation than the vast majority of believes. We must prepare ourselves for the difficult moments that could happen to us, so as to be faithful like the holy martyrs, who were faithful to Christ even to the point of shedding their blood.

Finally, before God, all of this carries as much weight as a spider web.

14.
THE CATHOLIC CHURCH: UNCONQUERABLE DEFENDER OF HUMAN LOVE

> "To be truly free means having the strength to choose the One for whom we were created and accepting his lordship over our lives. You perceive it in the depths of your heart: all that is good on earth, all professional success, even the human love that you dream of, can never fully satisfy your deepest and most intimate desires. Only an encounter with Jesus can give full meaning to your lives: 'for you made us for yourself, and our heart finds no peace until it rests in you.[483]
>
> *Message for the World Youth Day,*
> *March 4, 2004.*

The Church, defender of human love

At the end of the 20ᵗʰ and the beginning of the 21ˢᵗ century, the Catholic Church has stepped up as a firm and unconquerable defender of human love. In spite of the fact that defending authentic human love is unpopular in an era of enslavement to sex and pornography, and that the majority of society's means of communication—newspapers, magazines, books, TV, and the internet—are in the hands of those who are compulsively addicted to the momentary deviations of the majority, **the**

---

[483] SAINT AUGUSTINE, *The Confessions*, Book 1, Chapter 1.

Catholic Church serenely, joyfully, and firmly makes the greatest and best defense of human love.

The Church defends this intimate, constructive and distinctive gift in the face of mockery, corruption, and anti-Catholic campaigns on a worldwide level. The Church defends human love as a fruit of Christian love for the very people who have taken the wrong road, so that at least someone will treat them with true charity.

The Catholic Church, a specialist in humanity, could not refrain from testifying against the interests of the world's powers without seriously betraying the mission she was given by her founder, Jesus Christ.

She continues standing, like the standard over the nations that Isaiah had prophesized: *In that day the root of Jesse shall stand as an ensign to the peoples; him shall the nations seek, and his dwellings shall be glorious.*[484]

The Catholic Church, like her head and founder, Jesus Christ, is crucified for indissolubly uniting two things in her arms: the creative and unitive meanings of human love and virginity and marriage. For some people these two tenets have to be divided and separated because of the folly of the Hegelian dialectic that reigns in their minds. For others, they have to be divided and separated because of the powerful, dissolving, and destroying power of nihilism.

Rallying around the ten fronts of the battle

The Battle of the Church in defense of human love is fought on ten fronts, like the ten horns of the Beast that appears in the Apocalypse. They are expressed in these ways:

Contraception: is to make "love" without making a child;

---

[484] *Is* 11:10.

In vitro fertilization and **cloning:** to make a child without love;

Abortion: to unmake the child;

Euthanasia: to unmake the parents;

Pornography: to unmake love;

Homosexuality: (and therefore transexuality, and cross dressing), in the name of "love," to not want children of one's own flesh and blood (rather, in some cases, to adopt other children to help in old age);

Divorce: to definitely unmake love, and often, to not love one's children.

Contracepion, in-vitro fertilization, cloning, abortion, euthanasia, pornography, homosexuality, transexuality, and divorce are against the nature of authentic human love, because they are all forms of separating the creative and unitive meanings from love!

This is why the Pope has just reminded us that "the family is 'good news' to the extent that it accepts and makes its own the *perennial vocation* that God gave it at the beginning of humanity."

"But, *what family* is it referring to? Certainly not the inauthentic one based on individual egotisms. Experience shows such a 'caricature' of the family has no future and cannot ensure the future of any society."[485]

The attack against virginity and celibacy

With respect to the latter, the *Catechism of the Catholic Church* teaches: "Both the sacrament of Matrimony and virginity for the Kingdom of God come from the Lord himself. It is He who gives them meaning and grants them the grace which is indispensable for living them out in conformity with His will.

---

[485] Angelus message 1/26/2003.

Esteem of virginity for the sake of the kingdom and the Christian understanding of marriage are inseparable, and they reinforce each other: 'Whoever denigrates marriage also diminishes the glory of virginity. Whoever praises it makes virginity more admirable and resplendent...'"[486] For example, the words that are used in the sacred rite of the consecration of virgins wisely indicates that virginity testifies to the depth of marriage: "that there may exist more noble souls who disdain the marriage which consists in the bodily union of man and woman, but desire the mystery it enshrines, who reject its practice while loving its mystic signification,"[487] which is the union of Christ and the Church.

John Paul II teaches in *Familiaris consortio*: "Virginity or celibacy for the sake of the Kingdom of God not only does not contradict the dignity of marriage but presupposes it and confirms it. Marriage and virginity or celibacy are two ways of expressing and living the one mystery of the covenant of God with His people. When marriage is not esteemed, neither can consecrated virginity or celibacy exist; when human sexuality is not regarded as a great value given by the Creator, the renunciation of it for the sake of the Kingdom of Heaven loses its meaning. Rightly indeed does St. John Chrysostom say: 'Whoever denigrates marriage also diminishes the glory of virginity. Whoever praises it makes virginity more admirable and resplendent. What appears good only in comparison with evil would not be particularly good. It is something better than what is admitted to be good that is the most excellent good.'"[488] In virginity or celibacy, the human being is awaiting, in a bodily way, the eschatological marriage of Christ with the Church, giving himself or herself completely to the Church in the hope that Christ may give Himself to the Church in the full truth of eternal life. The celibate person thus anticipates in his or her flesh the

---

[486] CCC, 1620.

[487] PIUS XII, *Sacra Virginitatis*, 30—quoting from Pontificale Romanum: De benedictione et consecratione virginum.

[488] *La Virginidad*, X: PG 48. 540.

new world of the future resurrection.[489] By virtue of this witness, virginity or celibacy keeps alive in the Church a consciousness of the mystery of marriage and defends it from any reduction and impoverishment. Virginity or celibacy, by liberating the human heart[490] in a unique way, 'so as to make it burn with greater love for God and all humanity,'[491] bears witness that the Kingdom of God and His justice is that pearl of great price which is preferred to every other value no matter how great, and hence must be sought as the only definitive value. It is for this reason that the Church, throughout her history, has always defended the superiority of this charism to that of marriage, by reason of the wholly singular link which it has with the Kingdom of God [*Sacra Viginitas*, II]."[492]

On another occasion, he teaches: "The consecrated life must present to today's world examples of chastity lived by men and women who show balance, self-mastery, an enterprising spirit, and psychological and affective maturity. Thanks to this witness, human love is offered a stable point of reference: the pure love which consecrated persons draw from the contemplation of Trinitarian love, revealed to us in Christ. Precisely because they are immersed in this mystery, consecrated persons feel themselves capable of a radical and universal love, which gives them the strength for the self-mastery and discipline necessary in order not to fall under the domination of the senses and instincts. Consecrated chastity thus appears as a joyful and liberating experience. Enlightened by faith in the Risen Lord and by the prospect of the new heavens and the new earth,[493] it offers a priceless incentive in the task of educating to that chastity which corresponds to other states of life as well."[494]

---

[489] Cf. *Mt* 22:30.
[490] Cf. 1 *Cor* 7:32 ff.
[491] VATICAN II, *Perfectae caritatis*, 12.
[492] *Familiaris consortio*, 16.
[493] Cf. *Rev* 21:1.
[494] *Vita Consecrata*, 88.

The attack on celibacy is always an attack on the truth of marital love as God wants it to be.

The reality of pansexuality today

According to a recent news article, the word "sex" has always been the most searched for word on the internet. It constitutes a global obsession.

The news article is called "**Sex, the internet offers 167 million occasions**," by Beppe Severgnini.

Sex is what obsesses Rome and impassions Athens, stimulates Berlin and excites London (which isn't easily excited), intrigues Tokyo and delights Beijing, arouses Los Angeles and consoles Buenos Aires. It is not an opinion, but a statistical fact. "Sex" is the most searched for word on the most used search engine, *Google*. In one hundred countries and eighty-six languages, there are 150 million searches every day. Someone once defined that mass of information as "the collective conscience of the world."

And what does the collective conscience of the world search for, when it puts its fingers to the keyboard? Sex.

If we think about it, the whole thing is odd. The internet population is varied (transversal, as they say today), encompassing men and women, young and old, American and European, eastern and western, Christians and Muslims. The internet is the expression of an alert, curious, instructed and reasonably comfortable world. To be able to search for "sex" on the computer, one must have a computer and know how and where to connect to the internet. That these people would search for virtual sex as soon as they were left alone is not a given, but they did and they do.

Let us not judge, but rather explain this behavior. What motivated the *cyber-voyeurs* of the internet? Curiosity? Yes. For an Iraqi provided with a computer, the temptation to look at the women of "Baywatch" must be strong: at least they don't look like Saddam's billboards. But it is not the Arab countries that make up the majority of seachers on *Google*. It is in the Americas, Japan, and Europe where computers and web connections are most available. The question then remains: why do we write "sex" in the box when we are left alone? It is not because it is prohibited. In Italy, sex floods the TV, is poured out in advertisements, flares through conversations, slips out of corner stores, and winks from the navels of girls on the street. In spite of its prevalence, we also want it on the internet. And this is not something recent. Ten years ago, the Italian directors of *Lycos* showed me the list of the most common words on their search engine. Even then sex was at the top. Of the rest of the top ten words, five I cannot print here.

There is something disturbing and juvenile in these insatiable and solitary desires. And perhaps the explication is precisely here. The sex that surrounds us (TV, movies, advertisements, magazines) is not actually offered to us, but is behind a glass. Before that exposition we become—all of us, men and women—like insecure teenagers. Because of loneliness, shyness, incapacity, lack of time, moral scruples or health reasons, we seek the comfort of the internet. It is a new form of global impotence, which many seek because it is not difficult or contagious. Memories don't stick around in the heart and videocassettes don't stick around in the house. It is a light sex, "*a la carte.*" It is not eaten, it is tasted.

Clearly, it is a sex of escape. But many are contented by it. In the nights of the world millions of fingers move over keyboards. Search engine. Search with *Google*. "Sex." *Google* has searched for "sex" in the entire world-wide web. Time of the search: .07 seconds. Results: around 167,000,000. Just choose.[495]

In spite of the corruptions that sex without responsibility brings, sex as a work of the Creator is one of His great wonders. If God had not made it we would not have the wondrous proliferation of life: vegetal, animal, and human. Just as conjunctivitis doesn't cause us to think that eyes are evil, neither

---

[495] Cf. *Corriere della Sera,* December 1, 2002, 20.

should all the sexual deviations bring us to condemn sex, a creation that God Himself *saw was very good.*[496]

Faced with this world the Church steps up as a "sign of contradiction"

Who, unless assisted by supernatural help, would oppose such an unstoppable avalanche? Who without the help of God would give a witness different from what the world likes and wants to hear? How can we not realize that this firmness of doctrine provokes hatred from those who live controlled by their passions? Is this not one of the main reasons that they seek to silence the Catholic Church, so that she would not teach what God has revealed in the Bible? How can they not campaign against the buffets contemporary hedonism receives from virginity and celibacy? How can they not take psychological action against virginity and celibacy, minutely investigating anomalies—real or imaginary—in order to justify themselves? Can it be that today, as yesterday, it is the very "nature of man, inclined to vice, which wants to show that it not only has license, but also reason to sin,"[497] seeking to justify itself with the evil deeds—real or imaginary—of others?

Because of the lack of historical perspective, we are not aware of the seriousness of what is happening at our time in history, just as the Romans in their times were not aware that vomiting in order to continue to eat, was corrupt. With time, we become aware and condemn these practices and the current caricatures of true human love will be seen in the same way. The Church will rise like a standard over the nations for having been alone in coming out in defense of authentic love. Similarly, the consecrated virgins and those who remain celibate for the kingdom of Heaven, who do not give in, in spite of the

---

[496] Cf. *Gen* 1:31.

[497] LACTANCIO FIRMIANO, Divinar. Instit., Book 4; cf. Fray Luis de Granada, Los seis libros de la Rhetórica eclesiástica, Madrid 1793, 27. (Editorial translation).

destructive psychological pressures against them, will be considered heroes. They remained largely faithful, writing one of the most beautiful pages of the history of the Church and of the world. "In spite of painful negative cases,"[498] total consecration to God shines stronger and more beautifully than ever. Think of John Paul II, Mother Teresa of Calcutta, or the holy Padre Pio and the thousands of blesseds and saints raised to the honor of the altars in the last decades and in all of the history of the Church!

Benedict Groeschel[499] took upon himself the work of putting together a statistic. Out of 79 clerics jailed for pedophilia with children under 8 years of age in the United States, 40 were protestant ministers and the rest were divided between Catholics, orthodox, Jews, etc. The vast majority were not celibate. It is not celibacy that causes pedophilia; in fact, it is the lack of celibacy![500] And so, as a reaction, the number of priestly vocations in the United States has increased.

Furthermore, the accused that have already been declared innocent by justice are not reinstated as they should be, such as Cardinal Bernadin of Chicago, Archbishop Pell from Sydney, Father Grassi, and others.

---

[498] CONGREGATION FOR THE CLERGY, *Directory On The Ministry and Life of Priests*, 57.

[499] *An urgent appeal*, a conference held at Saint Casimir Church in Yonkers New York in September 2002.

[500] This epidemic is increasing throughout the world. Just think of the promotional tours featuring sex with children. Pedophilia online is a plague. In Italy 60,000 websites were monitored, resulting in the arrest of 90 people (Cf *Avvenire*, December 17, 2002, 11 and *L'Osservatore Romano*, Italian edition, December 18, 2002, 10). Milanese police investigated 462 people, spread through 77 provinces, confiscating 455 personal computers, 8,628 CDs, 7,800 floppy disks, hundreds of magazines and 300 DVDs. "In some rooms were also found video footage of a suspect abusing minors, and the torture of newborns was even filmed," *L'Osservatore Romano*, December 15, 2002, 10. Editorial translation.

In the end it is an attack against the Pope

The vicious attacks on human love and celibacy are aimed, indirectly, but truly, against the Pope, who is the firm defender of the truth regarding human love, virginity and ecclesiastic celibacy.

There are three examples that show the serious discrimination suffered by the Pope from the mass media:

1. Every technological advance that allows Professor Stephen Hawking to continue working from his wheel chair, communicating through a sophisticated system, is euphorically applauded. When the Pope used the Pope-mobile or a moving platform, some asked that he be removed from office. His incapacity was ridiculed and, in his sickness, he was attacked for what he taught and what he bore witness to.[501]

2. The Dalai Lama was never asked to step down.

3. King Fahd Al Saud of Saudi Arabia took a vacation in Marbella, Spain, accompanied by 1,200 members of his court. In addition to the seven Boeing 747s, they had three planes ready to leave at any moment to any place, 200 rented Merecedes Benz and 500 cellular phones for their use. Daily expenses are about 5,000,000 euros (or dollars).[502] The King, who is 81 years old, about the same age as the Pope, travels with a portable intensive therapy system but nobody tells him to step down from office! With $1,500,000 less than what King Saud spends *in one day*, the deficit of the Holy See could be paid for *356 days!*[503]

Dear Youth:

---

[501] Cf. *Palabra,* December 2002, 13.

[502] Cf. *La Nación,* August 18, 2002, 16.

[503] Consolidated balance of the Holy See and the State of the Vatican City in 2001. 1. The Holy See: Income 196,897,000 euros; Expenses 200,371,000; Deficit 3,474,000. (Between clergy, religious and laity, 2,671 people were employed until December 31, 2001; the expenses of the Nunciatures was $20,000,000). 2. The Vatican City had a surplus of 14,074,000 euros. Cf. *L'Osservatore Romano,* July 19, 2002, 2.

This is only a part of what the Pope has to pay for his valiant defense of the truth of human love and for being the Vicar of Jesus Christ.

"In spite of painful negative cases," [504] even in our own celibate lives, we will also have to pay something for announcing, celebrating and witnessing to the truth of human love and being faithful to Jesus Christ.

The world can defile human love more and more, but we will always have the witness of thousands and thousands of our brothers and sisters who, in the beautiful saying of Saint Augustine, "aged virgins"[505] because they truly gave themselves for the love of Jesus Christ. May the Virgin encourage us to rejoice in the Church of her Son who will raise an ensign for the nations.

---

[504] Congregation For The Clergy, *Directory On The Ministry and Life of Priests*, 57.

[505] ST. AUGUSTINE, *Confessions*; quoted in *Summa* II-II, 189, 10, ad 3.

15.
EUROPE AND CHRISTIANITY[506]

"The 'cement' of that extraordinary religious, cultural and civil patrimony which has given Europe its greatness down the centuries."

*Address to Italian parliament,
November 14, 2002.*

To recognize its Christian heritage in the beginning of the European Constitution would mean to recognize the very being of Europe; to do the contrary would mark its apostasy from Jesus Christ.

1. Pre-history

Europe, "the most beautiful of lands," as Pliny (23-79 AD) said, was for the Greeks, the Romans and the Middle Ages, one of the three parts of the world. The others were then called as they are now: Africa and Asia. The oldest records we have of this three-fold division of the globe are from Herodotus (480-424 BC), the "Father of History" and the first western writer to enrich this literary genre with his eloquence. But it was not him who gave Europe its name. He used it as something already known and declared that he did not know the origin of the name. There are no sources that specify where this name was' taken from, or who used it first.

---

[506] We closely follow what ex-president of the Spanish Senate, ANTONIO FONTÁN published in Madrid newspaper *ABC* on 2/10/2003, 3.

Before Herodotus, Europe, as a geographical name had been mentioned in the account of the voyage of the god Apollo through the Greek Lands. There, only continental Greece is called Europe.

In any case, the division of the world into three parts separated by the Don River, the Mediterranean Sea and the Nile River basin, was a common teaching among the Greeks from the fifth century before Christ. The Romans took it from them and the Romans passed it to the Europeans of the Dark Ages and the Middle Ages.

Already in 700 BC, there were Hellenic colonies on the coast of Anatolia and the Black Sea. However, that was not Europe, but Asia. After Alexander (356-323 BC), the Greeks and their culture took control of the dominions of the "Great King" and of Egypt. But these kingdoms belonged to Asia or Africa. On the other hand, the Italian peninsula, its islands, the Greek colonies, and the commercial centers of the western Mediterranean (Marseille, Ampurias, etc.) were in Europe.

2. The first Europe

The earliest Europe was Greek Europe, which ranged from the Greek lands in the east, reached Italy, the great colony of Marseille and the more modest colonies of Iberia. Later, Europe was the Europe of the Roman republic, the Greco-Roman culture in a Latin expression. With its center in Italy, the Roman republic reached from Thrace to the Alps, the south of current day France and the Spanish provinces, and was crowned with the conquest of the Gauls by Caesar and his landing in Britain. In the first years of the empire, the borders were the Rhine and the Danube Rivers, until it began to arrive in "Lower Germany" and Dacia. Finally, from the 4th century on, Christianized Europe would cover the entire continent in 600 years. This is the Europe that continued into the rest of the middle and modern ages through the present time, even though the people and governments of today are quite secularized.

3. A great event

An illustrious and accredited British historian who has recently passed away, John Morris Roberts, is the author of one of the best histories of Europe, published in Oxford in 1996. With the sober and direct style of the good Anglo-Saxon writers today, Professor Roberts likes to sprinkle his prose with rounded and expressive sentences.

In one of the first chapters of his book, he expounded on the inheritances that have given life and meaning to the continent. He wrote about an event that took place in the last years of the reign of Augustus that can be said to have had more repercussions in human existence than any other event. "It was" he says, "the birth of a Jew in Palestine who has entered history by the name of Jesus." For His followers, who shortly after were called Christians, the transcendence of this event is based on the fact that they understood Him to be a divine being. "One does not need to say much in order to stress the importance of that Jesus. All of history emphasizes it. His disciples were going to change the world. Concerning Europe, no other group of men or women has done more to change its history."

The English professor recognizes, "There have never ceased to be violent disagreements about who Jesus was, what He did and what He intended to do. But it is undeniable that His teaching has had greater influence than that of any other 'saint' of any time, because His followers saw Him crucified and then believed that He resurrected from among the dead...We are what we are," concludes Roberts, "and Europe is what it is, because a handful of Palestinian Jews gave testimony to these things."

4. Those who continued it

The disciples and successors of those Palestinians, in less than ten generations (or three centuries), in Greek and Latin, Christianized the Roman world and integrated the values, principles and history of Judaism into their religious message. The sacred books of Judaism would become part of Europe's spiritual and cultural patrimony, together with the books that refer to the life and teachings of Jesus (the Gospels) and the doctrinal writers of the first and most immediate followers of the Master.

Both series of works, known as the Old and the New Testaments, make up the Bible of the Christians.

From the fifth century on, Christianity spread to lands and people who were not Romanized (the Irish Celts, the Goths, the Franks, and other German invaders) thanks to the missionary action of the monks and the political work of the kings. Around the year 1,000, or a little after, Christianity arrived from the Latin side to Scandinavia and to the center of the continent to Poland. From the Byzantine side, with the Cyrillic alphabet and the old Slavic language, it took root in Bulgaria, in what is Ukraine today (*ukraina* means boarder) and in the Kievan Rus.

But at that time, Christianity had assimilated the philosophy and science of the Greeks, Roman concepts and principles of the person, equality and universality of the human race and the political organization of society, law and power. All of this content and doctrine was received by modernity through "Christian mediation."

5. History tells us all of this

Until the 20th century, the century of Nazi and Communist totalitarianism, everything—the good and the bad, wars and peace—had remained among Christians: orthodox or heterodox, from one or another profession or church, as had been happening since the Middle Ages; Dante and Boniface, Loyola and Luther, Trent and Calvin, Descartes and Kant, Galileo and Newton, Machiavelli and Erasmus, Shakespeare and Moliere, Dostoyevsky and Gogol, Thomas and Abelard, Benedict, Cyril and Methodius, Catherine of Siena and Bridget of Sweden, Copernicus and Newton, Constantine and Charlemagne, the hospitals and universities, the holy mountains and the guilds, the great cathedrals, the arts, and the great missionary voyages.

6. Sociology also

But speaking of Christianity and Europe, not everything is history. There is also sociology. The majority of the citizens of the European Union today are Christians. Assiduous or not in the practice of their respective professions of faith, Christians are over two-thirds of the population of "the fifteen." With ten new countries incorporated into the European Union, that number and proportion will increase. Even the calendar, holidays, weekly rest, and Sunday, are living inheritances from the Christian culture in Europe, along with the ideological and moral influence of the churches. For the most part, European families usually baptize their children and want Christian habits and traditions to be known among their family, friends, and in their countries. The anti-Christianism of Marxists and Nazis, conquered by history, has lowered its flags and put away its weapons. Religious liberty is a principle shared by believers and non-believers alike. Politics and religion are separate entities. In short, the principle expressed by Jesus of Nazareth, *render to Caesar the things that are Caesar's, and to God the things that are God's*,[507] has been accepted by all. In spite of the terrible influence of liberalism, we must realize that although politics and religion are separate realities, they should not be opposing realities, but rather cooperative. Caesar, insofar as he is Caesar, must also give to God what is God's, because Caesar is not God.

7. What some propose and what must be done

However, a new militant laicism that denies the history of people and social reality to the point of absurdity, seems to exist in some official doctrines of certain states and political systems.

On the contrary, it is not an anachronistic "confessionalism" to take up the Christian inheritance at the opening of the European Constitution. This would constitute recognition of the very being of Europe, its culture and that of the nations that form it at the height of the 21st century.

What will Europe do? Will it follow the road indicated by its elders, or will it continue choosing apostasy from Christ?

---

[507] *Lk* 20:25.

This choice interests us in the Americas, because we are a prolongation of Europe with our own characteristics that give us our identity.

Mary, you who have cradled Jesus, and have cradled us and our nations, keep us, who are at this crossroad, from falling into madness.

CHAPTER 6

The Responses of the Youth

"Lord...
You Know
that I Love You"
(Jn 21:15)

"Open trustingly your most intimate aspirations to the love of Christ, who waits for you in the Eucharist. You will find answers to all of your questions and with joy you will see that the coherence of life that he asks of you is the way to achieve the most noble desires of your young life."

Asunción, Paraguay, May 18, 1988.

1.

RISE WITH CHRIST

"He is not only your goal. He is also the path which leads you where you are going."[508]

Manila, Philippines, November 22, 1981.

Seek the things that are above, where Christ is, seated at the right hand of God. Set your minds on things that are above, not on things that are on earth.[509]

Dear young people: today many people only seek the things of here below!

What's more, today many do not want the things of Heaven; they only want the things of the earth. Man is the only upright animal capable of looking at heaven, but many people only look down.

Among other conditions of those who only look at the things of the earth, we have the sad phenomenon of **materialism.**

What is materialism? It is the belief that only material things exist, denying, therefore, spiritual things, including the existence of God, the angels, the human soul—spiritual and immortal— faith, hope, charity, sanctifying grace, and the power of the sacraments. For materialists, only what can be perceived by the senses, what can be seen, heard, smelled, tasted and touched, exists; the supernatural and naturally spiritual that cannot be

---

[508] Editorial translation.
[509] *Col* 3:1-2.

sensibly perceived do not exist. They forget that, as the Little Prince said: "What is essential is invisible to the eyes."[510] This is a truth that Saint Paul taught two thousands year ago: *for the things that are seen are transient, but the things that are unseen are eternal.*[511]

Materialism in this sense is an expression of the way that man lives and acts. It is a way of being that the material things, such as power, fame, money, and pleasure, are worth more than themselves and other people who are created in the image and likeness of God.

Today, because of materialism, we see some disturbing situations. For example, in Japan (with a GDP per capita of $27,000), a recent poll says that spouses dedicate a mere 26 minutes daily to housework and only 12 minutes to their children.[512] Is this human life? Is it not a life enslaved?

Don't misunderstand me; matter is not bad. On the contrary, matter is "very good" as God Himself calls it in the narration of the creation of the world in Genesis (3:1). What is bad is to live as if *only* matter existed. In addition to the material world that we see, there is another more important and beautiful world, the world of souls. The world of spiritual intelligence and will, science, liberty, love, conscience, the world of God, the eternal happiness of the angels and the saints, the world of Heaven—not the astronomical—but the Heaven of unceasing glory, the celestial world.

And so, I propose to you the clear teaching of the Apostle: *Seek the things that are above, where Christ is seated at the right hand of God. Set your minds on things that are above, not on things that are on earth.*[513]

---

510 Editorial Translation.
511 *2 Cor* 4:18.
512 *Noticias* Magazine, 12/23/94, 127.
513 *Col* 3:1-2.

The most important of these "things that are above" are the three divine Persons: The Person of the Father, the Person of the Son, Jesus Christ, and the Person of the Holy Spirit; the three divine Persons that are one true and living God.

May we always adore Jesus. Let us ask Him to teach us to adore Him because He is our Lord and God. For Him nothing is impossible. Let us ask Him for the grace to use the things of the world correctly, remembering the essential words of Saint Paul: *Seek the things that are above, where Christ is, seated at the right hand of God. Set your minds on things that are above, not on things that are on earth,* because *He who descended is he who also ascended.* He awaits us in Heaven. *He awaits us in our Home.*

2.
DO THIS!

"As I go to the altar, I wish...to offer up under the forms of bread and wine all that you, young men and women, carry in your hearts. The bread and wine will become, in the Eucharist, the Body and Blood of Christ. When you receive him in Holy Communion, may you have the courage to listen to his call."

Manila, Philippines, January 13, 1995.

Do this...! These are very clear and simple words: ***Do this...!***

Who said these words? Jesus Christ, our Lord said them.

When did He say them? He said them on Thursday the 13th of the Hebrew month of Nissan—which is the month of April— close to the full moon of the Spring equinox in the northern hemisphere, according to our calculations, in the year 33.

Where was Jesus? He was in the holy city of Jerusalem, in what, with the passing of time, would come to be called the Mount Zion of the Christians; more specifically, He was in an upper room used for eating. It was the place that Jesus, with the Twelve, the "dodeka," the twelve Apostles (apostle means "sent") met for the last time to eat dinner. The Apostles are those who were chosen by Jesus, and whom He later sent throughout the world to preach the Gospel.

They gathered there as He Himself had foreseen (in the same Upper Room that can be visited today). It was as we read in the

Gospel of Mark, *And he sent two of his disciples, and said to them, 'Go into the city, and a man carrying a jar of water will meet you.*[514] At that time, there was no running water and, they drew it from a well. In the case of Jerusalem, it was the Well of Gideon, which today is called The Fountain of the Virgin, because the Virgin drew water there. Even the Arabs and Muslims call it *Aim Siti Mariam*, Fountain of the Virgin. Jesus says to the twelve Apostles, who didn't know where this man carrying the jug of water on his shoulders was going, *follow him and wherever he enters, say to the householder, 'The Teacher says, Where is my guest room, where I am to eat the Passover with my disciples?' And he will show you a large upper room furnished and ready; there prepare for us.*[515]

What did the Apostles have to prepare? They had to prepare the Passover meal. The Passover lamb reminded them of the passing that the Jews, who had been slaves of the Egyptians, made when they passed through the Red Sea in a miraculous way, freeing themselves from the slavery of Pharaoh.

The twelve Apostles were with Jesus, including: Peter, Andrew, James, John, Phillip and Matthew…who wrote the first gospel in Hebrew because his Gospel, his good news, was dedicated to the Jews who had converted to Christianity.

What did Jesus do? He sang the Psalms called the *Hallel,*[516] Psalms that were always sung while eating the Passover lamb, as it says in the Gospel: *when they had sung a hymn.*[517] This corresponds to the first part of the Mass called the Liturgy of the Word, when the Bible is read. The Bible is the Word of God that elucidates what God wants from us.

What else did Our Lord do in the upper room? The Gospel says: *Now as they were eating, Jesus took bread, and blessed and broke it, and gave it to the disciples and said, 'Take, eat; this is my body.' And he*

---

[514] *Mk* 14:13.
[515] *Mk* 14:13-15.
[516] *Ps* 113-118.
[517] *Mt* 26:30; *Mk* 14:26.

took a cup, and when he had given thanks he gave it to them, saying, 'Drink of it, all of you; for this is my blood of the covenant, which is poured out for many for the forgiveness of sins'.[518]

And did he say anything else? Yes, He said something else: *Do this in remembrance of me.*[519] ***Do this!*** That is what He said to the Apostles, and not only to those twelve, but to all the successors of the Apostles: ***Do this!***

The successors of the Apostles are the Bishops, but all of us priests are also successors; as the Council of Trent says: "gave to the apostles (whom He then constituted priests of the New Testament)…He commanded them and their successors in the priesthood…to make offering,"[520] the consecrated bread and the consecrated wine.

What does "*this*" mean? "*This*," evidently is what Jesus said in the Upper Room, it is what Jesus did there, on Holy Thursday.

And what is it that He did?

-First, He transubstantiated the bread and wine into His Body and His Blood.

-Second, He perpetuated the sacrifice that he was going to make the next day on the cross. Just as the blood separated from His body on the cross, in the Upper Room the blood appears separated from the body in an anticipated way, in a sacramental form, as happens in every Mass. In the Upper Room, He clearly tells us that the Eucharist is a sacrifice.

-Third, Christ offered Himself at the Last Supper as He offered Himself on the cross, and as He offers Himself in every Mass, as a Victim for the salvation of all men. As He is on the cross, He is in the Mass, with arms out-stretched to embrace us all. Christ immolates Himself again in a sacramental way for all.

---

[518] *Mt* 26:26-28; cf. *Mk* 14:22-24; cf. *Lk* 22:15-20; cf. *1 Cor* 11:23-25.
[519] *Lk* 22:19; cf. *1 Cor* 11:24, 25.
[520] DZ, 938.

In order for the bread and the wine to be transubstantiated, i.e., the bread and the wine changed into the body and blood of Jesus, to bring about the same sacrifice of the cross in an efficacious way, to be offered to the Father as victim of expiation for all of humanity, He commanded the Apostles and their successors throughout history to do the same: *Do this...!* And He not only commanded them to do this, but He gave them the power to do what He Himself did there in the Upper Room, the power to work *in his name and in His memory: Do this in memory of Me.*

One of you could say: "Father, I understand this; if Jesus Christ taught it, and Jesus Christ is God, it is the truth; but this is only valid for the Apostles and the successors of the Apostles, the priests, who are successors in order to consecrate the body and blood of the Lord. But *Do this...* doesn't apply to me..."

We should respond to this by saying 'yes' and 'no.' Certainly when Jesus says *Do this...* it is primarily, directly, and fundamentally in reference to the Apostles. The successors of the Apostles are the only ones who, through the sacrament of Holy Orders, have the power to transubstantiate, and therefore, to liturgically offer the victim who immolates Himself again in a sacramental way in the Mass. In that sense it refers only to the Apostles, but in another sense, no. When He says *Do this...* He also refers to all the baptized because all the baptized, in their own way, *should offer the victim.* Each one of you, by the fact of your Baptism, has the power that Baptism gives to offer Jesus Christ, the victim who immolates Himself.

"And how, Father, do I have the power to do this?" In the first place: through the hands of the priest. The priest is the representative of the whole people and in the name of all the people, he offers the victim through his hands. Moreover, together with the priest, each one of you, by the fact of your Baptism, has the power to offer the victim who immolates Himself, together with the priest.

What victim? The victim is twofold: Jesus Christ under the appearance of bread and wine; and each one of you together with Jesus Christ, the victim who immolates Himself. This is said, for example, in the Second Vatican Council: the faithful, or the baptized, you, take "part **in the Eucharistic sacrifice**—the Mass—**they offer the Divine Victim**—Jesus Christ—**to God, and offer themselves**—each one of you—**along with It**."[521]

By offering to the Heavenly Father the victim, his Son, and ourselves together with the Son, we learn that man "cannot fully find himself except through a sincere gift of himself, (to others),"[522] as the Second Vatican Council also teaches.

Who are *the others*? God and our neighbor.

Do this... applies to all of the baptized, because all the baptized should participate in the Eucharist in a "full, conscious, and active"[523] way.

What does in an *active way* mean? It means that each person must put into the Mass what corresponds to him. This is why the priest says: *"Pray brethren, that my sacrifice and yours..."* Why yours? Because you also bring to the sacrifice what corresponds to you in an active way: responding to certain prayers, singing, with your posture (standing, sitting, kneeling), adoring, giving thanks, and in a special way—*actively*—offering the victim and offering yourselves together with the victim.

What does *in a conscious way* mean? It means that the participants must be conscious of what is happening. What is happening at Mass is no less than what happened at the Last Supper in the Upper Room or on the cross at Calvary! The blood is once again sacramentally separated from the body! That's what's happening!

What does *in a full way* mean? It means that I must dispose my soul, my heart, my mind, and my interior strength, to take advantage of what is going on, to receive the sacrifice of the cross

---

[521] *Lumen Gentium*, 11.

[522] *Gaudium et Spes*, 24.

[523] *Sacrosanctum Concilium*, 11, 14, 79; *Christus Dominus*, 30; *Gravissimum Educationis*, 4.

with fruit, and to enter into communication with God. And in a special way, it means to participate by communing with the victim, where we make ourselves *"the same body* and blood"[524] with Christ. This is why my soul must be cleansed from mortal sin in order to receive the victim.

All of this implies that we must *understand* the meaning of the rites, *participate* in the actions, allow that our "mind and voice may *accord together*,"[525] *harmonize* our own feelings with those of Christ, *prolong* in our lives what we live in the rite, and *connect* ordinary life with the liturgy.[526]

Look: what I have just told you is enough. If you can just remember that, I would be happy. And one more thing: In the liturgy, the true meaning of *feast* is really and profoundly expressed. You have to know that the ultimate meaning of a feast is not the music or the songs. They are things that contribute to the feast, but its ultimate meaning does not consist in them. You need to know this, because there are many, adults included, who do not know it. Even some parents do not know it. Not because they are bad, but because nobody taught it to them. The ultimate meaning of a feast is *the act of worship,* like the Mass.

What does worship mean? It means recognizing that God is God with one's mind, heart, and body.

God is good, and though this seems to be obvious, many don't know it. God is infinitely good. He is our Father, but an infinitely good Father, better than all the fathers on the earth. When I render worship to God, I am saying this to Him: "Lord, you are good." When I say that, I am also saying something else to Him: "Lord, your works, creation—the birds, the flowers, the plants, the human beings, the mountains, the snow, the water— are good because you made them, I thank you for that." Do you

---

[524] St. Cyril of Jerusalem, *Catechetical Lectures*, 22.
[525] Pius XII, *Mediator Dei*, 145, *The Rule of St. Benedict.*
[526] Cf. J.A. Abad Ibañez, M. Garrido Bonaño, OSB, *Iniciación a la liturgia de la Iglesia*, Ed. Palabra, Madrid, 1988, 49-58, especially 51-52.

understand? And when you all say, "Lord, you are good," "Your works are good," you are also saying something else: "Lord, I give You thanks because You created me and to have created me is a good thing, I give You thanks for my body and for my soul, I give You thanks for my intellect and for my will. I give You thanks because You have given me the capacity to think and the capacity for love. I give You thanks because I can contemplate creation, all of this beauty that You have made for me. I thank You, Lord." And that is what is done in an *act of worship*.

What is the act of worship of a Christian? The act of worship of a Christian is the Mass where the Christian adores God, gives Him praise and thanks (that is what Eucharist actually means), asks Him for forgiveness and asks Him for all the things that he needs. That is to say, he renders to Him worship and in rendering Him worship he sanctifies himself. So, if this is enough for you to understand what Our Lord said: *Do this...* (the Mass, the Eucharist), and if each one of you learns to participate more and more fully aware, actively engaged and enriched in the Mass, blessed be this day, and all the days that are to come! Because you will have learned that rendering worship to God is the most important thing that mankind has to do on the face of the earth. In this way, we learn the meaning of feasting: the rejoicing in love that feasting is, of recognizing all of the benefits, marvels, and goodness that exists in creation. And to also recognize that God has created me, loved me as His true son, has died for me on the cross, and that I am a living temple of the Holy Spirit, that I can call the Virgin my mother, and that I can receive the Lord in the Eucharist.

And so I ask again: what is it that makes a feast, a feast? What is the profound source that makes some determined days to be feasts? The ultimate source of the feast is: *Do this...*! It is the act of worship. To feast is to affirm that all that exists is good and it is good that it exists. To feast is to affirm that creation is good because God is good.

This is why man, male and female, adores God, praises Him, gives Him thanks, and worships Him. And it is by recognizing the love of God through worship that charity and joy reign in the genuine Christian feast: "where charity rejoices, there is the feast."[527] In the Mass, we crown everything, giving worship to our Father in heaven through Jesus Christ and in the Holy Spirit. And we do it by putting into practice what He taught us when He said: *Do this...*!

---

[527] Editorial Translation.

3.
FRIEND....

"Some of you may have known doubt and confusion; you may have experienced sadness and failure and serious sin. For all of you, however, this is an important time in your lives. It is a time of decision. It is a time to accept Christ: to accept his friendship and love."

Auckland, New Zealand, November 22, 1986.

There are few words as lovely as the word *friend*!

What is friendship?

Friendship, "benevolent love," is a special way of loving that consists in desiring the good of the other. When benevolence is mutual, there is true friendship.

Aristotle said of friendship: "It is most necessary for our life. For no one would choose to live without friends even if he had all the other goods."[528]

King David and Jonathan were great friends: *When he had finished speaking to Saul, the soul of Jonathan was knit to the soul of David, and Jonathan loved him as his own soul... And Jonathan made David swear again by his love for him; for he loved him as he loved his own soul.*[529]

---

[528] *Nicomachean Ethics*, Second Edition, trans, Terence Irwin, (Hackett Publishing Company: Indianapolis, 1999), Book VIII, 1, p. 119.
[529] *1 Sam* 18:1; 20:17.

Abraham and God: *Do not take away your mercy from us, for the sake of Abraham, your beloved.*[530]

1. Love of election

Therefore, "'when two go together...', they are more capable of understanding and acting."[531]   A friend is a gift from heaven.

A friend is found in the most unexpected and unique way, almost the same fortuitous way someone finds a treasure: *he that has found one has found a treasure.*[532]

Friendship is a love of predilection, a love that speaks face to face, as when Moses spoke with God: *Thus the LORD used to speak to Moses face to face, as a man speaks to his friend.*[533]

In this sense, what better friend can we have than Jesus Christ?   Jesus had many friends, and He made some of them closer to Him than the rest: *And he went up on the mountain, and called to him those whom he desired; and they came to him.   And he appointed twelve, to be with him.*[534]

Christ chose His friends. His friendship is a love of election: *You did not choose me, but I chose you.*[535] Christ is a true friend; He is the only friend who never fails.

We say that we have a friend, or that we are friends with someone, when that person is present together with us. However, a friend is not always there right when we need him; but Christ is always intimately present everywhere: *Even though I walk through the valley of the shadow of death, I fear no evil; for thou art with me.*[536]

---

[530] *Dan* 3:35.
[531] *Nichomachean Ethics,* Book VIII, 1, p. 119.
[532] *Sir* 6:14.
[533] *Ex* 33:11.
[534] *Mk* 3:13-14.
[535] *Jn* 15:16.
[536] *Ps* 23:4.

2. Without secrets

To converse with the friend is proper to friendship. Also, it is proper to friendship to reveal secrets because of the union between their hearts.[537] Therefore, friendship demands that all one has, he communicates it to his friend. This is why the most intimate secrets of the heart are revealed to one's friends.

Is this possible? Are there not things that are reserved for the absolute intimacy of a soul with God? Saint Augustine says: "When I see someone inflamed with Christian charity and I feel that by it he makes himself a faithful friend of mine, I make sure that all of the thoughts that I confide to him I am not confiding to a man, but to God, who abides in him; since 'God is love...and whoever remains in God, God is in him.'"[538]

God Himself is the friend of men with a heart of flesh. Christ is a true friend, because He communicated to us everything that He had: His divinity and His humanity. It is not in vain that Christ says to us: *No longer do I call you servants, for the servant does not know what his master is doing; but I have called you friends, for* ***all*** *that I have heard from my Father I have made known to you.*[539]

3. A friend makes us happy

It is proper of friendship to feel happy in the presence of the friend, rejoicing in his words and actions, and finding in him comfort in all afflictions. This is why we mainly seek the comfort of friends when we are sad.

The book of Proverbs says: *So a man's counsel is sweet to his friend.*[540] And a saint recommends seeking out a friend as a remedy for the bitterness of sadness, because: "in the very fact

---

[537] Cf. SAINT THOMAS, *Contra Gentiles,* IV, 21.

[538] We follow MIGUEL CRUZ in *Misterio de la amistad,* San Miguel de Tucumán, 1986, p 40. (Editorial translation).

[539] *Jn* 15:15.

[540] *Pr* 27:9 New American Standard Bible with Codes (1977).

that his friends will mourn with him, he knows that they love him."[541]

Christ is truly a friend because He says to us; *Come to me, all who labor and are heavy laden, and I will give you rest. Take my yoke upon you, and learn from me; for I am gentle and lowly in heart.*[542]

4. The faithfulness of a friend

"Every friend, entrusting himself to the other, creates an atmosphere of shared interiority with him. To break that, to open a breach, is to strip off and throw away the most intimate spaces of a soul."[543]

There is nothing as precious as a faithful friend, and no scales can measure his excellence. A faithful friend is an elixir of life; and those who fear the Lord will find him. Whoever fears the Lord directs his friendship aright, for as he is, so is his neighbor also.[544]

It is proper of friendship to consent to the desires of the friend, which therefore corresponds to the love with which we love God. We love God with the love of friendship, and follow His commandments because true love manifests and proves itself with works: *actions speak louder than words*. As Gregory the Great teaches, the love of friendship does great things: "Love is never idle. When it exists, it does great things; but if it does not act, love is not there."[545] As Saint John of the Cross says, love is creative: Where there is no love, bring love, and you will obtain love. Does it seem to you that you are not loved? Love! Does it seem to you that others don't notice you? Love them! Do you think that they forget you? Love them! That they don't understand you? Love them!

---

[541] SAINT THOMAS, cited by MIGUEL CRUZ *idem* 128. (Editorial translation).
[542] *Mt* 11:28-29.
[543] MIGUEL CRUZ, *Misterio de la amistad* 39. (Editorial translation).
[544] *Sir* 6:15-17.
[545] *Obras*, (Ed. B.A.C.: Madrid, 1958), *Homilías sobre el Evangelio*, 1. II, hom. 10 (30) p. 685. (Editorial translation).

5. To give one's life

Man considers his friend as another self. It is necessary, therefore, for a man to help his friend as he would help himself, having him take part in all of his things. And so, it is proper of friends to do good to their friends. True friendship is founded on love. The center of gravity of all love, in order to be eternal, must come from man, and attach itself to eternal truth: "the only one who cannot lose a friend is the one who has all his friendships in Him who cannot be lost,"[546] that is God Himself. Friendship is love for grown-ups, creatures who have developed through great effort, reaching the height of the cross.

This is true, above all, with Christ, *who having loved his own who were in the world, he loved them to the end.*[547] *Greater love has no man than this, that a man lay down his life for his friends.*[548]

6. The mystery of friendship

What is the root, the foundation of true friendship? What is it based on? True friendship consists in the melting of the heart, which is opposed to the cold or hardened heart. This melting of the heart implies a certain softening of the heart that makes a heart able to be penetrated by the beloved person. And so, when the beloved person is present and is spiritually possessed, fruition, joy and happiness are produced. But when the beloved is absent, two other passions result: sadness at the absence, or melancholy, and the ardent desire to be with the beloved person, or fervor.

As Saint Aelred of Rievaulx wrote: It is no small consolation in this life to have someone you can unite with you in an intimate affection and the embrace of a holy love, someone in whom your spirit can rest, to whom you can pour out your soul, to whose pleasant exchanges, as to soothing songs, you can fly in sorrow... with whose spiritual kisses, as with remedial salves, you may draw

---

[546] MIGUEL CRUZ, *Misterio de la amistad*, 112. (Editorial translation).
[547] *Jn* 13:1.
[548] *Jn* 15:13.

out all the weariness of your restless anxieties. A man who can shed tears with you in your worries, be happy with you when things go well, search out with you the answers to your problems, whom with the ties of charity you can lead into the depths of your heart; . . . where the sweetness of the Spirit flows between you, where you so join yourself and cleave to him that soul mingles with soul and two become one.[549]

And with these characteristics, do you know of a better friend than Jesus Christ?

---

[549] Cf. SAN ELREDO DE RIEDEVAL, *Caridad y Amistad*, Ed. Claretiana, 1982, p. 250.

4.

CREATIVITY AND FREE TIME

"Young people…Do not ever attempt
to ignore the irresistible force
that pushes you onward to the future."[550]

To the youth in Lima, Peru.

Creativity is a specifically human quality that abounds, or should abound, in youth.

God is the Creator. But man is the image of God, and therefore, is also a creator in a certain sense. He is "creator" in a similar way that God has creativity.

Let's look for a moment at creation. Isn't it marvelous? Look at the mountains with their peaks covered in eternal snows, the seas and oceans with the continual agitation of their gigantic waves, the courses of the heavenly bodies and the captivating sparkle of the luminosity of the stars. Look at the splendor and imposing energy of fire, together with the sweeping power of waterfalls and rapids, and the infinite wonders of the animal world…this, all of this, has been created. Or better yet, **it is being created**. If God stopped "thinking" of the universe for one moment, it would immediately cease to exist. And that means that in the enormous power and the subduing energy of the entire universe, a clean gaze and wise hands can "see" and "feel" the freshness of the omnipotence of God. With traces of His hands still on the roses, these hands are the ones that, with their ardor

---

[550] Editorial translation.

and light, sustain the mountains and move the waters of the sea with the tides, while carefully regulating the paths of the planets and the stars.

What grabs our attention is clearly the enormous power and the infinite force that is transmitted to all things and gives them an impressive dynamism.

Let's look for a minute at youth and see the enormous human potential that is hidden in the beating of their hearts, the energies hidden in the blood that circulates in their veins, the uncontainable vitality capable of moving their spirits into the most incredible adventures.... Let us look at all of this and discover the fresh, infinite current of the vitality that God the Creator communicates to men.

Youth are human beings who are images of God. They are "creators."

Obviously, no one can make something out of nothing, as God does, or sustain reality with his will or with his love, as God does. No one can decide who the new beings that come into the world will be, as God does. But youth can always do new things, transforming and changing the normal course of nature, and respecting her laws in order to collaborate with the creative work of God. Youth, like God, have intellect and will and the capacity to love. In fact, they do things that, if they had not willed them, would not have happened. They also have the capacity to conceive of and construct these things.

We already have the necessary elements to understand what it means for man to have creativity. It is very important to differentiate creativity from creation itself. To be Creator (to make something out of nothing) is proper to God only. God by His omnipotence and by His own will can create from nothing. Creativity is also something created by God. It is the quality by which He communicates to man (by giving him intellect and will) the capacity to combine existing elements to create something that did not previously exist. In creativity there is an elaboration, a production starting from something. Man is not capable of creating the same way that God does. But God has given man the capacity to imitate Him in His creative activity. He gave man a "spark" that makes him similar to His divinity: the intellect. With the intellect man delves deeply and scrutinizes the ultimate aspects of what he is. He has been given a memory in which he is able to store, as if it were a treasure chest, the incredible marvels of creation. He has been given an imagination so that, like God, he can "create."

✠   ✠   ✠

Creativity can be exercised in all the environments of the young person: the sciences, technology, art, history, architecture, medicine and leisure, but is not restricted to one field, certain people, social classes or cultures. If a person, whether young or old, rich or poor, says to himself: "Creativity is all well and good, but I am not creative. Nothing comes to mind," he would not be telling the truth. Every human being, by the mere fact of being human, has the ability to bring about (on a large or small scale) a "creative process," that will allow him to discover his potential and put it at the service of others.

Every person, therefore, has enormous potential that must be discovered and used. How is this done? It does not require great efforts or elaborate thought. Just let the mind explore in two directions: its own interior and in the exterior world. Mental exploration mainly refers to discovering the interior of what one possesses, has acquired with experience, or has stored in the memory. Exterior exploration should be mainly directed at nature. We know that the vast majority of inventions, such as the airplane, the automobile, or ships, have come from "technological copies" of what nature offers man. From those two directions data and images can be accumulated and stored for immediate or later use. The data that has been acquired with this "exploration" can be processed through a series of steps: combination, elaboration, elimination, modification, subtraction, and addition. This "exploration" is definitively creation, which is called "creativity" in human terms. In order to do this, man must use his memory, imagination, intellect and his fantasy. In this way, he is associated with the One who has the most beautiful and fruitful imagination: God.

Creativity itself reflects an activity of the spirit, and as such, should be used for what is noble and good. It can be oriented to merely material ends (such as an architecture workshop where what is created is sold), but the whole process would be weakened if personal creativity were to be put exclusively at the service of profit. A hard economic and materialist vision of the creative process will end up annihilating the aspect that makes man most like God when he creates: beauty. Man would remain, in that case, linked to other factors absolutely extrinsic, which contribute nothing to the process itself, and which, conditioning it from within, cause its abasement.

The possibility of producing something new from what already exists is a gift that comes from God. That creativity has to make itself a style of life. We must also live our own lives creatively by looking within ourselves and, above all, at Jesus Christ. In Him, the creativity of God reaches its highest point. If we imitate Him in our lives we will experience the meaning of the freshness of God's creativity and the plenitude of His youthfulness.

To be young can also be seen as a gift. The energy that makes our spirits a reflection of the eternal youthfulness of God is a gift.

"To be young means possessing within oneself an incessant newness of spirit, nourishing a continual quest for good, and persevering in reaching a goal. Being genuinely young in this sense is the way to prepare for your future, which is to fulfill your vocation as fully mature adults. Never try to ignore then the irresistible force that is driving you toward the future.

"The Church is not frightened at the intensity of your feelings. It is a sign of vitality."[551]

Is there anything more absurd than a bored young person incapable of creatively filling his free time? Why not read the

---

[551] JOHN PAUL II, Address to the Students of the University of Santo Tomas, Manila, February 18, 1981.

classics of universal literature? Why not pick a school of painting or a famous painter to get to know in a particular way? Why not learn to like classical music, bel canto, opera or ballet? Why not read the great playwrights of universal theater? Why not take advantage of good guides, or the World Wide Web to visit the great museums of the world? Why not do concrete works of charity with the poor, the sick, the lonely, or the needy? There are so many lovely and edifying things that could transform our lives. Why not change?

Youth maintains a very close connection with creativity. Behind creativity is a young soul. But a young person who is not creative is one who allows himself to be carried along by crowds and fads, doing what everyone else is doing and doing what is easiest. And if he is not creative, he is not truly young. He may seem young on the outside, but he carries around old age in his soul.

The heart of a young person beats with a powerful potency that must be well-channeled. If it is well-channeled and orientated toward what is new, toward the ongoing surpassing of the different barriers and difficulties that the world presents to us, this force will be capable of transforming the world from within and elevating it, like yeast hidden in the dough.

"Your dynamism, your imagination and your faith are able to move mountains."[552]

Dear young people, live your youth creatively and enable yourselves to give entirely to those things that are worthwhile. Throw yourselves into the adventure of the new, the unforeseen, and the unimagined.

To truly live this way we must always remember that only God can create out of nothing and that no man can create without depending on the immense current of energy that comes

[552] JOHN PAUL II in Yamoussoukro (Côte d'Ivoire), May 11, 1980. (Editorial translation).

from the hand of God. Consequently, dear young people, if you want to be always young, never go against the plan of God. Devote yourselves with all your strength to the impulses of the Spirit of God. With His strength you will transform the world, communicating new life to it.

5.

GOD OUR HOPE

"Man is the being who seeks God, because he seeks happiness... It can be said that man's whole life a nd the whole of human history is a great search for Jesus."

General Audience to youth,
December 27, 1978.

You will have often heard it said that the youth of today are the hope of tomorrow, that they are the hope for the future, or simply that our hope is in the youth.

Why are the youth so closely connected with hope? Is there something about hope that particularly belongs to the young?

Yes. Absolutely.

Just as the elderly are connected with wisdom or prudence, the fruits of life experience harvested with the passing of the years, youth are connected with hope because they have their whole lives ahead of them. Their unknown future is offered a true challenge, a perilous adventure and a battle still to fight.

For any conquest, battle or adventure, you need to be courageous and eager to compel yourselves towards the attainment of the proposed goal. Hope is all of this and more.

Youth, the time for responsibility

When Pope John Paul II considered what is meant by youthfulness, he responded: "It is not only a period of life that corresponds to a certain number of years, it is also *a time given by Providence to every person and given to him as a responsibility*."[553]

Since many young people do not take responsibility for their lives, or choose ideals that are false or live like old people, bored and bitter, they live a life without hope. And there are people who make this a way of thinking, which is to say, there are scholars who propose "theories" of despair because they are bitter and want to embitter the lives of others. Schopenhauer, for example, made the statement that "life is not worthy to be lived." Knowingly or not, youth who have these ideas as the first principle of their actions, are not truly young. They might have a young body, but their soul is decrepit.

However, people of an advanced age can have a young spirit. They are happy people who desire to do great things and to live fully. Youth, therefore, is a way of life rather than a stage of life.

What part does hope play in all this? Hope moves man toward what he hopes for. And the more elevated and noble that hope, the more elevated and noble the impulse that generates it. Thus motivated, he will work with greater sacrifice and energy to attain it. If the object of youthful aspirations is the greatest thing that there is, the highest, the most excellent, the best, the most important, the unimaginable...if that object is God, then that youth will be a youth of fire!

Hope is precisely a fire that invades the heart of youth with its strength, transforming, vivifying and filling it with energy. Hope fills the eyes with happiness and enthusiasm.

Youth without hope and noble ideals, will be youth without fire, without ardor and without happiness. "Light" youth cannot

---

[553] JOHN PAUL II, *Crossing the Threshold of Hope*, (Alfred A. Knopf: New York, 1994), 120-121.

change the world or conquer anything. They are like salt without flavor, which is useless.

Youth who truly respect their essence and the overflowing energy that God put in their hearts must forge great ideals for themselves. Ideals determine the measure of hope, the measure of fire that inflames a young soul.

Toward the conquest of ideals

Tell me what ideals you have and I will tell you what kind of person you are, young or old.

"What are the young people of today like and what are they looking for? It could be said that they are the same as ever. There is something in man which never changes...*today no less than yesterday, the idealism present in young people.*"[554]

And so I ask you, what are your ideals?

There is nothing as disappointing as seeing a young person without ideals, or with false ideals, with ideals that are deceptive, which make him tired of life.

Saying that youth is a way of life, does not exclude those who only recently began the journey of their personal history. In general, old men are not men of hope because very often they have experienced failures; or, since they have achieved some proposed temporal goals, they do not have this fire. And if their ideals are the things of earth, material things, then they will surely become sad and depressed, because they see with the passing of time what they have achieved will fall from their hands like sand through their fingers. And they discover that they do not have time to acquire many more things that perhaps they had hoped to have.

---

[554] JOHN PAUL II, *Crossing the Threshold of Hope*, (Alfred A. Knopf: New York, 1994), 118, 120.

To those who have recently gone into the world and begun to plan the life they want, a wide road to travel and an enormous horizon opens up before their gaze full of aspirations, plans, and goals. The longing for adventure beats in their hearts. A very wise man, Thomas Aquinas, once said: "Youth is a cause of hope…for youth has much of the future before it, and little of the past."[555]

The magnitude and fire of hope depends on that which is hoped for. This hope begets a joy that increases the closer one comes to the object of his hope.

But there is more.

There are two kinds of hope. One is completely natural and every person has it. For example, when we are going to embark on a voyage we *hope* to arrive. This is not the hope that is related to youth. The second kind of hope is supernatural, a gift that God has placed in our souls and that is, in a certain sense, as great as He is. It is with this hope that we hope to reach the promises of God, a hope that makes us young like God. And "God is younger than all else,"[556] as Saint Augustine says. It is hope that, therefore, makes us joyful like God, full of "drive" like Him, of fire like Him.

There are older people who are truly young because they did not put their hope in earthly things. When their days are coming to an end they do not despair because they know that even though their passage on the earth is over, their life is not over.

The saints were extraordinarily happy because they had hope. What were they hoping for?

The martyrs gladly gave their lives to the executioners. What were they hoping for?

---

[555] ST. THOMAS AQUINAS, *Summa Th.* I-II, 40, 6.
[556] ST. AUGUSTINE, quoted by Josef Pieper, *Faith, Hope and Love*, (Ignatius Press: San Francisco, 1997), 111.

Young missionary priests gladly left their native lands and their loved ones. What were they hoping for?

So many husbands and wives were faithful in spite of so many difficulties. What were they hoping for?

They were hoping for the definitive meeting with Jesus Christ.

Do you dare to be YOUNG?

Do you dare to be FIRE?

Do you dare to be a man of HOPE?

6.

MAGNANIMITY:
A VOCATION OF GREATNESS

*"Live for Jesus Christ
and your life will speak to the world."*[557]

*Brescia, Italy,
October 3, 1982.*

Pius XII once spoke with certainty of what he called the fatigue of the good.

It seems that the good people of today are tired and they feel that they lack the necessary strength to correct the disorders, errors, and sins of the world today.

Today we lack youth with great souls and with aspirations so enormous that the whole universe would fit inside of them. We lack youth with magnanimity, with the vocation to greatness. Youth who know how to raise their gaze above material things and discover that the history of humanity does not have meaning if it is not anchored in eternity. We lack magnanimous youth who seek to offer up their lives in witness to the primacy of the transcendent.

Instead, we have many youth who are fed up with everything and full of nothing. We see Catholics who limit themselves to the minimum, with people who cannot risk themselves for things that

---

[557] Editorial translation.

are worthwhile, and who are lukewarm and mediocre. God is also fed up: *So, because you are lukewarm, and neither cold nor hot, I will spew you out of my mouth.*[558]

Who is a magnanimous person?

A magnanimous person is a person of great soul, "anima magna," who dreams of great things and cultivates a broad vision, who does not drown in a puddle or live in a bubble and who is not satisfied with what satisfies the majority.

Most people say: "I'm good because I don't steal or kill." But to be good in this way is relatively easy. But the magnanimous person does not remain at the level of what is easy; rather he tends with great fervor to what is best, optimal, to perfection. The magnanimous person does not merely want to be a good worker, student, father or mother, priest or religious sister; he or she wants to be a saint by making the greatest possible effort to reach the maximum.

The magnanimous person will always be happy and enthusiastic because he is hopeful of reaching great things, and hope generates happiness. The magnanimous person knows that achieving the maximum—which surpasses the natural strength of men—is something that depends on Jesus Christ, who will never fail him. This is why his hope is full of confidence, and his happiness is gigantic.

The magnanimous person does not let himself be led around, there is an unmistakable style in his conduct: the style of Jesus Christ. He will not seek to please the masses, but will invariably tend to what is objectively better. Jesus Christ did not perform a miracle for Herod's enjoyment, even knowing that it might save His life. The magnanimous person does not fold when faced with adversity. He is unbeatable. *And do not fear those who kill the body but cannot kill the soul.*[559]

---

[558] *Rev* 3:16.
[559] *Mt* 10:28.

To remake all things

Greek mythology recounts that King Midas had a special gift: everything he touched turned into gold.

Something similar happens with a magnanimous young person. Since he *is* great and brings greatness to everything he does, he makes everything that he touches great. His ardor and youthful drive are contagious.

If a young person is truly magnanimous, he is continuously growing, and the things that he does grow with him. The whole world acquires a new dimension in the eyes of a magnanimous young person. Everything is greater. Everything is worth more.

The most radical example of a magnanimous young person is Jesus Christ. Jesus Christ is the very magnanimity of God incarnate. And in His eyes men are so valuable, that in a sense, their value is infinite. Because of this, the price of our ransom was no less than the very blood of God.

Like Jesus, the magnanimous person does great things in all virtue and does not worry about difficulties.

Caricatures of magnanimity

We will consider some aspects of false magnanimity that may appear separately or simultaneously.

We find false magnanimity in someone who proudly believes that he is great, without considering that he is only great in God, and that whatever greatness he has comes from God. This person is not magnanimous; he is puffed up, a showoff. These people are formalists who remain only in the exterior. They confuse "tending to greatness" with "showing off" or "striving for attention," and dedicate themselves to an infinite number of trivial things without making the smallest sacrifice for what truly matters.

This shows us the shades of vanity. Vain people are not magnanimous because they desire to appear well before others, and seek applause and human honors, loving the glory of men more than the glory of God. They do not have the spirit to do great things or to be constant in the fulfillment of what is good, because they fear the opinion of others. Therefore, they aspire to false greatness. They do not have upright or firm principles or devote themselves to the truth.

Another aspect mixed with pride is presumption. A presumptuous person is so puffed up that he believes that he can attain with his own strength what is only attainable with God's help. The fall of the presumptuous person is a clamorous one, and he ends up immersed in sadness.

Pusillanimity is the opposite of magnanimity, and means smallness of soul or stinginess, encompassing both of these aspects. Pusillanimity is proper to souls who, upon discovering their weakness in the face of failure, or because they do not tend toward greatness, close themselves up in stinginess, without developing the talents that God gave them and without asking God for the necessary help to achieve what is impossible without His help. He has a small soul and sees everything from his little "neck of the woods." He is only concerned with his own interests and cannot rise above adverse circumstances. He is not able to live or die for what he should.

Let us not grow tired

And so, dear youth, be magnanimous.

Be able to devote yourself to what is worthy. Be able to tend to the best. Be capable of greatness. Be able to put the style of Jesus Christ in your conduct. Be noble. Those who are noble are magnanimous.

To be noble is felt and not said. Nobility is proper to a young person of heart who has something for himself and something for others, who was born to be the lord of himself, capable of disciplining others and disciplining himself. A young person who is noble does not ask for false freedom, but lives freely in the truth and therefore loves and respects hierarchies. He knows how to lay down laws and how to follow them. A noble young person feels honor as he feels life, is master of himself and, because he possesses himself, is able to give himself to others. He knows how to abstain from things no one prohibits and gives things that no one is obligated to give. He knows, at every moment what the things are that he should be ready to die for.[560]

Youth, do not grow tired. Saint Bernard said that running after Jesus Christ is worth nothing if you do not reach Him. Run in such a way as to reach Him. Do not grow tired. Do not stop running until you reach Him.

A prayer to ask for magnanimity

Oh Christ, You are my King. Give me the noble heart of a knight for You.

Make me great in my life, choosing what elevates me and not what drags me down.

Make me great in my work, not seeing the load they impose on me, but the mission You entrust to me.

Make me great in my suffering, a true solider before my cross and a Simon of Cyrene for others.

Make me great with the world, forgiving its smallness without ceding anything to its deceits.

Make me great with men, loyal to all, servant to the needy, bringing those who love me to You.

Make me great with my leaders, seeing in their authority the beauty of Your fascinating face.

Make me great with myself, never closing up inside myself, grounding myself always in You.

Make me great with You, O Christ, happy to live to serve You, happy to die to see You. Amen.[561]

---

[560] Cf. LEONARDO CASTELLANI, *El nuevo gobierno de Sancho.*

[561] F. Tirso Arellano, S.J.

7.

HOW TO BE YOUTH
OF GREAT SOULS

*"The measure of man is God. This is why man must always
return to that source, the unique measure which is God incarnate in
Jesus Christ."*[562]

Audience, May 31, 1980.

1. His Holiness Pope John Paul II, in speaking to students,
magnificently summarized the goal of Catholic education: "the
goal of catholic education is to bring yourself to Christ, in order
that your attitude toward others may be that of Christ." [563]
Therefore, this is our principle objective: to form "other Christs"
who act like Christ.

2. To do this, a solid spiritual formation is not enough, but
demands a profound formation of the intellect, the will, creative
imagination and strong character, aesthetic sensitivity and
corporal agility, social solidarity and personal commitment,
responsibility and courtesy, dialogue and service, respect for
others and knowing how to give hope, the meaning of life,
inalienable liberty, the discipline that develops talents, the
hierarchy of values, nobility of soul, and a preferential love for

---

[562] Editorial translation.

[563] JOHN PAUL II, Discourse to students in Madison Square Garden,
10/03/1979. (Editorial translation).

the poor. Ultimately, it means to form youth with the *spirit of princes,* youth with principles, as King David asked.[564]

3. Youth must have an **integral** formation that is achieved by educating youth according to the natural order, which is parallel to "the order of natural inclinations."[565] This order means an inclination toward: the good of one's own nature (common to all beings); toward more particular goods according to one's specific nature (generation and education of offspring, etc.); and an inclination toward the good that corresponds to our rational nature, a specifically human inclination (the tendency to know divine truths, to live in society, etc.).

4. Youth must know that their personal constitution, their "human structure" is itself hierarchical and that if they truly want to be happy and live a full life, they must respect hierarchy and live with values that truly correspond to the reality of a human being, redeemed by Jesus Christ, who journeys toward heaven. They must, therefore, know that we are made to live, that **we live** in order to feel, that **we feel** in order to think, and **we think** in order to pray. In other words, what we have in common with minerals must be at the service of what we have in common with plants; and this, in turn, must be at the service of what we have in common with animals; and this must be at the service of what we have in common with angels; and this, finally, must be at the service of what we have in common with God. Each form, with its own laws, is not diluted or destroyed by the form above it; rather each form is elevated, dignified, perfected and ennobled. Thus we have the **body** *as matter and instrument of the soul,* moved by an exterior principle. **Vegetative** life is characterized by operations that are moved by an interior principle through a corporeal organ and by virtue of a corporeal quality. **Sensitive** life is characterized by operation through a corporeal organ without any corporeal quality. **Rational** life is characterized by operation that surpasses the corporeal nature and does not use a

---

[564] Cf. *Ps* 50.
[565] ST. THOMAS AQUINAS, *Summa Th.* I-II, 94, 2.

corporeal organ.[566] **Divine** life is characterized by sanctifying grace that makes us children of God. This is why the Greeks called man "microcosmos."

5. Living like this will stir up multifaceted vocational responses that tend to the development of all of youth's physical, aesthetic, social, artistic, literary, intellectual and cultural talents.

6. In summary, we consider that these points will give an orientation to "the social concern of the Church, directed towards an authentic development of man and society which would respect and promote all the dimensions of the human person."[567]

You must spread a culture of the truth and the good that can contribute to a fruitful cooperation between science and faith.

You must be youth who are capable of living with firm principles, coherent actions and charitable relationships.

What a beautiful plan of life for a young person!

1st- Be firm in principles;

2nd-Work in coherence with these principles;

3rd- Live in charity with everyone.

---

[566] Cf. St. Thomas Aquinas, *Summa Th.* I, 78, 1.
[567] John Paul II, *Sollicitudo rei socialis*, 1.

8.

OVERFLOWING JOY, TO LAUGH FOREVER!

"Please allow me to shout it aloud: 'It is time to return to God!' The person who does not yet have the joy of the faith is asked for the courage to seek it with confidence, perseverance and openness. Whoever has the grace of possessing it is asked to value it as the most treasured possession of his life, living it thoroughly and witnessing to it with passion...God alone can fully satisfy the desires of the human heart."

Angelus Message, March 7, 1993.

Magnanimity, hope, daring, freedom, life in plenitude...all of this causes joy. If you see a young person who does not have strength, who is left without answers and "without backup" when facing difficulties...if there is no true liberty, hope, daring, magnanimity...there will be no joy.

Joy is the unmistakable sign of great ideals. If you are full of depression and pessimism, and do not know how to step outside of yourself, or if you get down and do not have the spirit to truly rejoice in life, you are not truly happy. This means that you are not free and do not have great ideals. You do not have true hope nor do you know how to live your life creatively, throwing yourself into great adventures. And, definitely, you do not have the courage to make your own adventure of following Jesus Christ, the great adventurer.

Joy and youth: the adventure of newness

The virtues mentioned above are found in intimate connection with that way of life we have called "youth." Joy is the

373

sign, adornment, and "crown" of these qualities; it is proper to the young soul. It is impossible to live youthfully and not be happy. Sadness is an unmistakable sign of decrepitude, decadency, and defeat.

Joy, like creativity, has an aspect of perennial novelty. Joy means knowing how to appreciate with new eyes what we receive everyday, but is often neglected and treated as unimportant because it is so familiar to us.

For this reason joy always has something childlike about it, similar to God.

Chesterton says that God is like a child because children have the capacity to rejoice in the simple things, which are always new for them. God does too. Just as a child asks for "magic tricks" to be done over and over...God makes the sun rise over and over again...He is like a great magician. One of the things that excites Him the most is that eggs invariably become chickens and that little red balls come out of some pieces of wood with green fringes, which humans usually call apple trees.

Joy is creative. The joy of youth reflects the joy of God the Creator. And today the world needs this joy: "*We need the enthusiasm of the young. We need their joie de vivre. In youthful joy is reflected some of the original joy God had in creating man.*"[568]

God loves to repeat beautiful things and He rejoices each time as if it were the first time. Something similar happens in the Mass when Jesus Christ offers Himself for us as if it were the first time, *as if it were the only time.*

Joy and gratitude

It is proper of those who live with joy to be grateful. To receive every second of life with gratitude, every beat of the heart, the ongoing miracle of life:

---

[568] JOHN PAUL II, *Crossing the Threshold of Hope* (Alfred A. Knopf: New York, 1994), 125.

"You say grace before meals. All right.
But I say grace before the play and the opera,
And grace before the concert and pantomime,
And grace before I open a book,
And grace before sketching, painting,
Swimming, fencing, boxing, walking, playing, dancing;
And grace before I dip the pen in the ink."[569]

Unfortunately, there are a great number of people who are not capable of valuing the inestimable and most fundamental of gifts, which is life. Today the sad shadow of the culture of death is very widespread and threatens to invade the horizon that is opening up before us.

A world that does not love life is an old world, a "dead poets society" that is not capable of living opened to transcendence; a society that scorns and hates youth and joy. Our world is an old world that campaigns in favor of abortion, war, violence, misery and recklessness, dishonesty and corruption.

The world today needs true joy, not the cheap humor and empty smiles of advertisements and television programs or the superficiality of people who want to seem happy by laughing at any stupid thing. These empty people are not truly happy; they have as much happiness as an animated cartoon. They lack life, and creativity, letting time pass, doing nothing and not appreciating the gift of their lives.

The joyful young person has a great soul and celebrates life. He is always content and never gets down, because he knows that God exists and that Jesus Christ died for his sins and annihilated them. He is a young person who has experienced what the merciful love of God means, and what it means that God has poured out His blood for him. He knows that good is invariably stronger than evil and that those who follow Jesus Christ have the "upper hand" no matter what happens, they "have the ace of

---

[569] GILBERT KEITH CHESTERTON, (Maisie Ward, Rowman and Littlefield: 2005), 59. (Original Publisher: New York, Sheed & Ward, 1943).

spades." He knows that a person is worth more than things and the spirit more than matter. And so, he understands the true value of material things, enjoying and using them without ever enslaving himself to them.

The maximum paradigm of joy is Jesus Christ.

The Stoics, ancient philosophers, said that emotions were bad and should be hidden. For example, they did not show their tears. Jesus Christ did:

"He never concealed His tears; He showed them plainly on His open face at any daily sight, such as the far sight of His native city. Yet He concealed something...I say it with reverence; there was in that shattering personality a thread that must be called shyness. There was something that He hid from all men when He went up a mountain to pray. There was something that He covered constantly by abrupt silence or impetuous isolation. There was some one thing that was too great for God to show us when He walked upon our earth; and I have sometimes fancied that it was His mirth."[570]

We will not see the joy of Jesus Christ face to face here on earth. His smile is reserved for us in Heaven.

---

[570] G.K. CHESTERTON, *Orthodoxy* (Image Books: Garden City, NY, 1936), 160.

9.
WORK, SPORTS, STUDY

"True culture is humanizing, while non-cultures and false cultures are dehumanizing. In his choice of culture, man sets his destiny. Culture does not refer only to the spirit, nor only to the body. That 'ad unum' reduction always gives way to dehumanizing cultures."

Rio de Janeiro, Brazil,
July 1, 1980.[571]

What does it mean to form something or someone? It means to give form to something that is formless, to give the ground and foundations upon which to build.

A young person must form himself by seeking out principles of action that allow him to correctly direct himself in life. The physical actions, like walking, can be done thanks to those sandwiches, among other things, that we have eaten and digested for many years. We have digested and assimilated them and they are now part of us; we are able to act thanks to them. The same thing happens with principles: they are assimilated, digested, and become part of us. We don't remember what we ate seven years ago; likewise, we often don't remember or examine the principles that we have assimilated that cause us to act in certain ways. Nevertheless, we act and make decisions with these principles as our point of reference.

---

[571] Editorial translation.

It is crucial to *form ourselves* in order to forge an arsenal of right principles that guarantee the uprightness of our actions, and will re-direct us if we get off track.

"Formation" is a term, like so many others today, that has lost much of its meaning. Some believe that formation means to "let it be, let it happen," as if the maturing of a person were just a matter of time. This is where liberal youth come from, hippies, *light* youth…men and women without God, without a homeland, without personality, without great ideals. Others confuse *forming* with *formatting* or *informing*, and they think that it means to merely "fill up with contents" like downloading data onto a computer or filling a trashcan with trash. And this creates "intellectualoid" youth, who care more about their speculations than the truth; encyclopedic youth who know books full of facts, but ignore the book of life. They are the "very interesting" youth, the "robots," the "crowd" who do what everyone else does and say what everyone else says. Finally, many youth are formed by cultivating only one aspect of the person, to the detriment of other aspects that are often more important. And so we see athletes without brains, worthy only of admiration on the field; workers without heart, reduced to being one more cog in the huge production machines; students without hands, who spend time elaborating theories that have nothing to do with reality and are incapable of moving a finger to change what is truly wrong.

Youth like this have assimilated the false principles of an "un-transcendent" culture that soon becomes the culture of death, incapable of transcending quantity, mechanics and nature. That is to say, they do not have principles; they do not have a solid and true formation.

In spite of all the problems and inconveniences, the youth today still know how to recognize what is valuable when it is presented to them, and they realize, by contrast, that they have been deceived by false principles. I believe that it is worth the effort to introduce the *integral formation* that is offered by the "School of Jesus Christ." It brings together in an admirable harmony, the head, heart and hands of the youth, under one theme: *Magis*, which means *more, higher, greatness*.

In addition to everything that we have been presenting throughout the journey of this book, I believe that there are some other additional factors that, when well-directed, will contribute to the formation of the young. These *vital spaces* in which the young live and move are work, study and sports.

The formative value of work

Many young people today need to work, in order to continue their studies or out of the necessity for *survival.*

Even in these particular cases, we must take advantage of the fact that work is always, in one way or another, beneficial for forming character, creating strong habits, and structuring one's personality. To do this, it will be helpful to take some things into account:

1. Work allows man to develop himself and utilize his energies to transform nature in different ways. Therefore, man must not be at the service of work, but rather work at the service of man.

2. Work dignifies man, because it helps him to actualize himself, effectively and operatively, as the image of God the Creator. Through work man "collaborates" with God the Creator.

3. Jesus Christ was a carpenter. The Virgin Mary was a housewife. With any kind of work, even if it is the most humble, man does what God did: in Jesus Christ, God worked. He also worked as did the Mother of God.

4. Work always requires effort and patience, whether it is manual labor or office work. For this reason it serves two important purposes: as expiation for sins, which is penance; and as a means of strengthening the will through overcoming the inevitable obstacles.

5. Work enables us to fight against sloth and laziness, and consequently, to remove occasions of sin.

In all of this we can see that human work has a great value, especially for the young soul. Work is proper to generous souls and reveals the valor of those who are not afraid of sacrifice.

Work, young man, work without ceasing	*Trabaja, joven, sin cesar trabaja.*
The honored brow which sweat has been wetting	*La frente honrada que en sudor te moja*
Before another will never be found to be blushing	*Jamás ante otra frente se sonroja;*
Nor, before those who despise it, found groveling.	*Ni se rinde servil a quien la ultraja.*
From the snow of his years he is kept long,	*Tarde la nieve de los años cuaja*
He who from laziness keeps himself far	*Sobre quien lejos la indolencia arroja*
The strength of his body angers the strong,	*Su cuerpo, al roble, por lo fuerte, enoja,*
His soul from the world he has kept unmarred.	*Su alma, del mundo al ladozal no baja.*
The bread that work gives tastes far better	*El pan que da el trabajo es más sabroso*
Than hidden honey drawn with much effort	*Que la escondida miel que con empeño*
By the bee from a fragrant flower.	*Liba la abeja en el rosal frondoso.*
Eating this bread you will have self dominion	*Si comes ese pan serás tu dueño*
But laziness will lead to a pit of oblivion,	*Mas si del ocio ruedas al abismo,*
That way you could end up as anything save yourself.	*Todo serlo podrás, menos tú mismo.*

The formative value of study

Aristotle's *Metaphysics*, one of the most profound and beautiful books, begins thus: "All men by nature desire to know." This is a great truth. This is why newscasters are so famous; when something amazing happens, everyone wants to see and hear about it.

But sometimes the very noble desire to know can fall into mere curiosity. The "science of curiosity" does not form great leaders. Einstein didn't read *The Enquirer* to be a great scholar.

Study is a necessary activity. It is, in a sense, written into the very nature of man and has a high formative value. Study perfects the intelligence and gives, through "intellectual exercise," the treasures that are found hidden in things.

Like all training, like all perfecting activity, study must have an order. It is necessary to progress from simple things to more complex things and from what is known to what is unknown. Normally one cannot teach a six year old child the fundamental propositions of quantum physics.

Study also requires effort to acquire the habit or the custom of studying. Initially, it is not easy to set oneself to study. But once the habit is formed, it is no longer difficult and can even be joy filled.

To achieve the habit of studying is worth the effort, for many reasons. There are reasons known to everyone: "to get somewhere in life," "to get ahead in the work world," "to not fall behind." But there are more profound reasons.

The young person who can, but does not study, is easily manipulated and easily deceived. He who does not have passion to know the truth, will not show interest when the idea of "dying for the truth" is proposed to him. A person who does not study is easily influenced by the mass media and will believe just about anything. He is a young person without a mind equipped to read reality; he can be tricked and played for a fool.

It is difficult for youth who could study and do not do so to become virtuous. Usually they spend many lazy hours, losing a lot of time in front of the TV, which becomes a tyrant for their attention.

Youth who have the opportunity to study and take advantage of it, in general, have great dominion over themselves and over their time. They have strength of will and even find study to be an excellent way to distance themselves from temptation and to avoid occasions of sin.

What should we study?

Those who have no obstacle to going to school, or beginning a course of studies at a university, should study what corresponds to their circumstances. But everyone has to study, or at least to read something about the things of the faith, in order to know what we believe, to know how to explain what we believe to someone who might ask.[572] Since we study or read what interests us, if we study and read about the faith, we pay a courtesy to Jesus Christ.

There are very few young people who read, who seriously study. Certainly, the environment does not help. It is easier to avoid it, to keep watching TV, to just hang out or go out with friends…to let time slip between our fingers. This is easier. But we must make the effort. It is a big responsibility. If you study, you will be prepared for whatever comes to you. You have to conquer yourself in this also: conquer your distractions, your inclinations to comfort, to what is easy, conquer different obstacles…the harvest that you will reap in your future depends on the generosity of effort with which you have sown.

An open book is a doorway of light:
Child, if by this door you will enter,
God surely will be in your future
More visible and His power more bright.
An ignorant man lives in the desert,
Where water is scarce and the air is impure.
A grain makes his hesitating foot unsure,
He stumbles when walking, he lives as if dead!
In this, the flowering spring of your life
May your young heart these impressions receive
Like wax receives the touch of soft hands.

Es puerta de luz un libro abierto:
Entra por ella, niño, y de seguro
Que para ti serán en lo futuro
Dios más visible, su poder más cierto.
El ignorante vive en el desierto
Donde es el agua poca, el aire impuro;
Un grano le detiene el pie inseguro;
Camina tropezando, ¡vive muerto!
En ese de tu edad abril florido,
Recibe el corazón las impresiones,
Como la cera el toque de las manos.

---

[572] Cf. 1 *Pt* 3:15.

Study and then when you are grown
Neither a vulgar toy of the passions
Nor a servile slave of a tyrant
you'll be.

Estudia, y no serás, cuando crecido,
Si el juguete vulgar de las pasiones,
Si el esclavo servil de los tiranos.

The formative value of sports

"The Church (...) admires, approves, and esteems sports, discovering in them a gymnasium for body and spirit, a training for social relations founded on the respect of others and of oneself, and an element of social cohesion that favors friendly relations even in the international field."[573]

Sports have enormous formative power. Effort and pleasure, sacrifice and happiness come together to forge for youth a firm will. Sports are pleasurable and provide an effective antidote to sluggishness and the comfortable life by awakening within a person a sense of order. Sports can also aid in becoming a master of oneself by conquering fear or pusillanimity.

But, sometimes, the pleasure that is derived from sports becomes so dominating that they become an end in themselves rather than a means to cultivate the dignity and harmony of the body, health, vigor, agility, and recreation. This is a very common error and it is not unusual to see youth who passionately dedicate all of their interests and activity to sports. These are youth who give a bored and distracted attention to the important demands of their families, studies, and work. In fact, the home often becomes a hotel where the inhabitants are like guests, almost strangers, and all dialogue is broken.

Sports require great dedication and an ongoing desire to break the limits and surpass oneself. They are like art, because in sports you have to do exterior exercises in a creative way. Sports require greatness of soul, tenacity and fortitude to conquer all obstacles. Sports teach us to act as a team.

---

[573] JOHN PAUL II, OR n. 38, p.10, 1979. (Editorial translation).

Young people must be artists capable of transforming the world. And so they have to show their greatness in their dedication to work, to study and to sports.

10.

INTO THE DEEP.
DUC IN ALTUM!

*"This is not the moment for indecisiveness,
absences, or lack of commitment.
This is the hour of the daring, of those who hope,
those who aspire to live in the fullness of the Gospel, and those who
want to achieve it in the world today
and in the history that is still to come."*

Lima, Peru, 1985. [574]

The gospel of St. Luke recounts that, *While the people pressed upon him to hear the word of God, he was standing by the lake of Gennesaret…getting into one of the boats, which was Simon's, he asked him to put out a little from the land. And he sat down and taught the people from the boat. And when he had ceased speaking, he said to Simon, 'Put out into the deep!*[575]

Profound words of profound content, of deep mystic resonance…*Duc in altum! Put out into the deep!*

These are words that relate especially to youth who are full of great ideals and who do not want their lives to be a brief, grey, monotony.

These are words that youth of action, wide vision, decided and generous hearts understand, and who, because of the nobility of

---

[574] Editorial translation.
[575] *Lk* 5:1, 3-4.

their souls, smile with happiness to know that Jesus Himself said to them: "Duc in altum! Put out into the deep!"

These words are an invitation to carry out great works, extraordinary undertakings where there is adventure, vertigo and danger.

Young person: Put out into the deep! Where the waves strike the boat, the salty water sprays your face, where the prow opens its passage for the first time, where there is no trail and the stars are the only reference, where the keel is pounded by the whirling waters, where the full sails suffer the fury of the wind, where the masts creak...and the soul shivers...

Into the deep! Far from the shore and from the dry land of merely human thoughts, cold and calculating...where the water churns, the heart beats quickly, where the soul knows celestial raptures and fascinating joys.

It is to burn the ships, like Hernán Cortés, with Spanish arrogance...abandon everything.

To put into the deep is to take the demands of the Gospel seriously: *Go, sell what you possess.*[576]

It is the only adventure...

It is the longing to possess the infinite in our restless hearts...

It is proper to fishermen who are humble and hardworking, who do not fear danger and who are constant in going out to sea again and again, prudent in catching fish, hardened by the salt and the sun...It is to be rebellious against the spirit of the world for Christ.

Duc in altum! Live Christianity "to the max" in a mixture of bravery and courage that will captivate men, children and youth.

---

[576] *Mt* 19:21.

It means not to fear danger, and live in the free intrepidity of total, absolute, unrestricted and undivided love for God.

To live in a delirium of courage, to conquer the world, the flesh and the devil day by day, hour by hour.

To live with all of the passion of the saints and the martyrs, who gave **everything** for God.

To live always mocking the Antichrist. And if his dirty claw crushes us, to bellow, "Viva Cristo Rey!"…and spit on that scrap of human flesh.

And to do this it is necessary to break ties, sins, occasions, bad friendships…

Into the deep! In the abyss of unfathomable prayer with the Abyss.

It is to be disposed to die like the grain of wheat in order to see Christ in all things.

Into the deep!

11.

LIKE ANOTHER HUMANITY OF CHRIST

> *"Man-every man without any exception*
> *whatever-has been redeemed by Christ,*
> *and because with man, with each man*
> *without any exception whatever,*
> *Christ is in a way united,*
> *even when man is unaware of it."*

Redemptor Hominis, *14.*

Our Lord Jesus Christ is not only God, He is also man. That is why He appears more than eighty-four times in the Holy Gospels as the Son of Man, *the* man by antonomasia, and as such, the model for all men.

The Word, by assuming a perfect and individual human nature, uniting Himself to it in the unity of person, elevated man to the highest dignity and unsurpassable greatness. Christ the Man is, in Himself, the summit of humanity, that, "Only in the mystery of the Incarnate Word does the mystery of man take on light...[Jesus Christ] fully reveals man to man." [577] By His incarnation the Son of God has united Himself with every man. By His Incarnation He became our neighbor.

In the Incarnate Word, Jesus Christ, the meanings of life and love, work and rest, pain and death, are illuminated. This is why

---

[577] *Gadium et spes*, 22.

Pope John Paul II reminded us that: "No human action is foreign to the Gospel."

And Christ wants to prolong His Incarnation in each man.

1. In Christians

By Baptism the Christian is another Christ. To express this, Saint Paul invents words. He says that the baptized: *conmortui,*[578] we have died with Christ; *consepulti,*[579] buried...with Him; *conresuscitati,*[580] raised...up with Him; *convivificati,*[581] alive together with Christ; *complantati,*[582] united with Him, planted in him; *convivemus,*[583] live with Him; *consedere,*[584] *seated us with Him.*[585]

Furthermore, the Christian must be *alter Christus* (another Christ), in his endeavor to imitate the Lord: *Have this mind among yourselves, which is yours in Christ Jesus.*[586] Jesus says: *I have given you an example.*[587] By living the life of Christ, or rather that Christ lives His life in us: *it is no longer I who live, but Christ who lives in me.*[588] *For to me to live is Christ.*[589]

In this way the Christian is:

- *the aroma of Christ*[590];

- *ambassadors for Christ*[591]; *I am an ambassador (of the mystery of the Gospel)*[592];

---

[578] 2 *Tim* 2:11.
[579] *Rom* 6:4.
[580] *Eph* 2:6.
[581] *Eph* 2:5.
[582] *Rom* 6:5.
[583] 2 *Tim* 2:11.
[584] *Eph* 2:6.
[585] NAB Version.
[586] *Phil* 2:5.
[587] *Jn* 13:15.
[588] *Gal* 2:20.
[589] *Phil* 1:21.
[590] 2 *Cor* 2:15.

- a letter from Christ[593];

- clothed in Christ[594];

- predestined to be conformed to the image of his Son[595];

-to "reproduce" Christ, identifying the self with the exemplar;

-to configure and assimilate oneself to Christ by the practice of all the virtues, *becoming like him*[596];

-to reflect like mirrors...the glory of the Lord...*being transformed into the image that we reflect in brighter and brighter glory.*[597]

In the words of Blessed Elizabeth of the Trinity, the Christian is: "like a new Incarnation of the Word, in a way that the Father sees in Him nothing more than His beloved Son"; "like another humanity of Christ."

This is why Jesus identifies Himself with the apostles: *He who receives you receives me.*[598] And also with all Christians: *I in them*[599]*; I in him*[600]; asking Saul: *why do you persecute me?*[601]

Saint Augustine said: "We are Christ!"

2. In every man

Because Jesus Christ has become incarnate in a human nature, has poured out His blood for every man and because each man has a vocation to eternity, in some way every man represents

---

[591] 2 *Cor* 5:20.
[592] *Eph* 6:20.
[593] 2 *Cor* 3:3.
[594] *Gal* 3:27; NJB Version.
[595] *Rom* 8:29.
[596] *Phil* 3:10.
[597] 2 *Cor* 3:18.
[598] *Mt* 10:40.
[599] *Jn* 17:23.
[600] *Jn* 15:5.
[601] *Acts* 9:4.

Christ. Even the atheist and the sinner represent Christ. This is why all acts of fraternal charity truly affect Christ Himself.

The poor are Christ: "they represent the role of the Son of God."[602] Parents and husbands must be obeyed: *as to the Lord.*[603] Children: *Whoever receives one such child in my name receives me.*[604] Pilgrims: "In them more particularly, Christ is received."[605] Spouses must love each other *as Christ.*[606]

Saint Thomas Aquinas teaches that one loves one's neighbor either because God is in him, or so that God might be in him. Saint Therese of Lisieux said that she saw Christ hidden in the soul of one of her sisters (speaking of a religious who made her life impossible).

It is necessary, by faith, to see Christ Himself in every man and woman, young or old, even those who are deficient, have defects, are poor or deformed and to love them with the same consideration, respect, tenderness and generosity that we would feel if we were to meet Jesus and be allowed to help Him. We have this privilege within our reach because all men—all of our neighbors—are mystically Jesus. In this sense, John Paul II said: "Man, who is Christ."

Dear Youth:

We must love everyone. If we hate anyone, we are not Christians. Pilate presented Christ to the crowds saying: *Ecce homo, Behold the man!* He did not understand the depth of his words. Only in Christ is the complete truth of man's origin, mystery, and ultimate goal manifested. Do I know this? Everybody must be CHRIST for me. Do I live this out? At the end of life I will be

---

[602] SAINT VINCENT DE PAUL, *Cartas*, XI, 32; E.S. XI, 725. (Editorial translation).
[603] *Eph* 5:22; *Eph* 6:1; *Col* 3:20.
[604] *Mt* 18:5.
[605] SAINT BENEDICT, *The Rule of St. Benedict* in English, 53, 15.
[606] *Eph* 5:25.

judged on how much I love, as Saint John of the Cross says. Am I aware of this?

The urgent task of evangelization and catechesis that must begin in every family is none other than preparing the Incarnation of Christ in the souls of each one of His members. This is the work of the apostle: to form Christ in "each man," as Saint Paul said to the Galatians (4:19): *I am again in labor until Christ be formed in you!*[607]

May each one of us, with the help of the Blessed Virgin Mary, be able to say for the love of our neighbor: *Be imitators of me, as I am of Christ.*[608]

---

[607] *Gal* 4:9.
[608] 1 *Cor* 11:1.

12.
THE MADNESS OF BEING CHRISTIAN

"Since the Cross of Christ is the sign of love and salvation, we should not be surprised that all true love requires sacrifice. Do not be afraid, then, when love makes demands. Do not be afraid when love requires sacrifice. Do not be afraid of the Cross of Christ."

Auckland, New Zealand, November 22, 1986.

The saints are strange people and are often considered crazy: *This is the man whom we once held in derision and made a byword of reproach...we thought that his life was madness and that his end was without honor.*[609]

If we want the Christians who will be on the earth someday to celebrate us when celebrating All Saints Day, we must prepare ourselves by making sure that the world considers us to be "mad" now. Jesus Christ and His doctrine are "foolishness" for the world and for the worldly and, therefore, the true followers of Jesus Christ are held to be crazy.

1. The doctrine of Jesus Christ

There is no teaching more opposed to the world than the Beatitudes. What everyone flees from, the Lord presents to us as desirable, says Saint John Chrysostom. The world demands riches, Christ demands poverty; the world rewards the vindictive, Christ rewards the meek; the world celebrates carnal pleasure,

---

[609] *Wis* 5:4.

Christ requires mortification; the world calls the unjust clever, while Christ calls those who hunger and thirst for righteousness clever; the world considers the oppressive to be strong, Christ considers the merciful to be strong; the world exalts the lustful, Christ exalts the pure; the world admires the violent, Christ admires the peaceful; the world seeks comfort and "a good time," Christ seeks those who are having a hard time and those who suffer persecution.

Dedicated Catholics and genuine religious are considered crazy because they live in opposition to how the world wants to live. Their inclinations and their words and actions are in conflict with worldliness.

2. The example of Jesus Christ

Today we have lost the fire of the first Christians by living a comfortable and accommodating religion. We have become lazy and unconcerned about spreading the Kingdom of God. We have turned the religious life into something cold, lifeless, middleclass and calculating, into a religion of "old ladies."

True religion is completely different:

-it is fire: *I came to cast fire upon the earth*[610];

-it is a mighty wind, like on Pentecost;

-it is the awakening of life;

-it is fresh air;

-it is the dawn;

-it is red-hot iron that sparks;

-it is salt and yeast.

Because Christians live their religion this way, the world calls Christ and His followers, the saints, crazy.

---

[610] *Lk* 12:49.

When Jesus speaks about His resurrection, the Jews say: *He…is out of his mind.*[611] For many people whatever exceeds the capacity of human reason is madness.

When Paul preaches the resurrection of Christ, Festus the Pagan says: *You are out of your mind, Paul!*[612] For the pagans the faith is foolishness.

When the servant Rhoda believes in Peter's miraculous liberation from prison, she says to the incredulous Christians: *You are out of your mind!*[613] For some "Christians" miracles are a sign of craziness. As Saint Paul teaches, when the uninitiated or the unfaithful see the miraculous charisms, *will they not say that you are out of your mind?*[614]

If we were to live as true Christians and not the Christianity lived by hollow heads, empty hearts and full bellies…they would call us crazy.

The saints must desire to be considered crazy: *I desire to be accounted as worthless and a fool for Christ, rather than to be esteemed as wise and prudent in this world.*[615]

Do we truly follow Christ, He who has loved us to the point of foolishness, as Saint Catherine of Siena says, "O, You who are mad with love, why have You become so crazy? Because You have fallen in love with Your creature"; or do we follow the world?

---

[611] *Jn* 10:20; NAB Version.
[612] *Acts* 26:24; NJB Version.
[613] *Acts* 12:15; NAB Version.
[614] *1 Cor* 14:23.
[615] SAINT IGNATIUS OF LOYOLA, *The Spiritual Exercises of St. Ignatius: Based on Studies in the Language of the Autograph*, trans. Louis J. Puhl, S.J., (Loyola Press: Chicago, 1951), 167.

3. What is the madness of the Christians about?

First of all, there are two conditions for persecution to be evangelical: "namely, when what is said is false and when it is for God's sake."[616] To be worthily called crazy for Christ, we should be faithful to Him, never giving any occasion for others to think we are crazy, except for Christ Himself.

Christian madness consists in living in the *above* and the *beyond*, where calculations and all forms of give-and-take cease. Christianity begins when we no longer count, calculate, weigh or measure. Do you love only the one who loves you? Do you give only to the one who can return the favor? Do you do favors only for those who appreciate it? *Do not even the Gentiles do the same?*[617]

Holy madness consists in living the Beatitudes. If it is not mad to live according to the Beatitudes, then madness does not exist.

Blessed are those who are crazy for Christ! They will be pushed around and slandered in many ways; they will be laughed at, called stupid, slow and mentally unstable. The Kingdom of Heaven belongs to them!

Blessed! Because they live the madness of love without limits or measures, love that is stronger than blood: *If any one comes to me and does not hate his own father and mother and wife and children and brothers and sisters, yes, and even his own life, he cannot be my disciple.*[618] It is love that becomes a sword that cuts, that separates, that wounds, that disrupts false peace. It is Christ who brought this: *I have not come to bring peace, but a sword.*[619]

---

[616] SAINT JOHN CHRYSOSTOM, *Homily 15 on Matthew*, 11.
[617] *Mt* 5:47.
[618] *Lk* 14:26.
[619] *Mt* 10:34.

It is the madness of blessing those who persecute us[620] and to *repay no one evil for evil.*[621]

Blessed are those who are crazy for Christ because they have rid themselves of everything, even to the last thread; and they stand before God in all simplicity!

Blessed are those who are crazy for Christ because they are truly poor, they live triumphant poverty, they obey unto death, they live through Mary, with Mary, in Mary and for Mary!

Blessed are those who are crazy for Christ because no wisdom of the world could ever deceive them. They do not let themselves become infatuated with the empty blabber of men, even of those established in authority. They are the salt of the earth and the light of the world.

It is madness to say, after working all day for the Gospel: *We are unworthy servants; we have only done what was our duty.*[622] It is madness to know that *to him who has will more be given and he will have abundance; but from him who has not, even what he has will be taken away.*[623] It is madness to live entirely on Divine Providence: *Take nothing for your journey, no staff, nor bag, nor bread, nor money; and do not have two tunics.*[624] It is madness to seek the last place: *But many that are first will be last, and the last first*[625]; to be the slave of all: *but whoever would be great among you must be your servant*[626]; or to humble oneself: *For everyone who exalts himself will be humbled, and he who humbles himself will be exalted.*[627] This is the madness of forgiveness: *forgive them; for they know not what they do.*[628]

---

[620] cf. *Rom* 12:14.
[621] *Rom* 12:17.
[622] *Lk* 17:10.
[623] *Mt* 13:12.
[624] *Lk* 9:3.
[625] *Mt* 19:30.
[626] *Mk* 10:43.
[627] *Lk* 14:11.
[628] *Lk* 23:34.

My dear young people:

Let us not be afraid to be considered crazy for following Christ. Let us not betray the spirit of the Gospel.

When the world says: Look at those crazies! When rocks are thrown at them, they kiss the hands that throw them. When laughed at and made fun of, they will laugh along, like children who don't understand. When they are beaten and martyred, they give thanks to God for having been found worthy. When the world says this, it is a sign that we're doing well.

Look at our brothers and sisters, the saints in heaven. The world said to them:

-"Look at the crazies! They bless when they are cursed!"

-"Look at the crazies! They deny themselves and pick up their crosses every day. They do penance, they are infinitely happy, they are not afraid to call things what they are."

-"Look at the crazies! All kinds of nonsense are said about them and they don't care a whit! People try to load them down with heavy stones and they think they weigh as much as a spider's web. People plot and conspire against them, but for them their plots have less consistency than a bubble."

-Holy madness! Madness of love! But the madness of the cross is wiser than the wisdom of all men.

13.
OUR LORDSHIP

"Christ calls you to freedom, to truth, to love.
To the freedom that always becomes love through the truth…
He calls you to sanctity. Do not be afraid of that word!"

Mantua, Italy, June22, 1991.

One of the most beautiful titles of Jesus Christ is "the Lord." It indicates the characteristic freedom and the "dominating" attitude of the Spirit of Jesus Christ. In Greek it sounds lovely: *Kyrios*, Lord. The Lord.

All Christians, because they are Christians, must also be "lords," in imitation of the Lord…as if we were *other Christs*. In principle, we already are "Christ" by Baptism; but it is our task to be Him in plenitude, dying and living, as Saint Paul says: *So you also must consider yourselves dead to sin and alive to God in Christ Jesus,*[629] and as Saint Peter said: *He himself bore our sins in his body on the tree, that we might die to sin and live to righteousness.*[630]

Dying:

We must die:

-To sin and the works of the flesh, because *in Christ we have redemption through his blood, the forgiveness of our trespasses, according to*

---

[629] *Rom* 6:11.
[630] 1 *Pt* 2:24.

the riches of his grace.[631] And those who belong to Christ Jesus *have crucified the flesh with its passions and desires.*[632]

-To the pain of sin, the evil world: *I have overcome the world,*[633] *because before we were slaves to the elemental spirits of the universe*[634]; *and to hell, because at the name of Jesus every knee should bow......under the earth.*[635]

-To the fear of death, since the Son of God became man in order *to deliver all those who through fear of death were subject to lifelong bondage.*[636]

-To the power of the devil: *The reason the Son of God appeared was to destroy the works of the devil.*[637]

-To slavery to the old law: *Christ redeemed us from the curse of the law.*[638]

Living:

We must live:

-The priestly life of grace in fullness, since Christ has come in the flesh to bring us life and life in abundance. This life is the grace of God that makes us *partakers of the divine nature.*[639] It is the supernatural life of the theological virtues, the infused moral virtues and the gifts of the Holy Spirit.

-The prophetic life, by which we participate "in Christ's prophetic office"[640] giving testimony of faith and charity, offering

---

[631] *Eph* 1:7.
[632] *Gal* 5:24.
[633] *Jn* 16:33.
[634] *Gal* 4:3.
[635] *Phil* 2:10.
[636] *Heb* 2:15.
[637] 1 *Jn* 3:8.
[638] *Gal* 3:13.
[639] 2 *Pt* 1:4.
[640] VATICAN COUNCIL II, *Lumen Gentium*, 12.

to God the sacrifice of praise, teaching the Word in season and out of season, by preaching, teaching, writing or research, in evangelization or in catechesis.

Finally, truly living the life of lordship, implies a certain character of dominion.

A life of lords

What does this dominion mean? What do you have to do to truly be a "lord" or a "lady"?

We must work so that our will dominates four areas: ourselves, others, the world and the devil.

a) Lordship over oneself: Insofar as man triumphs over sin, he dominates the incentives of the flesh and governs his soul and his body. The youth, in submitting his soul to God, reaches a state of indifference and detachment to the things of the world. This does not produce powerlessness but rather the opposite, a dominated and free will, capable of dedicating itself to things without becoming dominated by them.

b) Lordship over men: Insofar as youth gives generously to the service of Jesus Christ, the only King that is worthy of being served, an effective spiritual royalty is acquired, over other men including those who have power and authority and even over those who abuse their power. Such youth take on themselves the burden of their sins and their sufferings by a humble love that can mean the possibility of sacrificing oneself.

c) *Lordship over the world* means two things:

-First, collaborating with the world of creation by work, and with the world of redemption by apostolate. In order for this spiritual royalty to be effective, disinterestedness and detachment from things is necessary. *From now on, let those who have wives live as though they had none, and those who mourn as though they were not mourning, and those who rejoice as though they were not rejoicing, and those who buy as though they had no goods, and those who deal with the world as though they had no dealings with it. For the form of this world is passing away.*[641]

-Second, rejecting the world, for the sake of loyalty to the world itself which must be held as a means and not as an end, and for the sake of loyalty to God, resisting concupiscences, the temptations and sins of the world. This means being independent from the slogans, mockeries, and persecutions of the world. We must learn to depend only on our right conscience, illuminated by faith and be ready for martyrdom for our loyalty to God. This is what constitutes the full and total rejection of the evil world.

d) Lordship over the devil: We need youth who are convinced that they have, by the grace of God, the power to resist the devil and the power to exorcise him, living as those who are resurrected: *seek the things that are above, where Christ is, seated at the right hand of God. Set your minds on things that are above, not on things that are on earth.*[642]

It is this four-fold lordship that allows us to live in the **liberty of the sons of God** who are not enslaved:

*by the elemental spirits of the universe[643];

*by the letter that brings death[644];

*by the spirit of the world.[645]

We should not submit ourselves to the yoke of slavery…(otherwise) Christ will be of no benefit to you. [646]

---

[641] 1 *Cor* 7:29-31.
[642] *Col* 3:1-2.
[643] *Gal* 4:3.
[644] cf. 2 *Cor* 2:6.
[645] 1 *Cor* 2:12.
[646] Cf. Gal 5:1-2.

We must be so docile to the Spirit that we can say: "My glory is to live as free as a bird in the sky; I do not make a nest on this ground."[647]

We owe nothing to the flesh, *for all flesh is like grass, and all its glory like the flower of the field,*[648] and if we live in the Spirit, let us also follow the Spirit,[649] because *What is born of flesh is flesh and what is born of spirit is spirit.*[650]

We must have, like Saint Teresa said, "an earnest and most determined determination not to halt until they reach their goal, whatever may come, whatever may happen to them, however hard they may have to labor, whoever may complain of them, whether they reach their goal or die on the road or have no heart to confront the trials which they meet, whether the very world dissolves before them."[651] What matters is to take a step and then another step.

You must follow the paths of lordship to the end, in such a way that you are firmly resolved to reach holiness. In Jesus Christ it is truly possible.

---

[647] Cf. JOSE HERNÁNDEZ, *El Gaucho Martín Fierro.* (Editorial translation).

[648] 1 *Pt* 1:24.

[649] *Gal* 5:25.

[650] *Jn* 3:6.

[651] ST. TERESA OF JESUS, *Way of Perfection,* Chapter 21

14.
EVEN IN THE EXTERIOR

*"Young men and women, have a great respect for your own
body and those of others! May your body be at the service of your
interior self. May your gestures, your looks, be always a reflection
of your soul! Adoration of the body? No, Never.
Degradation of the body? Nor this.
Dominion over the body? Yes!
Transfiguration of the body? Even better! "*

Paris, France, (OR),
June 15, 1980.

You have heard it said that the eyes are the mirror of the soul.
This means that the soul, spiritual and invisible, **is manifested** to
the bodily eyes through the body, its gestures and expressions, its
words and attitudes and looks, because exterior dispositions are
signs of interior dispositions. Thus, the face of the man of God
and the face of the vicious man reflect two opposed worlds.

Reciprocally, the exterior of the person **influences** the soul.
Every fault in exterior conduct has immediate repercussions on
character: vulgarity of manners, laziness in one's duties, coarse
vocabulary, lascivious glances, lewd poses, dirty or disorderly
clothes, frivolity in conversations, mediocre attitudes, uncouth
behavior and bad friendships: all diminish one's character and
destroy one's personality. Gradually, he who was born to be a
prince ends up being a pauper. This happens because the interior
sentiments follow in unison with the language one uses and the
habits with which one lives. He who habitually dresses like a bum
ends up living like one.

How sad it is to see a young man or woman lowering their expression of self in their way of dress or presentation before others in the desire to follow the fads and trends that the world imposes. On the contrary, how beautiful it is to meet a young person who is orderly, dignified, presentable and, at the same time, simple; one who is courteous, educated and speaks well. Dressing decently, not luxuriously, he promotes harmony in the exterior. For example, a mended garment does not tarnish one's image, but a dirty one does. This is why there are so many celebrities who in spite of dressing in the latest and most expensive clothing cannot hide the poverty and profound disorder in their souls.

How lovely it is to see a young woman who knows how to dress well! How beautiful are the souls of so many young women who know how to dress femininely! It expresses such modesty, simplicity, dominion and distinction, with simple tasteful details. They do not need to attract attention with sophisticated clothes, bold dresses or coarse posture, but they know how to hold themselves with grace, elegance and gentility.

Blessed Pier Giorgio Frassati[652] is an excellent example of this exterior harmony. This young man, a saint, was never hypocritical in his exterior manner. Just by looking at a picture of him, you can see perfect harmony between body, soul and God behind the manliness of his demeanor.

Dear youth, may you have perfect harmony of beauty and honor between God and soul, and between soul and body, for

---

[652] Blessed Pier Giorgio Frassati (1901-1925) is a young layman who died at the age of 24 and whom John Paul II, when beatifying him, gave as an example for the youth of our time. To get to know his spirit better, I recommend reading an account of his life. For now a passage from one of his letters should be enough: "You ask if I am happy. How could I not be while faith gives me strength? Sadness should be eradicated from the soul of a Catholic. Pain is not sadness, which is the most detestable of all illnesses. Such illness is almost always a product of atheism; but the end for which we were created points us towards a path, sown, if you may, with many thorns, but in no way sad. It is joyful even amidst pain." Letter from 3-14-1925. (Editorial translation).

the greater glory of God and for the good of the nation. As Pius XI said, "Flourish in beauty, so as to be fruitful in goodness!"

15.
CAN WE?

"The man who wishes to understand himself thoroughly-and not just in accordance with immediate, partial, often superficial, and even illusory standards and measures of his being-he must with his unrest, uncertainty and even his weakness and sinfulness, with his life and death, draw near to Christ. He must, so to speak, enter into him with all his own self, he must 'appropriate' and assimilate the whole of the reality of the Incarnation and Redemption in order to find himself."

Redemptor Hominis, 10.

I

People usually define themselves, even without meaning to, by some word or image. Consider the case of the apostles James and John, who are no exception to the rule. They define themselves with these words: WE CAN!

They were and are the first martyr Apostle and the first virgin Apostle. Jesus called them "Boanerges"[653] or "Sons of Thunder," for their impetuous spirits.

These words, **we can**,[654] are a beautiful definition of the life and work of the two brothers, the sons of Zebedee and Mary Salome, the *partners with Simon*,[655] as Saint Luke says.

---

[653] *Mk* 3:17.
[654] Cf. *Mt* 20:22.
[655] *Lk* 5:10.

411

II

Even today, our Lord Jesus Christ asks us: *Are you able to drink the cup that I am about to drink?*[656] As I see it, this is a question that encompasses the entire magnificent program that Jesus proposes to the youth when he calls them to follow Him more closely.

Can you renounce father, mother, brothers, sisters, and friends?

Can you renounce all material goods, comforts, conveniences, and plans?

Can you renounce your homeland, your language, your customs?

Can you renounce the use of sex, being virgin not only of body, but also, and above all, in your heart, if God calls you to the consecrated life?

Can you commit yourself to be faithful to your husband or your wife for your whole life?

Can you renounce your own judgment, your own will, your own honor and your own tastes?

We must respond: "We can! With grace we can do anything!"

III

Can you? This can also mean: Are you able to love me above all things, with all the strength of your mind, soul and heart?

Can you? Are you capable of spending your life, day by day, like the sanctuary lamp of the Blessed Sacrament that few, very few, people pay attention to?

---

[656] *Mt* 20:22.

Can you? Do you have enough courage to endure all kinds of calumnies, curses, mockery, injuries, rumors, scorn and persecutions?

Can you? Are you willing to burn yourself out, like incense or wood, as sacrifice seen only by God?

Can you? Are you ready to fight in order to live the authentic liberty of the sons of God, without allowing yourself to be enslaved by anything?

Can you? Are you ready never to let your right conscience waver for anything or anybody?

Can you? Are you ready to spiritually bear, with suffering, many children for God alone?

We must respond: "We can! With grace we can do anything!"

IV

Can you be faithful to the Church in spite of the bad testimony of many of its members?

Can you go *to all the world to preach the gospel,*[657] overcoming all geographical, cultural and linguistic barriers?

Can you drink from My chalice, immolating Me in the Mass, being authentic liturgists?

Can you form solid and fruitful Christian families?

Can you be capable of having dominion over all of human reality for My sake?

Can you work for the unity of all Christians, in spite of the almost insurmountable human obstacles?

Can you participate in interreligious dialogue, evangelize the culture, promote the family, the development of peoples, the

---

[657] Cf. *Mt* 16:15.

dignity of work, social justice, and the procurement of peace between nations and people?

Can you be saints?

We must respond: "We can! With grace we can do anything!"

A small unconquered fear can be the cause of a great defect.

"We can! With grace we can do anything!" Like Marcelo Javier Morsella said.[658]

That must be our firm conviction.

---

[658] Marcelo Javier Morsella was a young seminarian in the Institute of the Incarnate Word, who tragically died at 24 years of age on February 8, 1986. He was a dedicated young man, in love with God, very joyful...He left others an example of generous self-giving to the Lord, whom he wanted to serve as a missionary priest. He had offered himself to mission in Chad, Africa. Faced with great difficulties he liked to repeat with great spirit and confidence this phrase of the Boanerges apostles: **"We can!"** adding: **"With the grace of God we can do anything!"**

EPILOGUE
DO YOU LOVE ME MORE?

"This love, like other loves and yet even more so,
demands a response. After his resurrection,
Jesus asked Peter the basic question about love:
'Simon, son of John, do you love me more than these?'
And following his response Jesus entrusts Peter
with the mission: 'Feed my lambs.' [659]
Jesus first asks Peter if he loves him
so as to be able to entrust his flock to him.
However, in reality it was Christ's own love,
free and unsolicited, which gave rise to his question
to Peter and to his act of entrusting
'his' sheep to Peter."

Pastores Dabo Vobis, *25.*

This was now the third time that Jesus was revealed to the disciples after he was raised from the dead. *When they had finished breakfast, Jesus said to Simon Peter, 'Simon, son of John, do you love me more than these?' He said to him, 'Yes, Lord; you know that I love you.'*

He said to him, 'Feed my lambs.'

A second time he said to him, 'Simon, son of John, do you love me?'

He said to him, 'Yes, Lord; you know that I love you.' He said to him, 'Tend my sheep.'

He said to him the third time, 'Simon, son of John, do you love me?'

---

[659] *Jn* 21:15.

Peter was grieved because he said to him the third time, 'Do you love me?' And he said to him, 'Lord, you know everything; you know that I love you.' Jesus said to him, 'Feed my sheep.' [660]

Dear youth, today Jesus is asking you the same question that he asked Peter once...*do you love?*

1. ...*do you love...?*

We know that today's youth are not formed for true love. They are not taught to love and this lack of love in youth has various causes:

-a false rigidity, by which manliness is confused with a lack of sentiments and with the absence of an ardent will;

-they are not given an example of true love;

-the force of family problems, failure in love, not knowing that one is loved, etc.

This is why Jesus asks: *do you love?*

Which, in turn, provokes another question: what does it mean to love? To love implies an intense and vehement will. Cicero says: "loving consists only in delighting in the one you love, without seeking in the beloved any other advantage, which, nevertheless, is poured forth from the same friendship the less that you seek such advantage."[661]

Human love can be taken in two ways:

a- in the proper sense as a passion of the sensitive appetite, if it tends to the form of a desired sensible good;

b-in the analogous sense, as an act of the rational appetite, tending to the form of the rationally desired good.

---

[660] *Jn* 21:15-17.

[661] Editorial translation.

We must consider three things concerning tendency towards the beloved object.

1. The moving of the *a quo* term toward the *ad quem* (meaning, the movement from the point of departure to the point of arrival). In the appetite this corresponds *to love or simple volition*.

-Do you intensely strive to overcome idleness, laziness, lack of generosity, pusillanimity, fears and cowardice, lack of desire to serve, and lack of solidarity?

If you don't intensely strive to overcome lukewarmness and mediocrity, it is a sign that you do not love well.

-Have you not decided to leave behind the things of the flesh, your comforts, your self-love?

If you have not decided to leave behind your disorders, you lack growth in love.

2. The movement or effective transition from the *a quo* term to the *ad quem* term corresponds to the *desire or intention* in the appetite.

-Do you intensely seek sanctity, virtue, wisdom, prayer, and souls for Christ?

If you do not intensely seek to improve, it is a sign that you do not love well.

-Do you effectively seek the good of others?

If you do not put all of your effort in coming out of yourself, you lack growth in love.

3. The consequence of the movement or the arrival at the *ad quem* term corresponds to *pleasure, rest, or fruition* in the appetite.

-Do you take intense joy in mortifying and sacrificing yourself, imitating Jesus Christ, by crucifying yourself to reach great goals in study, sports, relations with others, and prayer through great effort?

-Do you tend, with effort, to seek the glory of God, the salvation of souls, the spreading of the Kingdom of God and His righteousness, the honor of Holy Mother Church, and sanctity?

-Do you know how to rest; do you reach tranquility in the beloved object?

I fear very much that, if you do not do these things, you do not yet know what love is.

There are young people who seem to have no blood in their veins; they are not disturbed by anything, they do not tremble for noble things, they are not excited about anything, for them everything is the same.

To faint, to dare, to be furious,	*Desmayarse, atreverse, estar furioso,*
Rough, tender, liberal, shy,	*Áspero, tierno, liberal, esquivo,*
Encouraged, fatal, dead, alive,	*Alentado, mortal, difunto, vivo,*
Loyal, traitor, coward and bold!	*Leal, traidor, cobarde y animoso!*
Not finding—apart from the good—	*No hallar fuera del bien centro y*
center or repose,	*reposo,*
Show oneself joyful, sad, humble,	*Mostrarse alegre, triste, humilde,*
haughty,	*altivo,*
Angry, valiant, fugitive, satisfied,	*Enojado, valiente, fugitivo, satisfecho,*
offended, suspicious;	*ofendido, receloso;*
Hiding one's face to obvious	*Huir el rostro al claro desengaño*
disappointment,	
Drinking poison as if smooth liquor,	*Beber veneno por licor suave,*
Forgetting the benefit, loving the harm;	*Olvidar el provecho, amar el daño;*
Believing that heavens fit in a hell,	*Creer que el cielo en un infierno cabe,*
Giving one's life and soul for a	*Dar la vida y el alma a un desengaño:*
disappointment:	
This is love; whoever has experienced it	*Esto es amor; quién lo probó lo sabe.*
knows.	
(Editorial Translation)	*(Lope de Vega)*

2. ...do you love more...?

Let us look at the effect of love:

1. *Simple Union:* The union of the lover with the beloved object, as contributing to his well-being.

-Are you united to your friends and family in this way?

-Do you understand their good as *your good?* When one loves, "he wills good to him, just as he wills good to himself...wherefore he apprehends him—poor, sinner, or enemy---as his other self,"[662] like "half of his soul." [663]

If you are not yet moved to desire and seek out the people whom you must love as belonging to yourself, then you do not yet *love more...*

2. *Mutual indwelling:* Every lover is in the beloved, and every beloved is in the lover. *I hold you in my heart*[664] said Saint Paul. Because he who truly loves "is not content with a superficial knowledge of the beloved, but makes an effort to study in depth everything about the beloved, so to penetrate to the interior,"[665] like the Holy Spirit, who is the love of God, who *searches everything, even the depths of God.*[666] In addition, the lover and the beloved are mutually present *"merely by the interior pleasure [the lover takes] in the beloved one,"* delighting in the beloved or in each other's goods. Lovers unite themselves to each other, penetrating to the interior of the beloved, judging as their own the goods or evils of the one loved and the will of the one loved as their own, so that they mutually seem to suffer the same evils and possess the same goods as the one loved. In addition, they mutually love each other, they mutually desire each other and mutually do each other good.

Do you love in this way, to the most interior point....Or are you contented with a superficial knowledge?

3. *Ecstasy:* Pseudo-Dionysius said, *"Love...produces ecstasy."* By this, he means that love places one outside of himself, because it

---

[662] SAINT THOMAS, *S. Th.* 1-2, 28, 1.

[663] SAINT AUGUSTINE, *Confessions*, Book 4; ARISTOTLE, *Ethics*, 9, c. 4, n. 5; SAINT THOMAS, *In Io.* 4, 10.

[664] *Phil* 1:7.

[665] SAINT THOMAS, *S. Th.* 1-2, 28, 2.

[666] 1 *Cor* 2:10.

elevates him to an understanding that exceeds the senses and reason, and by orienting oneself to the other, he comes out of himself in a sense. This is why the Second Vatican Council teaches that man: "can only fully discover his true self in a sincere giving of himself."[667] Love makes one meditate intensely on the beloved object, forgetting other things; and because love wants and efficaciously does good to loved ones, it introduces the cares, problems, and needs of the beloved causing one to come out of oneself.

-Do you really come out of yourself, giving yourself with sincerity to God and to your neighbor for God's sake?

-Do you still not know how to deny yourself? If the grain of wheat does not die, it does not love!

4. *Zeal*: *I the Lord your God am a jealous God*[668]; *the LORD, whose name is Jealous, is a jealous God*[669]; "on account of the great love that he has for what exists," as Pseudo-Dionysius says. Ordered zeal comes from the intensity of love. Zeal means ardor, fervor, intensity and vehemence in love. "He who loves intensely supports nothing that causes distaste to his love."[670] Perfect zeal is directed against those things that are in some way opposed to the good of the people loved. This is why when one rejects with strength, those things that are against the honor or the will of God, we say: *Zeal for thy house will consume me.*[671]

We should be able to say, *I have been most zealous for the LORD, the God of hosts.*[672]

-Is your life consumed by zeal for God? Or, on the contrary, are you consumed with jealousy?

---

667 VATICAN COUNCIL II, *Pastoral Constitution on the Church in the Modern World*, 24; cf. Lk 17:33.

668 *Ex* 20:5.

669 *Ex* 34:14.

670 SAINT THOMAS AQUINAS, *In Io*, chap. 2, lect. 2.

671 *Jn* 2:17.

672 1 *Kg* 19:14; NAB Version.

5. a. Wounding or vulnerability. He who loves is moved and is wounded by sympathy for the beloved. That is why it is said: *You have ravished my heart, my sister, my bride, you have ravished my heart with a glance of your eyes.*[673] Love wounds the heart like an arrow.

-Do you love to the point of feeling wounded in your heart? When you feel wounded, do you love even more?

b. *Ardor. The flash of it is a flash of fire, a flame of Yahweh himself.*[674] "So that it may boil, spill over itself and come out of itself."[675] A fire starts in the deepest part of a person, and from there it can only break out into inflamed words. This is why the saints do not bore, they convince.

c. *Softening or melting* of the heart occurs in order that the loved one might enter there, against the coldness, or hardness of heart. *My soul failed me when he spoke.*[676]

d. *Languishment.* This is why we must seek strength. *Strengthen me with raisin cakes, refresh me with apples, for I am faint with love.*[677] One suffers a certain sadness at the absence of the beloved: *I adjure you, O daughters of Jerusalem, if you find my beloved, that you tell him I am sick with love.*[678]

e. *Fruition.* When the beloved object is present and it is possessed, it causes pleasure. One feels the effects listed above and love dissolves into a sort of sweet intoxication: *I eat my honey and my honeycomb, I drink my wine and my milk. Eat, friends, and drink, drink deep, my dearest friends.*[679]

6. *Love is my weight.* Finally, love is the cause of everything that a lover does. Saint Augustine said: "My weight is my love, he

---

[673] *Song* 4:9.
[674] *Song* 8:6; NJB Version.
[675] SAINT THOMAS, In *Sent.* 3 d. 27 q.1 a.1 ad 4. (Editorial translation).
[676] *Song* 5:6.
[677] *Song* 2:5; NAB Version.
[678] *Song* 5:8.
[679] *Song* 5:1; NJB Version.

takes me wherever I am taken."[680] And elsewhere: "…souls tend to those things which they love, so as to arrive at them and rest."[681]

3. …do you love me more?…

But we would not respond to this question if we did not realize that this *love* refers to Jesus Himself. And we would not be aware of the deep significance of the words of Saint Paul: *I live by faith in the Son of God, who loved me.*[682] *Who shall separate us from the love of Christ?… we are more than conquerors through him who loved us.*[683]

4. Summarizing

*Am "I transforming" into Jesus, "in a way am I converting myself"[684] into Him? Can I say: *it is no longer I who live, but Christ who lives in me?*[685] Do I effectively seek to do this?

*Do I live in Him and He in me? *God is love, and he who abides in love abides in God, and God abides in Him.*[686] Or am I content with a superficial knowledge of the Beloved?

*Do I tend to Him by that "excess of the mind that is called ecstasy," in such a way that lower things are erased from my memory, as Saint Augustine says?[687] Do I do this with intensity and vehemence?

*Does zeal for the honor of His name devour me? Do I burn with His love?

---

[680] SAINT AUGUSTINE, *Confessions*, Book 13, chap. 9, n. 10. (Editorial translation).

[681] SAINT AUGUSTINE, *Epist.* 55. (Editorial translation).

[682] *Gal* 2:20.

[683] *Rom* 8:35, 37.

[684] Cf. SAINT THOMAS AQUINAS, *In Sent.* 3, d. 27, q. 1, a. 1, ad 2.

[685] *Gal* 2:20.

[686] 1 *Jn* 4:16.

[687] SAINT AUGUSTINE, *Enarratio 2 in Ps. 30*, serm. 2, n. 2.

*With Him, does my heart *rejoice, sweeten and pine after Him,* allowing Him to penetrate it? Am I *wounded* by the *fire* that He produces in me? Do I suffer *vulnerability* and *transfusion?* Do I find impenetrable serenity in Him?

*Can I truly say that "My weight is my love, he takes me wherever I am taken"? Do I enthusiastically take others to Him who takes me?

Dear Youth:

…do you love…?

…do you love more…?

…do you love Me more…?

May these questions and their answers, **the love of Christ,** be the great gift that this book leaves for you. May the sweeping strength of the love of Jesus Christ make you able to creatively live your youth, walking on the paths of the Lord and transforming the world that you must construct and build up for Him.

APPENDIX

A LETTER TO A SPIRITUAL SON IN THE YEAR 10,000

Because there is a need in my heart, I must write this letter to you. I do not know if the world will last for many more years. Maybe it will last for much longer. Anyway, I address myself to you whether you are from the twentieth, fiftieth, hundredth, or the thousandth century. But why do I write to you? Through my crosses, prayers, preaching, the apostolic zeal of one of my writings, the foundation of the Congregation of the Incarnate Word, the Servants of the Lord and the Virgin of Matará, or from the Third Order, or through one of its members, you have received the life that Jesus Christ brought to the world. I do not know the concrete and particular way the grace of God has related us to each other as a father to his child. I don't know if you are in America, Asia, Europe, Africa, Oceania, or on some other planet.

Nor do I know your name, age, history, culture or family. I do not know your gender, the color of your skin, or your face. But this is of little importance because it is enough to know that you are my son and, therefore, my glory and my crown. I trust that God who gave me the grace on Earth to be able to look into the eyes of many young people and love them, will give me in the Heaven I await (not by my merits, but only by His grace), the happiness of being able to know and love all those who, with the passage of time, will be considered my children. I believe that even in this case I have to trust more in you than in myself, as has already begun to happen to me while I am still in this world.

I believe that each time I see you I will feel a tingling joy at seeing the prolongation, in time and space, of myself; I will feel the indescribable joy of begetting and raising children knowing that we are of the same flesh and blood, the same spiritual family.

Do not think it is improper on my part that I attribute to myself a fatherhood which does not belong to me. Really, the only one who is Father, by essence, is God, and from Him proceeds all paternity (*cf. Eph* 3:15) by participation.

The true priest who authentically seeks the glory of God is supernaturally fruitful. He begets life and life in abundance because "the life of man is the glory of God" as Saint Irenaeus said.[688] Whoever seeks the Glory of God transmits life to man by it.

Because of this, let me say that **I love you** from the bottom of my heart. **I trust in you** in spite of your limitations and your sins. How could I not? If God trusts in me even though I have many more sins than you do, how could I not trust in you? I am convinced that you will be much better persons than I am and you will do greater things for the Glory of God. I am ashamed of myself, but God has given me the grace that, at least up until now, I never have had to be ashamed of an authentic son or daughter. I do not love you less because of your sins and your failures; rather I love you even more.

I cannot imagine what cities will be like in your century, or the transportation, communications, and other advances that will have taken place in medicine, computer technology, and energy. I cannot imagine which sports will be the most popular, what the organization of education will be, or the new nations that will exist in the world. How power will be redistributed or how new languages will emerge are unknown to me (I am sure you will laugh at my language, but people will do the same at yours later on). I cannot imagine what new pastoral techniques they will use...but the Catholic faith will be the same, and true love will be

---

[688] SAINT IRENAEUS, *Adversus Haereses*, book 4, chapter 20: 7.

the same, for *love never ends.*[689] And so, I aspire to love you with this love.

If this letter remains until the year 10,000, it will certainly be an archeological find. But faith and charity, together with hope, will always be what is most up to date, what is youngest, and newest. The world and its concupiscence are passing away, but God remains. What are 10,000 years in comparison to eternity? Not even an instant! And how foolish it is to lose eternity by attaching oneself to an instant. Heaven is the greatest thing, and in order to reach it, we have to arrange things on earth according to Christ.

What is it that is truly worth the most in the passing of the centuries while the world lasts? What is worth living for and worth dying for if necessary?

First of all, a right understanding of God, who is an infinitely perfect Being, "Ipsum Esse Subsistens," who is One in three distinct Persons, the Father, the Son, and the Holy Spirit. He governs Heaven and Earth and all they contain with His Providence, *in everything God works for the good with those who love him.*[690]

Secondly, faith in Jesus Christ our Lord, who is the Christ, *the Son of the living God,*[691] our Redeemer and Savior, *who was put to death for our trespasses and raised for our justification,*[692] the only One who has *the words of eternal life.*[693] He is the only thing that is truly new; the passing of the centuries since the moment of His redeeming Incarnation have not given Him even a touch of aging. *When He gave Himself, he gave novelty to all things.*[694] To be His disciple is nothing other than imitating Him to the point that you

---

[689] *1 Cor* 13:8.
[690] *Rom* 8:28.
[691] *Mt* 16:16.
[692] *Rom* 4:25.
[693] *Jn* 6:68.
[694] SAINT IRENAEUS, *Adversus Haereses*, Book 4, Chapter 34: 1.

can say *it is no longer I who live, but Christ who lives in me,*[695] and to try to always *seek first his kingdom and his righteousness, and all these things shall be yours as well.*[696]

Thirdly, Jesus Christ is prolonged and perpetuated in the Catholic Church, which He founded, and to whom He left as an inheritance the treasure of His Body and Blood and the perpetuation of His unique Sacrifice in the Eucharist *until He comes.*[697] He also left His Mother, Mary, as the Mother of the Church,[698] and He placed Peter, present in his successors, the Popes, Bishops of Rome, as the visible Head of the Church. In doctrine we must follow the Pope, who cannot err, and in life we must follow the saints, who have not erred. Only the Church that was founded upon Peter, the rock, will prevail against the gates of Hell (cf. *Mt* 16: 18). On the Vatican hill in Rome, the first Pope, Peter, the Fisherman, is buried. Do the columns of Bernini, the Egyptian obelisk, the facade of the Basilica of Maderno, and the dome of Michelangelo still exist? I celebrated Holy Mass there many times and I also prayed for you.

And so, in desiring for you true faith, I wish for you what is best. Faith is the beginning of the spiritual life and it is the path that leads to Jesus Christ, through real, true, and psychological contact, in spite of time and distance. Only He is *the Way, the Truth, and the Life.*[699] Commenting on this text, a classic for all times says:

"Without the way, no man can go;
without the truth, no man can know; and
without life, no man can live. I am the
way you must follow, the truth you must
believe, the life you must hope for. I am
the way secure from danger, the truth

---

[695] *Gal* 2:20.
[696] *Mt* 6:33.
[697] *1 Cor* 11:26.
[698] Cf. *Jn* 19:27.
[699] *Jn* 14:6.

that cannot deceive, and the life that will never end. I am the straightest way, the supreme truth, the genuine life, the blessed life, the uncreated life. If you keep to My way, you will know the truth and the truth will deliver you, and you will possess everlasting life."

I hope that you grow always in *hoping against hope*,[700] and that you may know *what is the hope to which he has called you.*[701]

Above all, I strongly recommend that you live the charity of Christ, the queen of all virtues, which *covers a multitude of sins,*[702] and *binds everything together in perfect harmony,*[703] and on which *depend all the law and the prophets.*[704] People should be able to say of you: "John is patient and kind; he is not jealous or boastful, arrogant, or rude; he does not insist on his own way; he is not irritable or resentful but rejoices in the right. He bears all things, believes all things, hopes all things, and endures all things."[705] And particularly he loves sinners, the poor, and his enemies.

Dedicate yourself to the propagation of the Gospel, so that someone could say of you: He was a preacher of the truth and an apostle of freedom.[706] Keep your faith pure and your conscience clean. May nothing human be foreign to you, so that you might raise it up to Christ. May Sacred Scripture always be your nourishment and the Eucharist your greatest love. Work for the increase and sanctification of vocations to the consecrated life. Feel the wind of Pentecost in your soul to inspire and remind you to: *Go into all the world and preach the gospel to the whole creation.*[707] Do

---

[700] *Rom* 4:18.
[701] *Eph* 1: 18.
[702] *1 Pt* 4:8.
[703] *Col* 3:14.
[704] *Mt* 22:40.
[705] Cf. 1 *Cor* 13:4-7.
[706] Cf. SAINT IRENAEUS, *Adversus haereses*, Book 3, Chapter 15, 3.
[707] *Mk* 16:15.

not forget that we are living instruments of Jesus Christ, but we are deficient and absolutely in need of His grace: *apart from me you can do nothing,*[708] the good works come from Him and only the mistakes are ours.

I hold you close to my heart, knowing that as we were united in the 20ᵗʰ century in the mind of God who has *arranged all things by measure and number and weight,*[709] we will be even more united in your century through grace and, still more, in the glory that we await. Forward, always forward! Ave Maria, and go forward! Give me your hand and a great hug! Full speed ahead until Heaven! I am proud of you.

---

[708] *Jn* 15:5.
[709] *Wis* 11:20.

New York – 2010